Concept of Gāyatrī in the Vedas and the Purāṇas

Concept of Gāyatrī in the Vedas and the Purāṇas

Prajna Paramita Das

2011

Kaveri Books

New Delhi - 110 002

First Published in 2011

ISBN : 978-81-7479-120-7

Published by

Kaveri Books

4832/24, Ansari Road,
New Delhi-110002 (India)

Tel: 011-4707 2321

E-mail : info@kaveribooks.com,
E-mail : kaveribooks@gmail.com
Web : www.kaveribooks.com

Printed at
G.S. Offset Printer, Delhi.

PRINTED IN INDIA

Dedicated to the

Memory of my

Father-in-law and Mother-in-law

Late Kailash Ch. Pattnayak

&

Smt. Nirmala Pattnayak

Foreword

Gāyatrī is the most popular metre in the a ancient Vedic literature which through the passage of time assumed the distinction of a prominent deity in the later literature, especially in the *Purāṇas*. Besides the metre, Gāyatrī as a mantra itself which occurs in the *Ṛgveda* (3.62.10) and many other later vedic texts is considered as the most sacred and powerful mantra and is often alluded as a wishyielding tree for attainment of almost everything in life.

Due to the importance of this mantra and the prominence of the mantra, Gāyatrī started to be narrated as *chandasām mātā* (*vedamata*), the mother Goddess the progenitor of the chandas or the Vedas. She is no other than Saraswati and Savitri too.

All her epithets, effulgent lustrous beauty, powers bounteousness etc., beginning from her origin, which are scattered in a vast arena of Vedic and Puranic literature has been put here at one place by the diligent and commendable endeavours of Dr. Prajna Paramita Das (Principal), Biswa Tarini Womens College in the Keonjhar District of Odisha for the quenching the thirst of knowledge of scholars, literatures as well as the devotees.

I am happy to write these few words to introduce this indispensable groundwork on the Vedic and mythological subject from which the young and old shall equally be benefited.

Dr. Raghunath Panda
Prof. & Former Head
P.G. Dept. of Sanskrit,
Utkal University
Bhubaneswar (Orissa)

Acknowledgement

'O Lord!
Give us great strength of body, mind and spirit
Free our intellect from all ills and pollutions,
O Lord! Guide us to glorify you
by treading the path of virtue.
Bestow us with fortitude in moments of grief and sorrow;
And give us wisdom to act righteously.
O Lord! guide us to keep in you faith unflinching, deep and true.'

At the outset I owe my deep sense of gratitude to all of the persons, institutions, librarians, revered teachers, friends, relatives, well-wishers and students, who have in some way or other extended their help, advice and co-operation for the successful completion of this thesis.

It is my privilege and solemn duty to express my deepest sense of gratitude to Dr. Raghunath Panda, professor, Postgraduate Dept. of Sanskrit, Utkal University, Bhubaneswar, under whose able guidance I carried out this work. In fact it is not possible for me to express in words my indebtedness to him for his valuable supervision, heartful co-operation and timely aid and advice till the completion of the thesis in spite of his pressing engagements.

I also thank my honourable teacher Prof. A.C. Sarangi, Head of the Department of Sanskrit, Utkal University, Prof. P.K. Mishra, Prof. G.K. Dash, Prof. R.M. Dash, Dr. S.C. Dash, Dr. D.B. Tripathy of our Department for their blessings in fulfilment of this endeavour. I am specially indebted and thankful to Dr. Mrs. P.M. Rath, Reader for providing me with some vedic materials.

I would like to express my deep sense of gratitude to Dr. Chaturbhuja Satapathy, Reader and H.O.D, Sanskrit, Nayagarh Autonomous College, Nayagarh, who has been kind enough to offer his valuable advice in some matters related to my study. I extend my sincere thanks to Mrs. Katyayani Mohapatra, Advocate, Orissa High Court, for giving the thesis a presentable form.

I accord my sincere thanks to all the librarians and staffs, Parija Library, Sri J.M. Acharya, P.G. Dept. of Sanskrit, Utkal University, Central Library, Cuttack, Gayatri Sakti Pitha Library Bhubaneswar, those have provided me adequate opportunities to utilize their materials.

I convey my gratefulness to Mrs. Kalpana Panda for her co-operation, encouragement and personal concern to finish this work. I can't forget the unconditional co-operation of my husband, Sri Sailendra Pattnaik, who is always like a fountainhead of inspiration for my academic progress.

I am indebted to my Father-in-Law, Sri Kailash Chandra Pattnaik and Mother-in-Law, Smt. Nirmala Pattnaik for their loving inspirations and encouragement. My two daughters Swati and Sraddha have extended their help to me at all stages of finishing this thesis. I feel gratified to have fulfilled the wish of my revered father, Late Purna Chandra Das, who would surely be happy in completion of this work. I am really grateful to the scholars in the field of religious oriental studies and researches by those esteemed and valuable works, I have been enlightened.

At last I convey my thanks to Mr. Ravindra K. Sil, Mr. Prasanta K. Mohapatra and Mr. Sivendranath Sahoo those who have devoted their valuable time to type the different chapters of this thesis within a very short span of time.

Prajnaparamita Das

Preface

Worshipping deities is our religious culture. Worshiping of "Shakti" in the from of mother deities undoubtedly comprises a significant part of this religious culture. In intellectual and spiritual discourses, one can find that neither the scholars nor the spiritualist have every shown the tendency of shying away from reflecting over the importance of worshipping Mother Power. Mother Goddess finds Numerous manifestations though the under-lying purposes may, when unraveled thread bare lead to one universal unity. Of the numerality of forms, "Vedamata" as Goddess Gāyatrī was known to the vedic people, finds Herself in twenty four forms. May be Gāyatrī Mantra or Gāyatrī Chanda (metre), as one may conveniently regard, finds different forms, the popularity and wholesome benefits that Gāyatrī bestows upon the devotees can never be put to question. Time is synonymous with flux. It flows from the ages of the veda(s) to the ages of computer(s), but the spiritual benefits of the Gāyatrī remain unquestionably the same. Moreover, Gāyatrī in Her different forms, has surpassed the frontiers of Hinduism and Gāyatrī now enjoys universal favour and appeal.

Given Universality of Gāyatrī, I am surprised to bring to the knowledge of my readers that few elite writers have made sparing references to Gāyatrī in their works. Apart from this, there is no literature on Gāyatrī. On personal level. I am brought up in a family of staunch followers of Hinduism and ardent believers of "Mother Power". Again, I am working as the Principal of a Women's College christened as Biswo Tarini Women's College. This Vaccum of literature on Gāyatrī and my religious fervour which I have imbibed from family faith and my profession, urged me to write a book on Gāyatrī. My main endeavour is to provide the scholars and devotee readers with information on Gāyatrī. I have ensured that apart from introducing the concept of Mother Goddess, accounts of the concept of Gāyatrī, its origin and significance in vedic as well as puranic literature contribute to the main fabric of the book. A complete chapter is dedicated to the discussion of forms of appearances and iconographical features of Gāyatrī. Gāyatrī as a metre, several forms of this metre in different purāṇas, and relationship of Gāyatrī with Sāvlitri constitute the centre of the chapter. Methods of Sandhya worship and Tantric mode of worshipping Gāyatrī forms the vital portion of the second half of the book. The chapter invested on tantric mode of Gāyatrī worship has its special significance in terms of the benefits that one derives by committing oneself to Gāyatrī Sādhanā. The conclusion reflects on a logical basis of the sustenance of Gāyatrī even in the teeth of rampart scientific developments. A number of iconographies of Gāyatrī of different ages have been included in the book for better perception of diverse manifestations of Gāyatrī in different ages of time. I hope the four appendices which contain the Analogus Gāyatrī mantra, Gāyatrī Sahasranāma, Sāvitri Astottarsa-tanāma and Glory and advantages of Gāyatrī-Japa would help the scholars and devotees immensely. This book contains eight chapters, including an introduction, which contains the concept of Mother Goddess in general, the Sakti, and its meaning and origin of Goddess Gāyatrī.

Chapter-1 contains the concept of Gāyatrī in the vedic literature and studies Gāyatrī as a sacred metre, its birth, appearance, divinity and application. Chapter-2 deals with the comparison of Gāyatrī with other deities. The Significance of Gāyatrī in Vedic literature is discussed in Chapter-3. Chapter-4 contains the origin and birth of Goddess Gāyatrī as it is described in Purānas. The forms, appearance and characteristics of Gāyatrī are dealt in the Chapter-5. Chapter-6 deals with the methods of *Sāndhya* worship of Gāyatrī, importance and glory of its *Mantra* and the advantages. The tantric mode of Gāyatrī is discussed in the Chapter-7. The Chapter-8 is named as the conclusion which, synthesizes the findings. Besides, the above chapters some more interesting features associated with the worship of the Goddess Gāyatrī has been given in the appendices. As usual a selected bibliography and a glossary of Sanskrit terms have been added for the better understanding and references.

The treatment and analysis of the Gāyatrī worship is quite extensive from the time of origin of the concept in the Vedas even up to the modern times including the vast Purānic literature.

I strongly believe that the chanting of

"Om Bhur, Bhuvah, Suvah
Tat Savitur Varenyam
Bhargo Devasya Dhimahi
Dhiyo yo Nah Prachodaya."

will benefit all and seek the indulgence of readers or errors, commi-ssions or omissions in the book. I invite constructive and corrective suggestions from one and all to make further improvements.

Contents

Abbreviations

AA – *Aitareya Āraṇyaka*

AB – *Aitareya Brāhmaṇa*

AG – *Āsvalāyana Gṛhya Sūtra*

AP – *Agni Purāṇa*

AP.GS – *Āpastamba Gṛhyasūtra*

AV – *Atharva Veda*

BDh – *Baudhāyana Dharma Sūtra*

BG – *Bhāgavad Gīta*

BhaP – *Bhāgavata Purāṇa*

BhavP – *Bhaviṣya Purāṇa*

BORI – Bhandarkar Oriental Research Institute

BrhU – *Brahadāraṇyaka Upaniṣad*

BVP – *Brahma Vaivarta Purāṇa*

ChU – *Chāndogya Upaniṣad*

DBP – *Devī Bhāgavata Purāṇa*

Ed. – Editor / Edition

GGS – *Gobhila Gṛhya Sūtra*

GB – *Gopatha Brāhmaṇa*

GRU – *Gāyatrī Rahasya Upaniṣad*

GP – *Guruḍa Puraṇa*

JUB – *Jaininiya Upaniṣad Brāhmana*

Kalila P – *Kalika Purāṇa*

Ka. – *Kathopaniṣad*

Kn. – *Kena Upaniṣad*

KP – *Kūrma Purāṇa*

KS	–	*Kauṣitaki Saṁhitā*
Linga P	–	*Linga Purāṇa*
Mahan U	–	*Mah Narāyaṇa Upaniṣad*
Mbh	–	*Mahābhārata*
MLBD	–	Motilal Banarsi Dass
MP	–	*Matsya Purāṇa*
MS	–	*Maitrāyaṇi Samhitā*
Nir	–	*Niruktam*
Pd P	–	*Padma Purāṇa*
Par G	–	*Parāśara Gṛhyasūtra*
Rv	–	*Ṛgveda*
SG	–	*Sānkhyāna Gṛhyasūtra*
SB	–	*Śatapatha Brāhmaṇa*
SkP	–	*Skanda Purāṇa*
SS	–	*Sānkhāyana Śrauta Sūtra*
SV	–	*Sāma Veda*
TA	–	*Taittirīya Āraṇyaka*
TB	–	*Taittirīya Brāhmaṇa*
TS	–	*Taittirīya Saṁhitā*
TandB	–	*Tāndya Brāhmaṇa*
Tr.	–	Translation
TU	–	*Taittirīya Upaniṣad*
YU	–	*Yajur Veda*
VarahaP	–	*Varāha Purāṇa*
VaP	–	*Vāyu Purāṇa*
VP	–	*Viṣṇu Purāṇa*
VS	–	*Vikrama Saṁvat*

Latin

etc.	–	*Etcetera* (and other things or and so on)
i.e.,	–	*id est* (That is or that means)

Transliteration

a	अ	ṭā	ट
ā	आ	ṭha	ठ
i	इ	ḍa	ड
ī	ई	ḍha	ढ
u	उ	ṇa	ण
ū	ऊ	ta	त
ṛ	ऋ	tha	थ
e	ए	da	द
ai	ऐ	dha	ध
o	ओ	ṅa	न
au	औ	pa	प
aṁ	अं	pha	फ
aḥ	अः	ba	ब
ka	क	bha	भ
kha	ख	ma	म
ga	ग	ya	य
gha	घ	ra	र
ṅa	ङ	la	ल
ca	च	va	व
cha	छ	śa	श
ja	ज	ṣa	ष
jha	झ	sa	स
ña	ञ		

1

Introduction

'Gāyatrī' is the title of the most sacred *mantra* of the Vedic Indians. The sage Viśvāmitra is the seer of this *mantra*. The deity, worshipped in this *mantra* has got the same name. This is perhaps the elevation of the principal *chandas* through which maximum number of hymns of the *Vedas* came into being. Hence, Gāyatrī, through the passing of the ages has been considered as the mother of the *Vedas* because the vedic *mantras* in large number were generated from this metre of twenty-four syllables.

Concept of Mother Goddess

The pantheon of *Hindu* deities has always included innumerable goddesses and goddess-worship has long been a significant aspect of the *Hindu* religious tradition. The vedic-tradition imagined the shape of the later Indian religion.

It is also significant to note that the present *Hinduism* owes not much to the Vedic religion and its roots may be traced far beyond the frontiers of Vedism namely, in the non-vedic popular cults and beliefs. However, due to want of strong evidence, this cannot be stated with emphasis. The Indus script has not been satisfactorily deciphered so far, for which it is difficult to assert on the exact nature of cults and religious beliefs, which had existed in India when the vedic people arrived in the region of the *Sapta-sindhu*[1]. But on the strength of important discoveries made at various archeological sites such as Harappa, Mahenjo-daro, Kot-Diji, Kalibangan and some other related places. Since 1922, as also on the basis of a comprehensive study of the *AV* which presumably mirrors the way of life and the thoughts of common people as against the hieratic religion of the *ṚV*. It may be assumed that the pre-vedic or non-Āryan religion and belief had been to an appreciable extent, a female-oriented one[2].

The mother-goddess cult, the fertility cult, the cult of guardian divinities and magical rites in all of which female divinities usually prevail, must have constituted the popular religious beliefs of common people of that period[3]. R.C. Hazra has opined, normally the female deities are of non-Āryan origin.[4] It is true that the female deity-worship was prevalent in the primitive tribes throughout the world. She is described as sitting on lions and is glorified as mountain mother or a vegetation deity. He has pointed out that the virginity of the female goddess is an essential factor. But in the *Purṇas* she is the *Prakṛti* who is married to the lord of Universe.

The word '*Gnā*' and '*Śacī*' are of common occurrence in *ṚV,* both of them are described as the wives of Indra. So Hazra's statement is to be restricted to the deities of primitive tribes only. In the *Purāṇas* and the *Upa-Purāṇas* many legends are devoted to the glorification of *Śakti* or *Devī*. She is regarded as the supreme creator, sustainer and destroyer of the Universe[5]. In the chapter entitled '*Doctrine of Śakti in the Devī Bhāgavata*' by P.G. Lalye, it is proved that the doctrine of *Śakti* was not unknown to the vedic people.

The term '*Śakti*' originates from the root '*Śak*' which means, to be able to have energy 'to do' or 'to act'. Thus, *Śakti*-worship is the worship of energy, which is personified as a female and is generally conceived as the all pervading mother goddess.[6]

The earliest reference to *Śakti*-manifestation is found in the *Vāgambhṛṇīya-sūkta* of the *ṚV.* We get therein the earliest glimpse of the omnipotence of a female deity called Vāk.[7] Many *Purāṇas* have also glorified the supreme powers *Śakti* or *Māyā* by virtue of which Śiva and Viṣṇu became the supreme Gods and could discharge their functions. Gradually, this *Śakti* assumed various names like Lakṣmī, Sarasvatī, Pārvatī etc. in various *Purāṇas*. Towards the end of the *purāṇic*-age, devotion towards the *Śakti* was considered to be more effective than devotion to its possessor, either Viṣṇu or Śiva. This change of emphasis appeared due to the growth of the *Tāntric* Systems. This *Śakti* was called '*Devī*'. Around this *Śakti,* a lot of mythologies grew up, resulting in the appearance of a *Pūrāṇa*, called *DBP*, exclusively devoted to the glorification of the *devī*.[8]

In some of the *Sūtras* the female deity is associated with Rudra.[9] In *BaudhDS,* details are given about the worship of a goddess called Durgā. It is one of the earliest references to the *devī* concept.

In many *Vaiṣṇava Saṁhitās* and *Purāṇas,* the female deity was described as the consort of Viṣṇu. In some *Vaiṣṇava Purāṇas, Śakti* is mentioned as the creative potentiality of Viṣṇu.[10] In the *Śaiva* works, Śiva's wife is variously called as Gaurī or Pārvatī. These works have used *Tāntric* expressions to glorify *Śakti.* The *Pūrāṇas* employed *Śakti*, the word, commonly used by the sectarian works to indicate the supreme power as wife of a particular male deity.

However, one of the most impressive characteristics of the ancient *Hindu* religious tradition is the importance of goddess-worship. A considerable number of goddesses are known in the earliest *Hindu*-scriptures and the vedic hymns.

The earliest evidences regarding the prevalence of the Mother Goddess worship have been traced from a larger number of inscriptions, clay-statues and seals which have been found from the Indus Valley, on the basis of which the history of the worshippers of the Mother Goddess has been traced. The possibility of the worship of the earth as a mother, as Sir John Marshall has pointed out is on the basis of seals obtained from Harappa.[11]

Although the mother-worship is evident from seals, figurines and statues etc. of the Indus valley, yet we rely upon the evidences furnished by the Vedas as those are the only earliest visible records. Generally, it is accepted by the scholars that the vedic people belonged to the patriarchal system of society and they gave more importance to male divinities like Agni, Indra and Soma. They are praised repeatedly throughout the *ṚV*. Among others Gods like Varuṇa, Mitra, Savitṛ also occupy significant position in the *ṚV.*

But we cannot deny the fact that the few female deities. described in the *ṚV* are of very interesting character. The most important one is 'Uṣas', the Goddess of the dawn.[12] She is conceived by the Vedic seers as the mother and the Supreme force.

Aditi is another important female deity. She is described as the all-prevading Goddess and is the mother of all the beings as well as the Gods too. She is praised in the *AV.*[13]

In the *ṚV*, Ila, Bhāratī and Sarasvatī are also praised as the three *Devīs.*[14] But among these three, Sarasvatī, the goddess of learning is invoked alone in many hymns. The goddess Pṛthvī too holds a prominent position in the *ṚV*.

Moreover, the goddess Rātrī is said to be the daughter of the heaven. She protects all beings from evils and gives them shelter in her lap just like an affectionate mother.[15]

We should therefore keep in mind while studying about the goddesses in the *ṚV*, that although there are many female deities, they do not either individually or collectively represent the centre of *Ṛg*-vedic religion. In most cases they are mentioned frequently and must have played minor roles when compared to the great male gods of the *ṚV*.

There is evidence that some of the vedic goddesses survived in the later *Hindu* tradition. *Pṛthvī* persists in later *Hinduism* and becomes associated with Lord Viṣṇu. She is often called Bhū-Devī. Although the goddess Vāk disappears in later *Hinduism,* Sarasvatī might be said to express Vāk's primary meaning as inspired speech.

In the vedic age the word Gāyatrī is known as a bird or a metre. This Mantra occurs in the *Trayī.*[16] The sage of this *Mantra* is Viśvāmitra and Savitṛ (sun) is the deity. It is called as Gāyatrī as it is composed in Gāyatrī metre. It is sometimes called as Sāvitrī after the name of the deity. This *Mantra* addressed to the God Sun, attained individuality in the later vedic literature and was the first deity, who played an important mythical role in it. Gāyatrī was just a metre, but the *Brāhmaṇa* authors considered it to be not merely the mechanical arrangement of the syllables but also a potential creativity.[17] The *ŚB* has called it energy of the life. Gāyatrī is full of *Tejas* and *Vīryas* because it is the special metre of Agni, who is produced along with her from the mouth of Prajāpati.[18]

The *TS* says that when there was the contest between the Gods and the *Asuras,* Gāyatrī withdrew into herself force, vigour, energy, progenitor etc. and stood apart.[19] She was identified with Sāvitrī, who also represented the quintessence of divine energy.

The goddess concept as a creating or generating force appeared in the epic and *purāṇic* literature in a more specific manner. She is generally accepted as a *devī* or goddess. The *PadP*, the *SkP*, the *AP*, the *GP*, the *MP*, the *VarāhaP,* the *VāP* and the *DBP* deal with several legends textured around Gāyatrī.

BṛhU says that Gāyatrī and Sāvitrī are one. Sāvitrī means that which is related to Savitṛ–

गायत्रीमेव सावित्रीमनुब्रुयात्

As such this favourable metre of the vedic *Samhitās* later assumed a form of a mother goddess in general and the mother of the vedic hymns in particular as Vedamātā Gāyatrī.

However, it may be pointed out that, the Gāyatrī is not treated as a mother goddess in the vedic literature. It is only in the *purāṇic* literature that her procreative nature is manifested along with Brahmā.[20] According to various sources Sāvitrī, Sarasvatī, Śatarupā, Gāyatrī, Brahmāṇī, Gaurī are the female offsprings of Brahmā.

Sāvitrī is a post-*Ṛg*-vedic name. In the *ṚV*, 'Sāvitṛ' is mentioned only once (*ṚV*, V - 5.4) and not Sāvitrī. But, after the post-vedic period, Sāvitrī has vividly been referred to in various contexts in the *Mahābhārata,* the *MP*, the *BrVaiP*, the *PadP* and the *SkP.*

Later on Sri Aurobindo also believes mother as the supreme poser and discusses the four aspects of the mother. He also believes in the four powers of the mother which are four outstanding personalities, portions and embodiments of her divinity through whom she acts on her creatures, orders and harmonises her creations in the worlds and directs the works of her thousand forces. For him, the mother is one but she comes before us with differing aspects, personalities, amanations and powers (*vibhutis*) that do her work in the universe. He regards the four aspects of the mother as Maheśvari, Mahākalī, Mahālaksmī and Mahā-Sarasvatī. This outlook is also influenced by vedic concept of mother-worship.[21]

As Sampurnānanda has pointed out that the deities are not separate entities as the ocean of power is indivisible. But it focalizes and polarizes itself according to the needs of the situation in various forms and various measures.[22]

Meaning

The word 'Gāyatrī' has been derived from the root '*Gai*' which means to sing. It contains three syllables. The word Gāyatrī has been derived from *Gāyatra*. So the term Gāyatrī has been traditionally derived from the two roots *i.e.,* '*gai*' and '*trai*'[23]. Thus it means an ascent responsible for both singing and protecting. Hence, speech is Gāyatrī. Gāyatrī protects the *gāyas*. The *gāyas* are the vital breaths (*Prāṇah*). To speak deductively it protects the vital breaths.[24] As Gāyatrī protects the *Prāṇa* (*gāyantam trāyate*[25]) so it is called Gāyatrī.[26]

Origin

The term 'Gāyatrī' denotes a particular metre in which a very larger number of vedic stanzas are composed. Among all these stanzas the most outstanding one is the stanza in *ṚV* (3.62.10) is about the seer Viśvāmitra and the deity is Savitṛ. This *Mantra* occurs in other *Veda Samhitās*, *Brāhamaṇa* texts, *Upaniṣads* and *Śrauta* texts. Several major *Upaniṣads* like *BṛhU* (6.3.7) explain the importance of the *Gāyatrī-Mantra* by stating 'If one sprinkles this, even on a dry stump, branches would grow and leaves spring forth'. This *Mantra* is used by a twice-born *Hindu* in his daily devotions and during special functions or worship. The *Gāyatrī-Mantra* is also called Sāvitrī and Sarasvatī in view of the fact that it is addressed to Savitṛ and worshipped also as Sarasvatī.

Exactly, on the same idea and verbal pattern, several other Gāyatrīs have come into vogue, although none of them has attained the same universality, sanctity and significance as the original Gāyatrī possesses, Never the less every holy formula cast in the mould of the first and foremost Gāyatrī has an outstanding part to play in the worship of that particular deity with which it is connected.

Now the original *Gāyatrī-mantra*, how it has been chanted, used, honoured and passed through the *Vedas* and *Purāṇas* and its over all significance draw our attention are to be discussed in the coming chapter.

References

1. R.N. Dandekar : *Some Aspects of the History of Hinduism,* Poona, 1967, p. 1-2.

   Hinduism appeared in the Historic Religions, Vol. II, 1971, p. 244.

   N.M. Bhattacharya : *Indian Mother Goddess,* Calcutta, 1971, p. 8, 103.
2. E.O. James : *The Cult of Mother Goddess,* London, 1959, 101f.

3. S.K. Lal : *Female Divinities in Hindu Mythology and Ritual,* University of Poona, 1980.
4. R.C. Hazra : *Studies in the Upapurāṇas*, Part-II, p. 16.
5. *Mbh,* p. 3.2-3b, 12, 15, 17b, 18.15-16, *DBP*, 1.2, 5.93, 9.40.
6. *Bṛhat Sanskṛtābhidhānam-Vācaspatyam,* Vol.-VI, p. 5074.

   Śabdārtha-cintāmaṇi, Vol.-IV, p. 491; *Śabdakalpadruma,* Vol. V, p. 4-5.
7. *ṚV,* x. 125, *ṚV. Samhitā,* Vaidika Samsodhana Mandala, Poona, 1963.
8. P.G. Layle : *Studies in Devi Bhāgavata,* Bombay, Popular Prakashan, p. 13-14.
9. *Sānkh. SS.* 29.1, *Baudh.DS.* 11.5.6.
10. *AP*, 26.3.1-6; *VP,* 1.17-30, *MP*, 164.27-28, 244, 16.26; *KP*, IV, 13.14.
11. Sri John Marshall : *Mohenjo-daro and Indus Civilization,* Vol. I, Pl.X. III. 12.
12. *ṚV*, I- 48, 49, 113, 124; IV-79; VII-75,76.81; X-172.
13. *AV*, VII-6.2, 6.4.
14. *ṚV*, I-142.9, 13.9; III-4.8; X-70.8.
15. *ṚV*, X-127.
16. *ṚV,* III-62.10; *YV*, III-35.30, II-36.3; *SV,* 13.3.2.
17. *TS,* V-1.3.
18. *ŚB*, 11.3.5.4, 1.3.5.15.
19. *TS*, 11.4.3.1.
20. *BrVaiP, SKP, Setu Mahatymam,* 40, 41-99.
21. Vidyadhara Sarmā Guleri : *Female Deities in Vedic and Epic Literature,* Nag Publishers.
22. Sampurnananda : *Evolution of Hindu Pantheon,* p. 24.
23. *Nir,* 1.3.3;

    The Nighantu and the Niruktam, Ed.; Lakshman Swarup, Oxford University Press, 1927.

    गायत्री गायतेः स्मुतिकर्मणः।
24. गायत्री त्रायते यस्मात् गायत्री तेन गायते-*Skada Puranam,* 8.59, Nag Publishers.

    यो वै प्राण अस्या या गायत्री - *ŚB*, 9.3.5.15.
25. *ŚB,* 94.8.15.7.
26. *BṛhU,* 5.14.4; *Eighteen Principal Upanisads,* Ed. : V.P. Limaye and R.D. Vadekar.

2

Concept of Gāyatrī in the Vedic Literature

Āryan ancestors were not only the framers of the first settled society but also created the most ancient literary works, the *Vedas*. The *Vedas* consist of four kinds of compilations *viz.*, the *Samhitās*, the *Brāhmaṇas*, the *Āraṇyakas* and the *Upaniṣads*. The *mantras*, revealed by those forefathers were collected in well defined disciplines and had been compiled under four titles *i.e.*, *Ṛk*, *Yajus*, *Sāman* and *Atharvan*. The *mantras*, recited all over India by the elites are found having some variations according to their times and locality.

The seers of the *Vedas* were all aware of the relation between human being and the rest of the universe or the nature. They perceived universal laws, practices and their concordances. They defined moral laws, meritorious works, virtues, righteousness, and destinations of life in the form of *Vargas*, that is why Maxmüller, a famous and learned scholar of 19th century describes his observations about them as "the fathers of most transparent methodologies, the genuine inventors of very subtle philosophies, the first workers in the construction of our fundamental concepts, the oldest ancestors that framed our first words and the most ancient poets of our thoughts.[1]

So the *Vedas* from the remote past to the modern age have miraculous power to influence human life and are therefore considered having eternal value.

The vedic religion, as it is commonly understood was a religion dominated by the cult of sacrifices. It was a sacredotal religion and it constituted the *Summum Bonum* of all the activities of the vedic society. The vedic hymns, are the prayers, addressed by the seers to the deities. various natural phenomena deified indicate a creative urge in the hearts of the sages. Apart from their lyrical character the hymns indicate the sort of intellectual activities flowing on the soil of the *Sapta-sindhu* for understanding the reality behind those phenomena. Though the hymns are mainly invocations to the gods, they represent the endeavour of the seers of the *Vedas* to comprehend the truth behind the regular recurrence of the natural phenomena.

The Vedic religion is characterised by the pre-eminence of male-gods where the female divinities may be said to be almost conspicuous by their absence or unimportance. The anthropologists and sociologists may say that, this is mainly due to the then prevailing patriarchal system in Indo-*Āryan* society. The female deities who made their appearance and were given secondary place are mainly Aditi, Pṛthvī, Sarasvatī and Rātrī. The female divinities in Vedic mythology may be broadly divided into three main groups. Benevolent, Malevolent and Abstract.[2]

The divinities of the benevolent nature mostly belong to the solar class. They are connected with Viṣṇu who is of the post-vedic and *purāṇic* literature and is regarded as a Sun-god.

The deities of malevolent nature on the other hand, came to be associated with Śiva, a god of Pre-*Aryan* time and connected with phallus-worship and fertility cult.

The abstract divinities, either remain aloof or have been artificially brought into contact with Pārvatī of the Rudra-group.

Genesis

The genesis of the solar female divinities, like their male counter-parts, ought to be sought in the eastern firmament every morning, which is the source of life. The Sun, the generator of life in the universe appears again and again in the east. In their deep pondering over the mysteries of the universe, the vedic seers derived a cue from this ever-recurring phenomenon of the eastern horizon. The Sun who is vivifying force, infuses and stimulates life in all beings. The physical Sun, however, did not appeal to the sound and deep thinking and brilliant imagination of vedic poets for long. They soon realised that there must have been some power, behind the Sun which causes him to rise and set every morning and evening and, which regulates his course.

It is probably at this stage that the concept of *Aditi* emerged especially due to the over-whelming and the very popular cult of the mother-goddess in the region of *Sapta-sindhu.* Besides, their attention must have also been drawn towards the procreative nature of the earthly women and there was evolved the concept of *Aditi*, endowed with motherhood. She is the mother of all Adityas. She is said to receive refulgent Agni in her womb. A very close connection of *Aditi* with *Ṛta* may also suggest her solar nature. *Ṛta*, too is said to have its source in the eastern direction. (*ṚV*, 10.68.4).

Like other female deities in *ṚV*, namely Pṛthvī, Sarasvatī and Rātrī have been earlier discussed.

The goddess Gāyatrī or Sāvitrī has been delineated as belonging to the solar-divinity (Savitṛ). The forms of Gāyatrī namely, Brhāmī , Sāvitrī and Sarasvatī represent respectively three junctions of the Sun, in the morning, at noon and in the evening. They are said to follow the course of the Sun diligently.[3]

She is described as a luminous, lustrous and bright divinity[4]. The close nexus between Gāyatrī on one hand with Sāvitrī and Agni on the other hand also testifies to the fact that Gāyatrī belongs to the solar class. The various aspects of this Gāyatrī are discussed in the ensuing pages.

The *Mantra* is as :

तत्सवितुर्वरेण्यं भर्गो देवस्य धीमहि। धियो यो नः प्रचोदयात्।।

This *Mantra* occurs not only in *RV* (3.62.10) but also in *YV* (3.6.3). *SV* (2.81.2), *VS* (3.35, 22.9, 36.3), *TS* (1.56.4, 8.4, 4.1.1.1), *MS*(4.10.3, 149.14), *MU* (6.7.34-38), *AB* (4.32.2, 5.5.6, 1.3.8), *BṛhU* (6.3, 6-7) and *GRU*. Such frequent use of *Sāvitrī Mantra* signifies deep concern with natural religion in India or in vedic thought. Such interpretations of this *mantra* are elucidated in many texts of the vedic literature.

Gāyatrī is also the name of the metre in which *Gāyatrī-mantra* was revealed to Viśvāmitra. So it is pertinent to discuss first, *Gāyatrī* as a metre, than Gāyatrī as a *mantra* and Gāyatrī as a divinity, in the vedic literature.

Gāyatrī as a Metre (*Chandas*) and its Application

The text of the *Vedas* is a reflection of the intellectual activity of the ancient people of India. A long interval might have elapsed between the composition and compilation of these hymns, as it was gradual built up of ideas of those people. Maxmüller divides the *Samhita* period into two phases *i.e.* the *chandas* (Metre) period and the *Mantra* period. The hymns were composed in the *chandas,* which is a particular way of composition. The pure emotions have explored themselves in songs and thus a creative poetry began. The *mantras* are *Ṛks*, used for praising different divinities and also constitute the body of them. *Ṛks* must have *pādas,* which help us in undertaking them and *pādas* must have *chandas* such as Gāyatrī, Uṣṇik, Anuṣtup, Bṛhatī, Paṅkti, Triṣtup and Jagatī. One cannot study the *Vedas* or perform vedic rituals without sufficient knowledge of *chandas Ṛsis* are the seers of the *mantras* (ऋषयो मन्त्रद्रष्टार:). This revelation is always associated with some appropriate *chandas.*

Now a few words about *chandas* particularly, as we find in the *Vedas,* may be hinted here. *Chandas* (metres) is defined in various ways. It is the support of the *Vedas,* the very feet (छन्द: पादौ तु वेदस्य)-*Paṇinīya Śiksā,* 41.

Chandas is also defined as a covering - छदांसि छादनात् - (*Nir*, VIII, 3.11). To understand the *mantra*, the cover concealing it should be removed. This can be done only with the knowledge of *chandas.* The deities are covered by *mantras* and the *mantras* are covered by the *chandas.*

Again *chandas* is supposed to strengthen the meaning of the *mantra*. It gives life and joy - छन्दयति आह्लादयतीति छन्द: (*Amarakosa,* 3.20).

Chandas is the combination of number of letters in the *mantra.* छन्दोऽक्षरसंख्यावच्छेदकमुच्यते - (*Atharva Bṛhat Sarvanukramaṇikā*).

यदक्षरपरिमाणं तच्छन्द: (*Ṛk Sarvānukramaṇikā* 2.6). चतुर्विंशत्यक्षरादीनि चतुरुत्तराणि गायत्र्यादीनि छन्दांसि। (*Yujurveda Sarvānukramaṇikā,* Ch. V.)[5]

It starts with twenty-four letters in the *Gāyatrī Mantra* and by adding four letters successively to this we get other *chandas*. Generally, the number of letters, linked in a particular way and constituting the *mantra* decides the greatness of the *mantra*. But Gāyatrī is a *mantra* for invocation; it is a metre, which has become great with just eight letters in a foot and with three feet (अष्टाक्षरा त्रिपदा गायत्री). It removes ignorance and reveal the truth. The use of the *mantra* with a particular *chandas* in a vedic rituals depends upon the mental composition of a person who is performing the ritual. *AV* starts with the *mantras* in Gāyatrī metre. Many *Ṛks* in *ṚV* are included in the *SV*m and are chanted musically. These *Ṛks* are in Gāyatrī metre. गायन्ति त्वा गायत्रिणः (*Ṛk-Samhitā*, 1.10.1), which means "O Indra! *Ṛtviks,* who chant the *Rks* in the Gāyatrī metre are chanting *Sāma*-Vedic hymns.

The *Ṛks* in Gāyatrī *chandas* are prescribed for a *brāhmaṇa,* whereas there are *ṛks* in Triṣtup for a *ksatriya,* and those in Jagatī are for a *Vaiśya.* The prescription of different chandas for different persons is due to the difference in their aspirations. Gāyatrī *chandas* is prescribed for one with the highest aspiration for spiritual bliss. Triṣtup gives valour and energy while Jagatī gives cattle and wealth. Gāyatrī is said to be the mother of all *chandas* (छन्दसां माता).

In *ṚV*, the Gāyatrī metre has been celebrated as the foremost among all the metres.[6] The poet exhorts the singers to sing a song in the Gāyatrī metre.

मिमीहि श्लोकमास्ये पर्जन्य इव ततनः, गाय गायत्रमुक्थ्यम्।
(*ṚV*, 1.38.14)

"Form in thy mouth the hymn of praise expand thee like a rainy cloud. Sing forth thee method eulogy." Gāyatrī excels in majesty and vigour as stated –

गायत्रस्य समिधस्तिस्र आहुस्ततो मह्ना प्ररिरियेमहित्वा। (*ṚV* - 1.64.25)

It is said that she permits all other metres.

कथं गायत्री त्रिवृतं व्यापि कथं विष्टुप् पञ्चदशेन कल्पते
त्रयस्त्रिंशेन जगती कथमनुष्टुप् कथमेकविंशः। (*AV*. 8.9.20)

All other metres are obtained by adding four syllables to the Gāyatrī metre.

सप्तच्छदांसि चतुरुतराण्यन्यां अन्यसिमन्य अध्यर्पितानि। (*AV.* 8.9.19.)

According to *ŚB* (4.3.2.10), it is Gāyatrī alone, who when increased, itself gets transformed into metres like Triṣtup and Jagatī. *ŚB* illustrates the episode in the form of an anecdote that, in the beginning, the metres consisted of four syllables only. The gods asked them to bring Soma from heaven. At first, Jagatī flew-up, but she came back without getting the same and she left behind three syllables. Then Triṣtup flew up and she too came back without Soma and left behind one syllable. Then, when Gāyatrī flew up for Soma, she returned with Soma and also brought those four syllables, those were left behind by Jagatī and Triṣtup. Therefore, Gāyatrī consists of eight syllables in a *pāda* and it is only Gāyatrī, which transforms itself into other metres by adding four syllables, step by step.

It is further said in *AB* (XIII - 28) that, when Gāyatrī gathered the four syllables, left by Triṣtup and Jagatī, there arose a quarrel among the three. Jagatī and Triṣtup claimed to Gāyatrī that she had taken their property and that she ought to return their syllables to them. Gāyatrī reconciled with the matter. Gāyatrī, by means of her eight syllables was able to support the morning, pressed the Soma and said to her "*let there be a portion for me in the mid-day pressing and I will join you.*" Triṣtup agreed and asked Gāyatrī to unite with her eight syllables. Gāyatrī did so and Triṣtup became eleven syllabled (8 + 3) and was able to support the mid-day-pressing. Similarly, Jagatī, having only one syllable was unable to support the evening's pressing. Gāyatrī said to her "*Let there be a portion for me in the evening's pressing and I will join you.*" Jagatī agreed and asked Gāyatrī to unite with her. Gāyatrī united with Jagatī and the latter, becoming a metre of twelve syllables (*i.e.,* eleven of Triṣtup, three of Triṣtup, which were gathered by Gāyatrī plus eight of the Gāyatrī, one syllable of her own), was able to support the evening pressing.

The same context is also seen in *TS.*[7] The main purpose of this legend is only to emphasize that it is the Gāyatrī, who runs through the Triṣtup and Jagatī. This is the reason for which Gāyatrī is regarded as having multiple forms as stated in *MS* (3.16.4) and *KS* (22.14).

Although Gāyatrī is the smallest among all the metres, she is the most glorious as referred to in *TS* (6.1.6.3-4) and in *SB* (1.3.4.6).

गायत्र्या गायत्रीमेवैत्समिन्धे सा गायत्री समिद्धाऽन्यानि छन्दांसि समिन्ध छन्दांसि समिद्धानि देवेभ्या यज्ञं व्यूहन्ति॥ (*ŚB*, 1.3.4.6)

TB says Gāyatrī alone represents all the metres.

अग्निना तपोऽन्वभवद् वा या ब्रह्म मणिनां रुपाणींन्द्रेण देवान् वातेन प्राणान्सूर्येण द्यां चन्द्रमसा नक्षत्राणि यमेन पितृन् राज्ञा मनुष्यान् फलेन नादेयान् अजगरेण सर्पान् व्याघ्रेणारण्यान् पशूक्रुछेयेनेन पतत्रिणो। यवेनैषधींन्यग्रोधेन वनस्पतींन्नुदुम्वरेणोज गायत्रिणा छन्दांसि त्रिवृता स्तोमान् ब्राह्मणेन वाचम्।

(*TS*, 7.3.14. I)

By means of Gāyatrī metre, the performer of a sacrifice ascends to the heaven.[8]

In connection with the laying down of the *chandasyā* bricks on the fifth layer of the fire-altar in the *Agnicayana,* and among them the Gāyatrī bricks (three in number) at the east of the spine of the altar, it is said that the Gāyatrī verses are the head of the fire-altar[9] and she is regarded as the first metre among all the metres.[10]

According to *RV,* Gāyatrī is described as a hawk or *Śyena.* This may be a bird or *Maruts* or be pre-eminent over other hawks, since with a wheel-less car. When the bird Gāyatrī frightening its guardians carried off Soma, it was flying so speedily as though it was alone on the vast path. It went rapidly with the sweet Soma plant and the hawks hence-forth acquired celebrity status in the world. The straight-forward hawk or Gāyatrī, conveying the some plant from long distance attended by the gods brought the adorable exhilarating soma, having taken it from that lofty heaven.

According to Macdonell, the word *Śyena,* the name in the *RV*[11] is a strong bird of prey, most probably eagle, it seems to mean the falcon or hawk. It is the swiftest of birds and a source of terror to smaller birds. It is the strongest of all and even attacks herds. This strongest bird or hawk brings soma from heaven. (Macdonell, A and Berriedale Keith; *Vedic Index of Names and Subjects,* Vol. II, MLBD, 1958).

The story as told in *TS* is slightly different from as it is described in *RV.* Once Kadru and Suparṇī had a contest as to who was more beautiful. Kadru managed to win and made the vanquished Suparṇī her slave. Kadru told Suparṇī that there was soma in the third part of the heaven. She would get her freedom if soma would be brought to her (Kadru). Kadru is, this earth. Suparṇī is the middle region. *Chandas* (metres) are Suparṇī's children. Suparṇī told her children that they should get soma for Kadru, so that she might get her freedom. Then fourteen-lettered Jagatī-metre flew to the skies, but was unable to get soma. Jagatī lost two letters, but got the sacrificial animals. This is the reason that Jagatī metre is prescribed for the *Vaiśyas* in sacrifices. They get cattle and wealth by means of doing this.

The Triṣtup metre, with thirteen letters flew to the sky. It could not procure soma. It lost two letters. But it returned with sacrificial fees (दक्षिणा) and articles required for *tapas*.

Then four-lettered Gāyatrī flew with a goat in the form of light. This goat helped Gāyatrī to get the soma. Gāyatrī brought the soma and while returning, brought the four (2 + 2) letters, those were left behind by its predecessors. Gāyatrī added these four letters to itself and became eight-lettered *chandas*. This is the reason that Gāyatrī became the prominent even though it had only the minimum number of letters for its *chandas*. Bringing Soma to help a sacrifice is considered as a great act.

It is said in the *ŚB* that Gāyatrī has nine letters.[12] One is Praṇava (ओं). The remaining eight forms the Gāyatrī. In the entire sacrifice, Gāyatrī is the most important one.

> शिरो वै यज्ञस्यातिथ्यं नवाक्षरा वै गायत्री अष्टौ तानि यान्यन्वाह प्रणवो नवमः पूर्वार्धो वै यज्ञस्य गायत्री।

While bringing the Soma, Gāyatrī brought in the grip of its feet two *savanas* of soma, whereas, it brought one soma in its mouth. It drank the soma, brought in its mouth. Soma, which was brought by Gāyatrī in its right-foot, became *Prātas-savana* and Gāyatrī is established in this. There are similar stories in *AB*.

The eagle that is reffered to in the stories is Gāyatrī. Soma may be taken to mean the effulgence of Āditya. Āditya is the *Paramātman*. Gāyatrī is Agni. That is why, for us Agni is important for a sacrifice so is Gāyatrī (गायत्री वा अग्निः गायत्रोऽग्निः, अग्निर्वै गायत्री गायत्रमग्नेश्छन्दः - *SB*, 6.1.3-19). Gāyatrī as Agni brought the soma. So it helped the performance of the sacrifice. If soma is considered as a symbol for the effulgence of Āditya, this episode of Gāyatrī's bringing soma may mean that through Gāyatrī alone, we can realise Āditya or *Brahman*. If soma is considered as an article of worship in a sacrifice, then the episode means Gāyatrī is the direct means for realisation and also the important means for the completion of the *Yajña* or sacrifice, which leads to realisation.[13] With the help of the commentary of Sāyaṇa, one can go through the body of the vedic literature and come to correct conclusions as regards the meaning of the terms, Agni, Śyena (eagle), Suparṇa (*Paramātman*), Āditya and Gāyatrī.[14]

Explaining the Superiority of Gāyatrī over other metres *ŚB* (8.2.3.9, 14) says–when Prajāpati was relaxing, the cattle becane metres and deserted him. Gāyatrī as a metre overtook them all by her vigour and quickness and so Prajāpati in the form of the Gāyatrī and by the dint of his vigour it overtook these cattle.

Once, when the gods and the *asuras* were in conflict, Gāyatrī snatched their force, might, power, strength, offspring and cattle and remained away. The gods and the *asuras* became feeble. The gods eulogized her 'Thou art force, thou art strength, thou art might, thou art blazing, thou art the home of the gods, thou art all, thou art everything, thou art of every life, the overcoming.[15] She was pleased and returned to them their strength, off spring, cattle etc.

AĀ states that Gāyatrī is like the head in the body. It is the greatest among all *chandas*.

अथातः शिरः तद् गायत्रीषु भवत्यग्रं वै छन्दसां गायत्यग्रमङ्गानां शिरः।

According to *JB* (2.13), Gāyatrī is the mouth of all the metres.

As Gāyatrī is the base and all the other metres have their structures built there on, Gāyatrī has been called as the mother of all metres in the *AĀ* Passage (x. 4-1).

इतरेषां छन्दसामस्यैव चतुश्यतुरक्षराद्दिकयम् तत्तच्छन्दोऽभिः प्रतिमिमीते- Sāyaṇācharya says 'The structural form of each one of the other metres is fashioned after this (*i.e.,* Gāyatrī) by the recurring addition in each case of four letters'. It is thus-

Gāyatrī (8×3)	=	24 letters.
Uṣṇik (24+4)	=	28 letters.

Anuṣṭup (24+4+4)	=	32 letters.
Bṛhatī (24+4+4+4)	=	36 letters.
Paṇkti (24+4+4+4+4)	=	40 letters.
Triṣtup (24+4+4+4+4+4)	=	44 letters.
Jagatī (24+4+4+4+4+4+4)	=	48 letters.

Since all other metres are derived from Gāyatrī it is the first and foremost of all metres in the fullest sense.

All the other metres can confer only temporal benefits. Gāyatrī alone can lead to the attainment of that eternal wealth called the *Brahman*. There in, lies the unique potency and greatness of Gāyatrī. The difference between Gāyatrī and the other metres is explained clearly in many passages. The *Pra-u-ga Śāstra* passage in *AĀ* is one of the such passages.

The question which arises there is that which one of the metres is to be resorted to the recitation of the *Pra-u-ga-Śāstra.* The unique merit of Gāyatrī is explained considerably in detail to answer to this inquiry. The Gāyatrī metre is replete with the almighty vigour and the resplendent effulgence of the *Brahman* Himself. In this context, we can not say that the other metres are useless. Those have their own value and importance. If the '*Pra-u-ga-Śāstra*' is recited by the performer of the sacrifice in the Uṣnik metre which has the nature of the vital principle, he will acquire longevity. But if this *śāstra* is composed in the vigorous Anuṣṭup metre, then the sacrificer, who recites, acquires vigour. If the *śāstra* is composed in the wealth giving Bṛhatī metre, the sacrificer gains great wealth. Similarly, the Paṅki metre confers food, the Triṣṭup confers physical might and the Jagatī metre confers live-stock.

Thus all the metres are undoubtedly beneficial. Yet all the forms of wealth like food are of transient by nature and value. Gāyatrī, on the contrary, has the nature of the *Brahman* himself. Hence, it is only if the *Pra-u-ga-Śāstra* composed in the Gāyatrī metre is recited at the sacrifice that the sacrificer will be able to realise the *Brahman.* Such is the unequivocal declaration made in this *AĀ* passage.

Gāyatri alone is chanted for *Prātas-savana* (morning libation). Where as Triṣtup with Gāyatrī and other metres are chanted for

Mādhyandina-savana (mid-day libation) and Jagatī with Gāyatrī and other metres is chanted for evening libation (Tṛtīya). This accounts for Gāyatrī pervading all the three *Savanas*[16] united with the *Sāman,* the *Sāman* with the heaven, heaven with Sūrya, Sūrya with rays, rays with the rain, the rain with herbs and trees, and trees with animals, animals with work, work with austerity, austerity with truth, truth with *Brahman,* the *Brahman* with the *Brāhmaṇa,* and the *Brāhmaṇa* with the vow.

It may be pointed out that the deification of Gāyatrī has been based on her solar character. The sun symbolizes the cosmic vital force, '*prāṇa*' and it is the sun, who permeates in all living organism. Sāvitrī does the same.

According to *TS* (5.4.10.4), (6.1.27), (7.3.22) Gāyatrī has eight letters in each *pada*.

किमष्टमेनेत्दष्टाक्षरां गायत्रीमिति किं नवमेनेति त्रिवृतं... (*TS*. 7.3.2.2)

Yet another explanation is given in the "*Female Divinities in Hindu Mythology and Ritual*" under the context of Gāyatrī - Sāvitrī. According to it, Prajāpati conquered this universe by means of the three-fold knowledge (*Vedas*). He thought that if other gods also performed sacrifices by means of that three-fold knowledge, they would obtain the victory, which was of him. He took out the three-fold knowledge. By muttering *bhūs* he took the shape of *RV*, that becomes this earth. The shape of it, which streamed forth became Agni. He uttered *bhuvas* and thereby he took out the shape of *YV*. That becomes this mid-region. The shape of it, which streamed from became *Vāyu*. He uttered *svaḥ* and thereby he took out the shape of the *SV*. That became founder sky. The shape of it, which streamed forth became Āditya. Now, there was one syllable that was not able to take out the shape, is *AUM*. They also represent three *Vedas,* the first *pāda* of Gāyatrī is the *RV*, the second *pāda* is the *YV*, and the third *pāda* is the *SV*.[17]

If the *Vyāhṛtis*[18] are added to it, Gāyatrī becomes four - footed.[19] These four-feet of Gāyatrī are presided over by Viranci, Viṣṇu, Rudra and Īśa respectively. Explaining the connection of the three *Vedas* with the three feet of Gāyatrī, *GB* says that Savitṛ (of the first pada of Gāyatrī) united with *ṛk*, the *ṛk* with the earth, the earth with Agni, Agni with prosperity, prosperity with woman, woman with pairing, pairing with offspring, offspring with work, work with austerity, austerity with truth, truth with *Brahman* and the *Brahman* with the vow.

Similarly, Savitṛ (of the second *pada* of Gāyatrī) united with the *Yajus*, the *Yajus* with the mid-region, mid-region with Vāyu, Vāyu with cloud, cloud with rain, rain with herbs and trees, herbs and trees with animals, animals with work, work with austerity, austerity with truth, truth with the *Brahman,* the *Brahman* with the *Brāhmaṇa* and the *Brāhmaṇa* with the vow.[20]

Like wise, Sāvitrī is of the third *pāda* of Gāyatrī. It is also said that by employing Gāyatri in the three *Trirātra*-rites, the sacrifice is, as it were, started, established and concluded with splendour, or eye (*caksu*) is, as it were put in the beginning, in the middle and at the end.[21]

This three-fold connection of Gāyatrī with the three pressings and *trirātra*-rites has probably risen in the post-vedic literature, to the concept of three Gāyatrī's belonging to the three junctions of the Sun *i.e.,* the morning, the mid-day and the evening. *SkP, Āvantya Khanda* and *Revā Khanda* also said that Gāyatrī is known as Gāyatrī in the morning in the eastern direction; she is known as Sāvitrī at the noon in the mid-sky, and she is known as Sarasvatī in the evening the west. The three Gāyatrīs are also known as Brāhmi, Māhesvarī and Vaiṣṇavi respectively.

According to *RV* the three-fold character of Gāyatrī is also employed in explaining the three *padas* of Gāyatrī : गायत्रस्य समिध स्तिस्र आहु – स्ततो महना प्ररिरिदे महित्वा. – (*RV*, 1.164.25) mentions that Gāyatrī has three fuel sticks.

The three feet of Gāyatrī are also said to represent the three worlds.

गायत्रीमनुवाककककयामन्वाह त्रिपदा वै गायत्री त्रय इमे लोका...

(*SB*, 11.2.2.1)

It has been pointed out that Gāyatrī is associated with the three pressing in the soma-sacrifice. In the same way, Gāyatrī is connected with the *trirātra*-rite of the *dvādasāha.*

According to *TāṇḍB*[22] the first *trirātra*-rite has Gāyatrī at the beginning, the second *trirātra* has Gāyatrī in the middle, and the third *trirātra* has Gāyatrī at the end. The three *trirātra* represent respectively Agni, Vāyu and Sūrya. It is further said that because the first *trirātra* has Gāyatrī at the beginning, therefore Agni goes upward, the second *trirātra* has Gāyatrī in the middle, hence Vāyu blows horizontally, and the third *trirātra* has Gāyatrī at the end, therefore Sūrya sends its rays downwards.[23]

The metres of the morning pressing are (*i*) Gāyatrī, (*ii*) Triṣtup and (*iii*) Jagatī are in ascending order. The metres of the mid-day pressing are Jagatī, Gāyatrī and Triṣtup *i.e.,* in the middle traverse and the metres of the third pressing are Triṣtup, Jagatī and Gāyatrī in the descending order. In other words, in the first pressing, Gāyatrī is at the beginning, in the second pressing, she is in the middle and in the third pressing she is at the end.

AA, (3.13) says that Prajāpati allotted to the Gods for the sacrifice the metres in different portions. He assigned the Gāyatrī metre to Agni and the Vasus at the morning pressing. Vasus are regarded as *prāṇa*, they are connected with the morning-pressing.[24]

JUB (1.4.4.1-4) has the following legend that Prajāpati created Gods and Death. Gods were afraid of death. They approached Prajāpati. Prajāpati asked them to bring the metres and enter into them. The Vasus brought Gāyatrī. They entered into her, and thus they were saved from death. There are eight Vasus; those are the eight syllables of Gāyatrī (*IS.* 3.8.9.7).

There are many passages in the *Upaniṣads* dealing with *Gāyatrī-chandas.* The *ChU* and the *BṛhU* deal with the philosophy of Gāyatrī in various ways.

देवा वै मृत्योर्बिभ्यतस्त्रयीं विद्यां प्रविशंस्ते छन्दोभिराच्छादयन् यदेभिराच्छायन् स्तच्छन्दसां छन्दत्वम्। (*ChU,* 1.4.2) This *Mantra* speaks of the *chandas* in general. *Devas* were afraid of death. The knowledge of the three *Vedas* embodied as *trayī-vidyā* covered them with *chandas* and thus hid them from death. The three-feet (*padas*) of Gāyatrī speaks of lower knowledge (अपरतत्त्व), and the fourth foot speaks of the transcendental truth (परतत्त्व).[25]

भूमिरन्तरिक्षं द्यौरित्यष्टावक्षराणि। अष्टाक्षरं ह वा एकं गायतयै पदं। एतदुहैवास्या एतदेवं पदं वेद। (*BrhU.* 5.14.1). भूमि, अन्तरिक्ष and द्यौ: are the eight letters. This is the first *pāda* of *Gāyatrī*. One who knows this truth earns the wealth of the three worlds.

ऋचो यजुङ्षि सामानि इत्यष्टावक्षराणि। अष्टाक्षरं ह वा एकं गायत्र्यै पदं। एतदुहैवास्या एतत्। स यावतीयं त्रयी विद्या तावद्ध जयति योऽस्यां एतदेतं पदं वेद. (*BrU,* 6.14.2).

ऋच: (*Ṛk*) यजूङ्षि (*Yajus*) सामानि (*Sāmāni*) are the eight letters, which form the second *pada* of Gāyatrī. One who knows this truth gets all the knowledge in the three *Vedas*.

प्राणोऽपानो व्यान इत्यष्टावक्षराणि. अष्टाक्षरं वा एकं गायत्र्यै पदं...।
(*BrU*, 6.14.3)

Prāṇa, Apāna and *Vyāna* are the eight syllables of the third *pada* of Gāyatrī. One, who knows this truth wins the living beings. Āditya, who is self-effulgent, and who is seen by all the three worlds as such is the fourth *pada.*

सैषा गायत्री तस्मिंस्तुरीयें दर्शते पदे परोरजसि प्रतिष्ठिता। चक्षुर्वै सत्यं। चक्षुर्हिवै सत्यं... एवं वैषा गायत्र्यध्यात्मं प्रतिष्ठिता। (*BrU,* 5.14.4).

Gāyatrī is established in the fourth *pāda*, which is seen and is called as परोरजस्। Gāyatrī is established in truth.

तां हैतमेके सावित्रीमनुष्टभमन्वाहु:. वागमनुष्टुप्..... गायत्रीमेव सावित्रीमनुब्रूयात्।
(*BrU*, 5.14.5)

Vāk (expression/speech) could be in the form of अनुष्टुप् metre and also in Gāyatrī metre. One should instruct Sāvitrī in Gāyatrī metre. So, one who knows this truth even if he accepts a lot of wealth, it will not be equal with one *pāda* of Gāyatrī.

Śri Śankara says – तस्माद् गायत्री एवं प्रकारोपास्या। So, one should get the full realisation of Gāyatrī only by means of meditation.

एतं हैनैवंविद् यद्यपि बहविव कुरुते सर्वमेवैत्संप्साय शुद्धः पूतोऽजरोऽमृत: संभवति। (*BrU,* 5.14.8)

One who knows this Gāyatrī fully, even if he happens to commit sinful acts, will be able to burn away the sins and becomes pure, undecaying, and immortal. However, the prominence, given to Gāyatrī is guided by three considerations.

(*i*) Gāyatrī (*chandas*) brought soma and gave it to gods. Soma is a very important material. Other metres could not bring the nector-like somas.

(*ii*) Gāyatrī absorbed the letters of other metres and pervaded all metres.

(*iii*) Gāyatrī is used for all the three *savanas*. It is like a mother essential for all those who aspire for spiritual life like *Brāhmaṇas*. The knowledge of *Brahman* is possible only through Gāyatrī.

Gāyatrī as a *chanda*, is very important in a sacrifice and sacrifice itself is identified with Prajāpati. So Gāyatrī is an effective means to acquire the knowledge of *Brahman*. But the question arises that how do we say Gāyatrī is *Brāhaman?* Śri Śankara takes up this question and states the view in *Brahma-sūtra Sānkara Bhāṣya* (1-i-25).

ChU says that the Gāyatrī metre is everything in this world.

गायत्री वा इदं सर्वं भूतं यदिदं कस्य वाग्वै–गायत्री वाग्वा इदं सर्वं भूतं गायति च त्रायते। (*ChU*, 3.12.1)

The word '*vai*' is used for emphasis on '*sarvam*' (all), *bhūtam*; this totality of living things, moving or not moving, all that is Gāyatrī itself. *ChU* presents Gāyatrī as Vāk (speech which is the source of Gāyatrī and which is of the nature of sound. Thus one is protected by speech being forbidden from all kinds of fear; the term Gāyatrī denotes *gāna* (singing) and *trāṇa* (protecting). As Gāyatrī is connected with beings through singing and protecting, the earth is similarly connected with beings because of their habitation therein, So Gāyatrī is earth.

या वै सा गायत्रीयं वाव सा सेयं पुथिव्यस्यां हीदं सर्वं भूतं प्रतिष्ठितमेतामेव नातिशीयते। (*ChU*, 3.12.2).

However, it may be concluded that *Brahman* is the essence of Gāyatrī. Gāyatrī is not merely an aggregate of letters. Letters can never be 'all this' (सर्वं भूतं), which is said in the context of Gāyatrī. *Brahman* is the cause and Gāyatrī is its effect. The cause and effect are not essentially different. This is made clear in *Brahman-sūtra* तदनन्यत्वमारम्भणशब्दादिभ्यः (2.1.14). *AA* (3.2.3) says that we should approach the cause through the effect which is tangible.

सर्वेषु भूतेषु एतमेव ब्रह्मेत्याचक्षते। स एष संवत्सरसमानश्वक्षुर्मयः श्रोत्रमयश्छन्दोमयो मनोमयो वाङ्मय आत्मा स एवमेतं..... शंसति।

Eyes, ears and metres etc. are the effects of the casual substance, *Brahman*. This *Brahman* should be meditated upon (उपासनं) in the form of metre.

In *MNU* it is stated that may the boon confirming divine Gāyatrī come to us in order to instruct about the imperishable *Brahman,* who is determined by the *Vedanta.* May Gāyatrī, the mother of the metres, favour us with the supreme *Brahman.*

आयातु वरदा देवी अखरं ब्रह्म सम्मितम्।
गायत्री छन्दसां मातेदं ब्रह्म जुषस्व न।। (*MNU,* 34.1)

The metres, playing such an important part in the mysticism of ritual, consider the divine beings. They even receive oblations that mythology concerns itself with them, especially with the Gāyatrī, which in the form of a bird fetches the soma from heaven that they are created like other beings by Prajāpati.[26]

All these indicate the great age of these metres, which were thought to have originated since times immemorial. Thus the age of metres is also of the hymns themselves.[27] The significance of *Gāyatrī-Mantra* will be discussed in a separately.

Birth of Gāyatrī

Gāyatrī has a noble birth. The *Brāhmaṇa* texts give details about the birth of Gāyatrī.

Setting forth the sequential process of the creation *ŚB* (6.1.31-5) and (6.1.3.6) says that, in the beginning Prajāpati alone desired to reproduce himself. Then he toiled, practised austerity or became heated. From that heated person the water was created.

The water said "what is to become of us? Ye shall be heated foam. Then then foam is heated and when it floats on the water, covering it and when one beats upon it, becomes clay.

They clay said "what is to become of me? Thou shalt be heated! he said. It was heated and produced sand. For this clay becomes indeed heated when they plough it, and if only they plough very fine then it becomes, as it were, sandy.

From the sand he created the pebble. When sand finally indeed becomes a pebble then from the pebble it was stone, from the stone metal ore, whence from stone they smelt ore. Whence ore much smelted comes, as it were, to have the appearance of gold. Now whatever Prajāpati created was as if flowing (*akṣarat-vksarttaīí*), thus a syllable *akṣara* was born, and as it flowed eight times, the octo-syllable Gāyatrī was produced.

The *GRU*, (p. 405) states that '*Ka*' is the name of *Svayambhū-puruṣa*. He twisted his fingers, there from water was produced; from the water foam and from the foam bubble was produced. That bubble became the mundane egg. From that egg *Brahma was born*. Vāyu came forth from *Brahma*. From Vāyu, Agni came forth. *Oṁkāra* came forth from Agni. From *Omkāra* were produced the *Vyāhṛtis* and from the *Vyahṛtis* was produced the Gāyatrī.[28]

Similarly the *GChU*, (p. 69) says that in the beginning there was water, Prajāpati performed penance, he saw *Omkāra*, from *Omkāra* were produced the *Vyahṛtis*, from the *Vyahṛtis* was produced the Gāyatrī.

According to *TS*, (7.1.1.4) Prajāpati measured out the *Trivṛt Sāman* from his mouth with a view to having progeny. First, Agni among the gods, Gāyatrī among the metres, *Rathantara* among the *Sāmans*, *Brāhmaṇa* among men and the goat among the cattles were created. Agni etc. are the chief in their respective categories, for they were produced from the mouth of Prajāpti.

प्रजापतिरकामयत प्र जायेयेति स मुखतस्त्रिवृतं निरमिमीत तमग्निर्देवताऽन्वसृजयत गायत्री छन्दो रथन्तर.... साम ब्राह्मणो मनुष्याणामजः पशूनां तस्मात् ते मुख्या मुख्यतोऽसृज्यन्तो। (*TS* 7.1.1.4)

TāṇḍB, (6.1.6) and *JB*, (1.68) state that Prajāpati wished : 'May I create the sacrifice'. Out of his mouth, he created the nine-fold (nine-versed) '*stoma*'; along with it, there came in to existence Gāyatrī as the first among the metres; Agni the first among the deities; *Brāhmaṇa* as the first among men; the Spring as the first among the seasons, and so on. Therefore, Gāyatrī is the mouth of the metres, Agni of deities, *Brāhmaṇa* of men, and the Spring of the seasons.

सोऽकामयत यज्ञ सृज्येति स मुख्यत एवं त्रिवृतमसृजत तं गायत्रीच्छन्दोऽन्व-सृज्यताऽग्निर्देवता ब्राह्मणो मनुष्यो व्यसन्त ऋतुस्तस्मात् त्रिवृत्स्तोमानां मुखं गायत्री... व्वीर्य्यङ्करोति मुखतो हि सृष्टः। (*TanB*, 6.1.6)

In another context in the birth of Gāyatrī it is also mentioned that Prajāpati, after creating *Brahma,* water, triple sciences, Agni, Aśva, Rāṣabha and Aja wished to generate the earth from the waters. He squeezed the mundane egg. The juice which flowed from it became a tortoise. He again toiled and practised austerity; foam was produced. Again he practiced penance and created clay, mud, saline soil, sand, gravel (pebble), rock ore, gold, plants, and trees. Then Prajāpati thought that this earth has become a proper foundation (*bhū*); hence the earth is called *bhūmi.* The earth thought herself to be quite perfect and out of joy, she sang; because she sang, she is called Gāyatrī.

The earth is identified with Gāyatrī in many references likely in *TS* (1.7.54), (5.2.1.1); *MS* (1.5.10); *KS* (19.1); *SB* (1.7.2.15), (4.3.4.9), (5.2.35); *TāṇḍB* (7.3.11). (14.14); *AA* (1.4.3), and *JB* (3.214).

With reference to *ŚB* (4.3.4.9) that, in *Agni-stoma* sacrifice the sacrificer offers with this Gāyatrī verse. *VS* (7.41) and उदुत्यं जातवेदसं देवं वूहन्ति केतवः दृशे विश्वाय सूर्यम् (*RV*, 1.50.1). The lights bear on high that divine knower of beings, Sūrya, that all may see him. For the Gāyatrī in this earth and she is a safe resting place, Hence he thereby stands firmly on his safe resting place.

स जुहोति। उदुत्यं जानवेदसं देवं व्यूहन्ति कतव. दुशे विश्वाय सूर्य्यं स्वाहेत्येतमा गायत्री वा इयं पृथिवी सेयं प्रतिष्ठा .... (*ŚB*, 4.3.4.9)

Though it is a cake on eight pot sheds the Gāyatrī consists of eight syllables and this earth is Gāyatrī as mentioned in *ŚB*, (5.2.35) with reference to *Ṛajasuya*-sacrifice.

ŚB (1.4.1.34) states that the gods and the *asuras* both sprang from Prajāpati and were contending for superiority over each other when they were thus vying with each other Gāyatrī stood between them. Gāyatrī was the same as this earth, and this earth indeed lay between them. Both of them knew that whoever were favoured by her would be victorious in the contest. Both parties then invited her secretly, to come to them. Agni acted as a messenger of the gods and she allowed Agni. However, it is said that she was not content with the earth and hence goes aloft to the sky (*AB*, 3.39).

Further it is also mentioned in *ŚB*, (8.1.1.5) that Prajāpati fashioned the breath (*Prāṇa*); from out of the breath he fashioned the spring season; and from out of the spring season he fashioned the Gāyatrī metre.

It is also found that she is said to have been born from the spring season as mentioned in *TS*, (4.3.21); *MS* (2.7.19); *KS*, (16.19), and also in *VS*, (13.54).

अयं पुरो भुवस्तस्य प्राणो भौवायनो वसन्तः प्राणायनो गायत्री वासन्ती गायत्र्यै गायत्रम् गायत्यादुपांशुरुपा ..... प्राणं गृहणामि प्रजाभ्यः।

Forms and Appearances of Gāyatrī

The vedic literature personified Gāyatrī not as a metre but celebrated it as a female divinity. Gāyatrī as a *mantra* occurs in the *Trayi i.e.,* in *RV* (3.62.10); *YV* (3.35-30), (2.36.3) and *SV* (13.3.2) that has been discussed in earlier. This *mantra* addressed to the god, Sun attained individuality in the later vedic literature and was the first deity, who played an important mythical role in it. Gāyatrī was just a metre, but the *brāhmaṇa* authors considered it to be not merely the mechanical arrangement of the syllables, but also a potential creativity.[29] Little account of the *brāhmaṇical* texts express the forms and appearance of Gāyatrī as a divinity.

AB (4.23) says that the Gāyatrī is possessed of wings, eyes, light and brilliance. According to *GB* (1.38.10) she is regarded as '*Jyotiṣ pakśā*' having wings of light as in *TB* -

गायत्री वा एतां ज्योतिः पक्षा मासते यदेतं द्वादशाहमष्टौ – मध्य उक्था..... ब्रह्मद्यमन्नमवि दीप्यमानः। (*TB*, 10.4.5)

गायत्रीं ज्योतिः पक्षा वेद ज्योतिषा भासा सुवर्गं लोकमेति .... स आत्मैषा वै गायत्री ज्योतिः पक्षा च एवं भासा स्वर्गलोकमेति। (*TS*, 7.2.9.2)

KS (34.8), (21.10), (22-6) also expresses this thing in equal manner.

In the *Rājasūya*-sacrifice, when the sacrificer figuratively ascends all the directions, Gāyatrī is invoked to protect him in the east as mentioned in *TS* (1.8.13.1) and *SB* (5.4.1.3).[30]

Gāyatrī has the fiercely brilliant lustre as mentioned in *TandB* (6.9.25) and (12.1.12).

दविद्युतती वै गायत्री परिष्टोभन्ती त्रिष्टुव्गवाशी जर्जगती त्रीणि रूपाणि समारभते त्रिरात्रस्याऽविस्रसाय। (*TandB*, 6.9.25)

दविद्युतत्या रुचेति वै गायत्र्या रुपं परिष्टोभन्त्येति त्रिष्टुभः कृपत्येनुष्टुभः सोमाः शुक्रा गवाशिर .... प्रतिपद्मभवति स्वेनैवैना स्त द्रुपेण समर्द्धयति।
(*TāṇḍB*, 12.1.12)

According to *GB* (1.5.15) Gāyatrī is light. The darkness of the night is evil. By means of Gāyatrī the gods smite away the evil, darkness.

Gāyatrī is vigour (*ŚB*, 1.9.1.17). As we discussed above it is said in *TāṇḍB* (12.1.12) that, she is fiercely brilliant. Gāyatrī envelops the three *triratras* by her splendour.

तेजसा वै गायत्री प्रथमं त्रिरात्रं दाधार पदैर्द्वितीयमक्षरैस्तृतीयम्।
(*TāṇḍB*, 10.5.3)

The frequent references to the association of Gāyatrī with the morning-pressing may also be deemed as emphasizing her luminous character as found in *TS* (3.2.9.1), (5.6.5.1), (6.4.5.1); *ŚB* (4.1.1.8), (4.3.2.8); *TāṇḍB* (9.7.2), *GB* (2.3.10) and *JB* (1.3.21).

This three-fold connection of Gāyatrī with the three pressings and three *trirātra*-rites has probably given rise, in the post-vedic literature, to the concept of three Gayatrīs belonging to the three junctions of the Sun, the morning, the midday and the evening as we find in *GRU*.

It is said in *GRU*, (p. 406) that Gāyatrī is known as Gāyatrī in the morning in the eastern direction. She is known as Sāvitrī at noon in the middle-sky, and she is known as Sarasvatī in the evening in the west. पूर्वायां भवतु गायत्री। मध्यमायां भवतु सावित्री। पश्चिमायां भवतु सरस्वती। The three Gāyatrīs are also known as Brahmī, Maheśvarī and Vaiṣṇavī respectively. The following is the description of the three Gāyatrīs.

Gāyatrī in the Morning known as Brāhmī

A young girl with red complexion like the morning Sun, red garment, red garland, and red sandal paste, has three heads and four hands, respectively bearing a *pāsa*, a goad, a rosary and a *kamaṇdalu*, mounting on a swan, is associated with *Brahmā* and the *ṚV* she with all these follows the track of the Sun, and is connected with the *bhūloka*.

पूर्वाह्णकालिका संन्ध्या गायत्री कुमारी रक्ता रक्तांङ्गी रक्तवासिनी रक्तगन्ध-माल्यानुलेपनी पाशांङ्कुशाक्षमाला कमण्डलुवरहस्ता हंसारूढा ब्रह्मदैवतया ऋग्वेदसहिता आदित्यपथगामिनी भूमण्डलवासिनी।

Gāyatrī in the Mid-day known as Sāvitri or Māheśvarī

A young woman with white complexion like moon of conch, white clothes, white garland, and white paste, two hands, bearing a trident and a *ḍamaru,* is associated with Rudra and the *YV*, also follows the path of the Sun, and represents *bhuvaḥ-loka.*

मध्याह्नकालिका सन्ध्या सावित्री युवती श्वेतांङ्गी श्वेतवासिनी श्वेतगन्धमाल्यानु-लेपनी त्रिशुलडमरुहस्ता बृषभारुढ़ा रुद्रदैवत्या यजुवेदसहिता आदित्यपथगामिनी भूवोलोके व्यवस्थिता।

Gāyatrī in the Evening known as Sarasvatī or Vaiṣṇavī

An old woman with black complexion, black dress, black garland, and black paste, four hands; left hand bearing a conch, one of the right hands, a disc, and a club and the fourth show in the *abhaya* pose, mounts on Garuḍa, is connected with Viṣṇu and the *SV*, also follows the path of the Sun and represents *svargaloka.*

सायं सन्ध्या सरस्वती बृद्धा कृष्णांङ्गी कृष्णवासिनी कृष्णगन्धमाल्यानुलेपना शङ्खचक्रगदाभयहस्ता गरुडारुढ़ा विष्णुदैवत्या सामवेदसहिता आदित्यपथगामिनी स्वर्गलोके व्यवस्थिता।

These three forms of Gāyatrī are said also to represent respectively, (*i*) Agni, (*ii*) Vāyu, (*iii*) Sūrya or (*i*) Āhavanīya, (*ii*) Gārhapatya, (*iii*) Dakśiṇāgni or (*i*) Ṛk, (*ii*) Yajus, (*iii*) Sāman or (*i*) Bhūh, (*ii*) Bhuvah, (*iii*) Svah or the three pressings; (*i*) Prātah, (*ii*) Madhyāhṇa, (*iii*) Sāyam or (*i*) Sattva, (*ii*) Rajas, (*iii*) Tamas or (*i*) Jāgrat, (*ii*) Svapna, (*iii*) Suṣupta or (*i*) Āditya, (*ii*) Rudra, (*iii*) Vasu or (*i*) Brahmā, (*ii*) Śankara, (*iii*) Viṣṇu or (*i*) Icchā, (*ii*) Jnāna, (*iii*) Kriyā.[31]

Gāyatrī as a Deity

The Vedic literature personified Gāyatrī not as a metre but celebrating it as a female divinity.

The three verses of the hymn *ṚV* (3.62 namely 10-12) of which the famous *Gāyatrī-mantra* forms a part, extol Savitṛ.

देवस्य सवितुर्वयं वाजयन्तः पुरंध्या भगस्य रातिमीमहे। (*RV*, 3.62.11)

With understanding, earnestly, of Savitṛ the god we crave our portion of prosperity.

देवं नरः सवितारं विप्रा यज्ञैः सुवृक्तिभिः नमस्यन्ति धियेषिता।
(*RV*, 3.62.12)

Men, singers worship Savitṛ the god with hymn and holy rites, urged by the impulse of their thoughts. In view of the popularity and sanctity of the *Vedas,* a conceptual mother of the *Vedas* '*vedamātṛ*' (*AV*, 19.7.1) is conceived as a deity in the *AV*. The *Veda* is the mother of all. She possesses the boon-giving power. She is invoked to fulfil all desires. She bestows long life, breath, progeny, cattle, fame, wealth and vedic splendour.

स्तुता मया वरदा वेदमाता प्रचोदयन्तम् पवमानी द्विजानाम्।
आयुः प्राणम् प्रजाम् पशुम् कीर्तिम् द्रविणम् ब्रह्मवर्चसम्। (*AV*, 19.7.1)

Hence, Gāyatrī is regarded as a luminous, lustrous and bright divinity. It is repeatedly said in different *brāhmaṇa-* texts like *TS*, (1.5.8.3), (3.2.9.3), (5.1.3.5), (5.1.3.81), (6.3.3.7), (4.3.27); *MS*, (3.2.6), (4.2.11); *GB*, (2.5); *AA* (1.1.3) and *JB*, (2.89), (3.110); *The TāndB,* (4.25) says that-

चतुर्विंशत्यक्षरा गायत्री तेजो ब्रह्मवर्चसंङ्गायत्री तेज एवं ब्रह्मवर्चसमारभ्य प्रयन्ति गायत्री तेज एव ब्रह्मवर्चसमवरुन्धे। (8.10.2)

In *VS* (38.18), it is mentioned that the divine light (*diyā suk*) of the *gharma* (a vessel used in the *pravargya* Ceremony) has entered into the Gāyatrī metre and has made it effulgent.

Gāyatrī is the lustre of the metres as described in *TāṇḍB* (13.7.2), (15.10.6).

ज्योतिर्वै गायत्री छन्दसां ज्योतिः .... ज्योतिरेव तत्सम्यक् सन्दधात्यपि ह पुत्रस्य पुत्रो ज्योतिष्मान् भवति। (*TāṇḍB,* 13.7.2)

गायत्री वै रथन्तरस्य योनि ...... रथन्तरं प्रतिष्ठापयति। (*TāṇḍB,* 15.10.6)

AV (8.9.14) portrays her as the bringer of heaven. She is prayed to protect the sacrificer. She yields all the sacrificer's wishes, and she is beseeched to fulfil the desires of the sacrificer as mentioned in *SB*. (4.2.4.21-22).

गायत्र्यै यज्ञो वै गायत्री द्वादश स्तोत्राणि द्वादश शस्त्राणि चतुर्विंशत्यक्षरा वै गायत्री .... यजमानाय सर्व्वान्निकामान्दोहाता इति। (*SB*, 4.2.4.21)

गोपयति अवनयति गायत्री मेवैतत्प्रस्रावयति .... यजमानाय सर्वान्निकामान्दोहाता इति। (*SB,* 4.2.4.22)

She produces offspring and cattle for the sacrificer. According to *TāṇḍB* she is the means of procreation.

तेजो ब्रह्मवर्च्चसं गायत्री तेज एव ब्रह्मवर्च्चसमवरुन्धे प्राणो गायत्री प्रजननं प्राणादेव गायत्र्याः प्रजायते। (*TāṇḍB*, 16.14.15)

प्राणो गायत्री प्रजननं प्राणादेव गायत्र्याः प्रजायते। (*TāṇḍB*. 19.5.9)

गायत्री सम्पद्यते तेजो ब्रह्मवर्च्चसं गायत्री तेज एव ब्रह्मवर्च्चसमवरुन्ध प्राणो गायत्री प्रजननं प्राणादेव गायत्र्याः प्रजायते। (*TāṇḍB,* 19.7.7)

माध्यन्दिनेन वै पवमानेन देवाः स्वर्गं .... स्वर्गस्यऽऽक्रान्त्यै चतुर्विंशत्यक्षरा गायत्री तेजो ब्रह्मवर्च्चसं गायत्री तेज एव ब्रह्मवर्च्चसमवरुन्धे प्राणो गायत्री प्रजननं प्राणादेव गायत्र्याः प्रजायते। (*TāṇḍB,* 19.11.9)

चतुर्विशं वर्हिष्यपवमानं भवयुत्तरस्याऽह्नश्चतुर्वित्यक्षरा गायत्री प्रजननं गायत्री प्रजात्यै। (*TāṇḍB*, 20.11.9)

चतुर्विंशाः पवमाना भवन्ति चतुर्विंशत्यक्षरा गायत्री प्रजननं गायत्री प्रजात्यै। (*TāṇḍB*, 21.9.4)

Gāyatrī who produces nectar in the heaven, is asked to bring the gods to the sacrifice, for, she knows them. Homage is paid to her in the *Aśvamedha.* (*KS*, 43.2, 51.1). The Gāyatrī verses are the head of the fire-alter (*SB* 8.6.2.3, 6, 10.2-2.1, 11.4.1.16). She is the bearer of the *havis,* offerings to the gods. (P 5.14.3).

व्वेदिरेव गायत्री तस्यै अष्टौ पुरस्तादाज्जयभागा स तक्षिणो .... पक्षै .... सैषा गायत्री हरिणी ज्योतिष्पक्षमा यजमान स्वर्गलोकमभिव्हनि। (*ŚB*, 11.4.1.16)

गायत्रीमनुवाककयामन्वाह। त्रिपदा वै गायत्री त्रय इमे लोका .... प्रत्यष्टापयन्। (11.2.2.1)

She is the mouth of the sacrifice as mentioned in *TS* (5.3.3.4), (6.3.3.7); *MS* (3.1.1); *KS* (8.8) and *TāṇḍB* (7.3.7). In the *Devikā* rites, offerings are made to the four lunar female divinities. Among them *Anumatī* is identified with Gāyatrī.

आत्मा वै यज्ञस्य पवमानो मुखं गायत्री प्राणो गायत्रं यद्गायत्र्यां गायत्रेण स्तुवन्ति मुखत एष तत्प्राणान् दधति।। (*TāṇḍB,* 7.3.7)

A few references in the vedic literature indicate the motherly aspect of Gāyatrī.[32] Gāyatrī is the womb of the immortal Sun (*AV*, 13.3.20).

Out of the Gāyatrī womb, Prajāpati created the *Pṛṣthas.*

प्रजापतिर्ता एतां गायत्रीं योनिमपश्यत्स आदीधीतास्माद्योनेः पृष्टानि सुजा इति। (*TāṇḍB,* 15.10.6)

She is also the womb of *Rathantara.*

गायत्री वै रथन्तरस्य योनिः स्वयमेव तद्योनौ रथन्तरं प्रतिष्ठापयति। (*TāṇḍB*, 15.10.6)

She forms a pair with Manas, Agni, Vāyu, Aditya, Moon, Day, Heat, Cloud, Lightning, Life, *Vedas* and *Yajña* in the forms of Vāk, earth, firmament, sky, constellation, night coolness, rain, thunder, food, metres and *Daksiṇā* respectively for the viable creation.[33]

Indeed, every letter of the Gāyatrī *Mantra* is regarded as a divinity. The following is the list of *Ṛsi, Devatā*, etc. of Gāyatrī *Mantra.*[34]

List of Ṛsi, Devatā, Chandas etc. Gāyatrī-Mantra

	Akśara	*Ṛsi*	*Chandas*	*Devatā*	*Śakti*	*Varṇa*
1.	Tat	Vāmadeva	Gāyatrī	Agni	Vāmadevī	Campaka
2.	Sa	Atri	Uṣṇik	Prajāpati	Priyā	Atasi
3.	Vi	Vaśiṣtha	Anuṣtup	Soma	Satyā	Vidruma
4.	Tu	Śukra	Vṛhatī	Īśāna	Viśvā	Sphātika
5.	Va	Kaṇva	Paṅkti	Savitṛ	Bhadravilāsinī	Padma
6.	Re	Parāśara	Triṣtubh	Āditya	Prabhāvatī	Āditya
7.	Ni	Viśvāmitra	Jagatī	Bṛhaṣpati	Jayā	Indu
8.	Yam	Kapila	Ati-jagatī	Maitrā-varuṇa	Śāmtā	Padma-patra
9.	Bha	Śaunaka	Śākkvarī	Bhaga	Kāmitā	Padmarāga
10.	rgo	Vājna-valkya	Ati-śākkvarī	Āryaman	Durgā	Indranila
11.	De	Bharadvāja	Dhṛti	Gaṇeśa	Sarasvatī	Muktā
12.	Va	Jāmadagni	Ati-dhṛti	Tvastṛ	Vidrumā	Kuṁkuma
13.	Sya	Goutama	Virāt	Puṣan	Viśāleśā	Anjana
14.	Dhi	Mudgala	Prastara	Indrāgni	Vyāpinī	Rakta
15.	Ma	Vedavyāsa	Paṅkti	Vāyu	Vimalā	Vaidurya
16.	Hi	Lomaśa	Kṛti	Vāmadeva	Tamopahārinī	Kśaudra
17.	Dhi	Agastya	Prakṛti	Maitrā-varuṇa	Sūkśmā	Haridrā
18.	Yo	Kauśika	Ākṛti	Viśvadevah	Viśvayonih	Kuṇda
19.	Yo	Vatsa	Vikṛti	Mātṛka	Jāyā	Dugdha
20.	Nah	Pulatsya	Samskṛti	Viṛṇu	Vaijnā	Ravi
21.	Pra	Manduka	Samskṛti	Vāsudeva	Padmamālyā	Śukapucha
22.	Co	Durvāsā	Samskṛti	Rudra	Parā	Ketakī
23.	Da	Nārada	Samskṛti	Kuvera	Sobhā	Mallikā
24.	Yat	Kaśyapa	Samskṛti	Aśvina	Bhadrā	Karavīra

An Assimilation

Gāyatrī as a divinity, does not play any important role in the *Śrauta* or *Gṛhya* ritual. The Gāyatrī *Mantra* is employed in the *Upanayana* Ceremony.[35] The *mantra,* Gāyatrī and the goddess, Gāyatrī are usually regarded as one entity and they are accorded worship as such. Gāyatrī is regarded as a supreme goddess who combines in her all gods and goddesses.

References

1. Joshi Mahādeva Nārāyana : *Gāyatrī in Ṛg Veda,* Roopa Publications, Dharwad, (2001), p. 1.
2. S.K. Lal : *Female Divinity in Vedic Mythology and Ritual,* p. 241.
3. *GRU,* p. 406, *SkP, Avanti Khanda, Revā Khanda,* 200 *Gāyatri Mantrārtha Bhāskara of Mithila Pandita,* Bahunananandana, Bombay, 1418.
4. *TS,* 1.5.8.3, 3.2.9.3, 5.1.3.5; *MS*, 3.2.6.3, 2.4; *AB*, 1.5; *GB,* 2.5.3, *AA*, 1.1.3; *JB*, 2.89.
5. References to the source are as given in Chandas in Silbamu in Telugu by Dr. P. Madhava Sharma (1966), quoted from Swami Amṛtananda: *Rgvedic Sūktas*, p. 4.
6. Visva Vandhu, Gāyatrī Research Bulletin, No. 13., Punjab University, 195, believes that the words - स्तुता मया वरदा वेदमाता (*AV* 19.71.1) referred to Gāyatrī; *Franklin Edgerton* : '*AV*, 13.1.10'; Indological Study in honour of W. Norman Brown, 1962 opines that, the word *Gāyatrī* in *AV,* 13.1.10 referred to the celebrated stanza of *RV*, 3.62.10.
7. *TS*, 6.1.63; tr. : A.B. Keith, Delhi.
8. *ŚB*, 1.7.3.23.
9. *ŚB*, 8.6.2.3.6
10. *ŚB*, 1.8.2.10.
11. *RV*, 32.14.33
12. *SB*, 3.4.1.15.
13. Swami Amrtananda : *Rgvedic Sūktas, Gāyatrī and Others,* Sri Ramakrishna Math, Mylapore, Chennai.
14. *Ibid.*
15. *TS*, 2.4.3.1-2, The prayer is as under-

    ओजोऽसि सहोऽसि बलमसि भ्राजोऽसि देवानां धाम।
    नामासि विश्वमसि विश्वायुः सर्वमसि सर्वायुरभिभूयेयम्।

    Mahānārāyoṇopaniṣat (14.1)
16. *SB*, 4.2.5, 20-22.
17. *GRU,* p. 406, *Upaniṣad Saṁgrahah,* Pdt. Jagadis Sastri, MLBD, Delhi, 1970.
18. *Oum bhūh bhuvah svah, KP,* 2.14.53.

19. It is said that in '*japa*', '*Tri-padā-Gāyatrī*' is uttered and in '*pujā*' '*Catus-padā-Gayatri*' is recited.—*GP*, 1.35.4.
20. *GB,* 1.1.34-36, Rajendra Lal Mitra, Varanasi, 1972.
21. तेजसा वा एते प्रयन्ति तेजो मध्ये दधति तेजोऽभ्युद्यन्ति ज्योतिषा – *TāndB,* 10.55.
22. त्रयो वा एते त्रिरात्रा यदेष द्वादशाहो गायत्रमुखः
प्रथमो गायत्रमध्यो द्वितीयो गायत्रोत्तमस्तृतीयः।
यस्माद् गायत्रमुखः प्रथमः तसमादुर्ध्वोग्निर्दीर्घाय
यस्माद् गायत्रमध्यो द्वितीयस्तस्मात्तिर्य्यह्ल् वायुः पवते
यस्माद् गायत्रोत्तमस्तृतीयः तसमाद्वाह्ल् दित्यस्तपति। – *TB*, 10.5.1, *Ibid.,* 10.5.
23. *JB*, 3.6; *AB* 4.25.
24. *JB*, 1.10; *ChU,* 3.16.1.
25. Swami Amṛtananda : *Rgvedic Sūktas,* p. 28-29.
26. *BrU*, 5.1.15.
27. Mourice Winternitz : *A History of Indian Literature,* Vol. I, Printed by V.K. Batra at Pearl Offset Press, 5/33, Vstria Area, New Delhi (1972).
28. को नमा स्वयम्भूः पुरुष इति। तेनङ्गुलि–मथ्यमानात् सलिलमभवत्। सलिलात् फेनमीवत्। फेनाद्बुद्बुदमभवत्। अण्डात् ब्रह्मा भवेत्। ब्रह्मणो वायुरभवत्। वायोरग्निरभवत्। अग्नेरोंङ्कारोऽभवत्। ओंकारात् व्याहृतिरभवत्। व्याहृत्याः गायत्र्यभवत्। *GRU,* p. 406.
29. *TS*, 5.1.3.4.
30. शमिध मा तिष्ठ गायत्री छन्दसामवतु...। (*TS*, 1.8.13.1); प्राचीमारोह गायत्रीत्वाऽवतु रथन्तर साम त्रिवृत्स्तोमो वसन्तऋतुर्ब्रह्म द्रविणम्। (*SB*, 5.4.13.)
31. *TS*, (1.5.6.4); *SS*, (2-12.7); *GRU*, p. 407.
32. J.E. Carpenter : *Theism In Medieval India,* p. 2785.
33. *GB*, 1.33
34. *GRU*, p. 405/7; *DBP*, 12.1.2; *Gāyatrī Tantram* 1.22F44; *Gāyatrī Mantrārthabhāskara,* p. 40; *GP.* 1.35.4.
35. *Gobhila G* 2.10.38; *HirkG* 1.6.6; *ApG* 4.11.9; *SG* 2.5.4-12; *AGS* 1.21.5; *Par.G* 2.3.3; Krishna Lal : *Sāvitrī from Samhitās to Gṛhya Sūtras*, ABORI, 52; pts. I-IV, 1971, p. 225-229.

3

Gāyatrī in Comparison with Other Deities in Vedic Literature

Identification of Gāyatrī with Other Deities

The vedic people invoked a large number of gods to accept their offerings in the fire and their songs of praise. Sometimes they offered only songs without any oblations. The vedic people were clearly aware of the fact that all the various gods whom they invoke were really representations of a single one. It was only a difference on aspects, and as such a difference in name. The various Gods were associated with great qualities of power, brilliance, wisdom, friendliness, protection against enemies, liberality, and bestowal of immense wealth and granting of happiness in life etc.

Similarly, Gāyatrī is associated with various gods namely Brahman, Agni, Soma and other deities also.

Gāyatrī and *Lord Brahma*

The relationship of Gāyatrī with Lord Brahmā is noteworthy. This effulgent aspect of Gāyatrī led to her identification with *Brahman*. Gāyatrī herself is regarded as *Brahman* as we find in *KS* (19.3, 37.2); *MS* (3.4.4, 4.7.3); (*ŚB* 1.35.5, 4.1.1.14); (13.6.2-7) (अष्टाक्षरा गायत्री ब्रम्हा गायत्री तद्ब्रह्मैवैतदस्य सर्वस्योत्तमंङ्करोति तस्माद्ब्रह्मस्य सर्वस्योत्तममित्याहु); *AĀ* (1.1.1; 5.1) *JB* (1.263; 2.89, 4.15).

She is *Brahman*-splendour as (ब्रह्मवर्चस) is mentioned in different *Brāhmaṇa* texts like *KS* (34.9), *TS* (2.2.5.3: 5.10.2; 3; 7.1.4.2; 26.2.3; 4.1.3; 2.5;); *MS* (3.2.6; 3.2); *AB* (1.5; 28; 3.34; 4.11); *KB* (3.5; 7.10; 17.2.9;) *TāṇḍB* (4.25; 5.1.9; 6.9.2; 8.10.2; 11.11.9; 12.9.23; 13.3.2; 25; 28; 14.5.30; 11.38; 15.18; 5.37; 16.14.5; 16.6;

19.5.8; 9; 7.7.8.2); *GB* (2.5.5); *TāṇḍB* (2.7.3.3); *AĀ* (1.1.3) and; *JB* (3.110; 1.142).

In *TS* she is described as *Brahmvarcas.*

ब्रह्मवर्चसमस्त्विति गायत्रिणा परिदध्या ब्रह्मवर्चसं वै गायत्री ब्रह्मवर्चसमेव भवति। (2.5.10.1)

चतुर्विंशत्यक्षरा गायत्री ब्रह्मवर्चसं गायत्रियैवास्मै ब्रह्मवर्चसमवरुन्धे। (2.5.10.2)

TāṇḍB describes as follows–

चतुर्विंशत्यक्षरा गायत्री तेजो ब्रह्मवर्चसङ्गायत्री तेज एव ब्रह्मवर्चसमारभ्य प्रयन्ति। (4.25)

अन्नं वा अर्को ब्रह्मवर्चसं गायत्रन्नाद्यं ये तेभ्यो ब्रह्मवर्चसस्य मुखतो दधाति। (5.1.9)

तेजो ब्रह्मवर्चसं गायत्री तेज एव ब्रह्मवर्चसमवरुन्धे। (8.10.2)

ब्रह्म वै पूर्वमहः क्षत्रं द्वितीयं यद्गायत्रीषु ब्रह्मसामभवति ब्रह्म तद्यशसार्द्धयति ब्रह्म हि गायत्री। (11.11.9)

गायत्रीषु स्तुवन्ति प्रतिष्ठायै ब्रह्मवर्चसाय येनैव प्राणेन प्रयन्ति तमभ्युद्यन्ति। (12-9.23)

ब्रह वै गायत्री यज्ञो विष्णुर्ब्रह्मण्येव तद्यज्ञं प्रतिष्ठापयति। (13.3.2)

गायत्रिषु स्तुवनित प्रतिष्टायै ब्रह्मवर्चसाय चेनैव प्राणेन प्रयन्ति तमभ्युद्यन्ति। (13.3.25; 14.11.38; 14.5.30)

तेजो ब्रह्मवर्चसं गायत्री तेज एव ब्रह्मवर्चसमवरुन्धे, प्राणो गायत्री प्रजननं प्राणादेव गायत्र्याः प्रजायते। (16.14.5)

गायत्री सम्पद्यते तेजो ब्रह्मवर्च्यसां गायत्री तेज एव ब्रह्मवर्च्यसमवरुन्धे। (16.16.6)

चतुर्विंशोऽग्निष्टोम यतुर्विंशत्यक्षरा गायत्री तेजो ब्रह्मवर्च्चसं गायत्री तेज एव ब्रह्मवर्च्चसमवरुन्धे। (19.5.8)

A person who desires spiritual lustre should lead the *ukthya* lauds with the Gāyatrī verses.

गायत्रीषु ब्रह्मबर्च्यसकामायोक्थ्यानि प्रणयेयुर्गायत्र्या।
ब्रह्मसामाऽनुष्टुभयच्छावाक् साम सैषा गायत्री सम्पद्यते। (8.10.1)

Bṛhaspati obtained *Brahman* splendour by means of *Aṣṭarātra*. The *Aṣṭarātra* rite is compared to Gāyatrī, for Gāyatrī has eight syllables, as said in *TS*.

गायत्री ब्रह्मबर्चसं गायत्रियैत ब्रह्मबर्चसमबरुन्ध अष्टरात्रो भबति। (*TS*, 7.2.3.1)

AB (1.5) says that if a person wants to possess lustre and *Brahman*-splendour he should employ Gāyatrī verses as *Yājna* and *Puronuvākya* in the *Sviṣṭakṛt* offerings.

Similarly, if one wants holy-power, he should recite the *Samidheni* verses in the Gāyatrī metre as in *TS* (2.5.10.2-3).

Most of the *Brāhmaṇa* texts including *TS, MS, AB, TB* described Gāyatrī as being the *Brāhmaṇa,* the representative of *Brahman* on the earth.

The concept of *Brahmā* in the *Purānic* literature is identified with the concept of Prajāpati (ŚB 11.I, 6.I) or *Brahman* in the *upaniṣadas* like *BṛhU, ChU, KaU, KnU.*

ॐ आप्यायन्तु ममाङ्गानि वाक्प्राणश्चक्षुः श्रोत्रमथोबलामिन्द्रियाणि च सर्वाणि सर्वं ब्रह्मोपनिषदं माहं ब्रह्म .... ते मयि सन्तु। (*KnU,* 4.1)

यदा सर्वे प्रभिद्यन्ते हुदयस्येह ग्रन्थयः, अथ मयाुऽमुतो भवत्येतावद्धनुशासनम्।
(*KaU*, 2.16)

It has been said earlier that Gāyatrī has been connected with *Brāhman* in the *brāhmaṇa* texts. The purāṇic literature it seems clear regarded her as the wife of Lord Brahmā. But in vedic period there is not any special reference regarding this context.

Gāyatrī and Savitṛ Deva

There are two gods in the *RV* with whom she has a close nexus. They are Savitṛ, and Agni. With a view to explaining this connection, it is imperative to study in brief the character and functions of these two divinities in the vedic literature.

Savitṛ is intimately connected with sacrifices. He is the presiding deity of the sacrifice either of morning or evening.

In Gāyatrī *Mantra*, Savitṛ is connected with wisdom and intelligence. He is the divine object of meditation. The *mantra* is associated with Savitṛ who has been invoked as the Supreme God, the creator and preserver of the universe. He is praised by all gods. He is referred to as (*Visvarupa*) and Prajāpati which proves the supremacy of Sāvitrī.

BṛhU says that Gāyatrī and Sāvitrī are one. Sāvitrī means that which is related to Savitṛ (गायत्रीमेव सावित्रीमनुब्रूयात्). Sāyaṇa says Sāvitrī means *Para-brahman.* This is the stand of the *Vedas.* This point is discussed in the *Brahmasūtras* where the objection raised is that, Gāyatrī is only a *chanda* and indicates Sāvitrī. How can it mean *Para-brahman?* Western scholars believe that Mitra, Varuṇa etc. are personifications of natural phenomena. Savitṛ is the youngest to be added to this group.

The following statements taken from *Nir* and *Ṛksamhitā* substantiate the statement that it is all one principle and manifestations are many.

देवताया एक आत्मा बहुधा स्तूयते।
एकस्य आत्मनः अन्ये देवाः प्रत्यांङ्गानि भवन्ति। (*Nir*, 14)

यो नः पिता जनिता यो विधाता धामानि वेद भुवनानि विश्वा।
यो देवानां नामधा एक एव तं सप्रश्नं भुवना यन्त्यन्या। (*ṚV,* 10.82.3)

देवस्त्वष्टा सविता विश्वरूपः पूपोष प्रजाः पुरुधा जजान।
इमा च विश्वा भुवनान्यस्य महद्देवानामसुरत्वमेकम्। (*ṚV,* 3.55.19)

Savitṛ is regarded as the most auspicious and prominent solar deity in the *RV*. This is confirmed by the statement in *Nir* (सविता सर्वस्य प्रसविता) *i.e.,* Savitā is the progenitor of the entire creation. In the IIIrd *Maṇḍal* of *ṚV Samhitā,* there occurs a statement (देवत्स्वष्टा सविता विश्वरूपः) god Tvashtā of cosmic form, is also called Savitā (*RV*, 3.55.19). In the Xth *Maṇḍala,* the same is confirmed in the following statement–'Good Tvashtā, also called Savitā, who is of cosmic form, is indeed the creator and progenitor (*ṚV* X.10.5). This leads us to the fact that Prajāpati is the cause and creator of the universe. He is the reality behind all. He manifests in diversity of forms. He has many names according to the functions discharged by each. Āditya, Varyṇa, Sūrya, Indra and Savitā etc., are all names of gods in the creation of universe, being assigned with different functions. The supreme reality is called Savitā. Savitā is Āditya and also the supreme being in Āditya. The name Savitṛ is derived from the root which has two meanings *i.e.,* (*i*) षु प्रेरणे and (*ii*) सूङ् प्राणि-गर्भ-विमोचने। The meanings of Savitṛ therefore include–one who inspires and one who creates.[1]

Savitṛ has been delineated as a radiant divinity in the *ṚV*. Savitā in *ṚV* is pre-eminently a *Hiraṇyadevatā.* Savitṛ is golden-eyed, golden-handed and golden-fingered. He is a golden-handed *Asura* and his hair is golden.

हिरण्याक्षः सविता देव आगात्। (*ṚV,* 1.35.8)

हिरण्यापाणिः सविता विचर्षणिः। (*ṚV,* 1.35.9)

हिरण्यहस्ता असुरः सूनीथः। (*ṚV,* 1.35.10)

हिरण्यजिह्वः सविताय नव्यसे। (*ṚV,* 6.71.3)

with him three-fold light he brightens up the three regions, the terrestrial, region, the midregion and the heaven.

उता यासि सवितस्त्रीणि रोचनोत सूर्यस्य रश्मिभिः समुच्चसि।
(*ṚV,* 5.81.4)

The maintenance and regularisation of the universe is his foremost duty. He has golden tongue. He spreads his golden lustre all around him.

उदष्य देवः सविता ययाम हिरण्ययीममतिं यामशिश्रेत्।
नूनं भगो हव्यो मानुषेभि-वियो रत्ना पुरुवसुर्दधाति।। (7.38.1)

He protects the mortals and celestial dames. It is through Savitṛ's favour that mankind attains bliss and wealth.

यः पार्थिवानि विममे स एतशो रजांसि देवः सविता महित्वना। (5.91.3)

His lustre illuminates all the regions far and wide.

उदस्य वाहु शिथिरा बृहन्ता हिरण्ययां दिवो अन्ता अनष्टाम्।
नूनं सो अस्य महिमा पनिष्ट सूरश्चिदस्मा अनुदादपस्याम्। (*ṚV,* 7.45.2)

(Golden, sublime and easy in their motion, his arms extend into the bounds of heaven. Now shall that mightness of him be lauded. Even *sura* yields to him in active vigour).

ṚV literature in particular and vedic literature in general recognise Savitṛ as another name of the sun–the light of all lights. He is considered as the stimulative aspect of the sun. He is the spiritual power of sun. Unlike Sūrya, he is considered a more abstract deity. He is also intimately connected with the sacred rites of sacrifice.

Among the solar deities Sūrya is the most luminous. There are references in the *ṚV* to the rising, mounting and setting Sūrya. Sūrya is the personified form of the sun. He is for-seeing and all-seeing, born from the eye of the *Puruṣa.* He is Āditya or Āditeya and is the son of Aditi. He is the dispeller of darkness and bestower of light. He is a moral force also. सत्येनोत्तभिता भूमिः सूर्येनोत्तभिता द्यौः as said in ṚV means earth is upheld by truth and heaven is upheld by Sūrya. He is purity incarnate. He has the ability to ward off all impurities, evil spirits and influences. He rouses mankind to pursue their vocations and perform their rightful duties and to seek peace and prosperity. All these qualities of Sūrya are fully developed in the personality of Savitṛ.

These attributes can well be applied to the sun, yet Savitṛ does not represent the physical sun, for it is said that he bids the sun to approach.

हिरण्मयेन सविता रथेना देवो याति भुवनानि पश्यन्।
याति देवः प्रवता यात्युद्वता याति शुभ्राभ्यां यजतो हरिभ्याम्। (*ṚV,* 1.35.2)

So, in the *ṚV* Savitṛ and Sūrya are mentioned as identical. Savitṛ himself is described as one having rays like the sun.

सूर्यरश्मिमर्हरिकेशः पुरस्तात् सविता ज्योतिरुदर्या अजस्त्रम्।
तस्य पूषा प्रस्वे याति विद्वान्स्तंपश्यन् विश्वा भुवनानि गोपा। (10.139.1)

"Savitṛ golden haired, hath lifted eastward bright with sun-beams, his eternal lustre. He is whose energy with *Puṣan* marches, surveying all existence like a herdsman".

In some other places there is a slight different between the two. It is said that god Savitṛ has raised aloft his brilliance making light for the whole world. Sūrya shifting brightly has filled the heaven, earth and air with his rays (*ṚV*, 4.11.2). There is also a mention of Savitṛ shining the rays of Sūrya. The adjective of Sūrya-*raśmi* is used for him and Savitā spreads his effulgence from the eastern horizon.

Savitṛ has two fold function-he brings life and as well as rest to all the animate and inanimate creation. He also wards off evil dreams and makes men sinless.

बृहत्सुम्नः प्रसविता निवेशनो जगतः स्थातुरुभयस्यथो वशी।

He is known as the divinity of Light. He has power to disperse darkness from the world. He is invoked as the sun who follows Uṣā with the dawn he is supposed to have illumined the heaven. He is expected to spread light over the earth and heaven. (*ṚV,* 6.71.2). He invigorates men through rays and lights.

आगान् देव ऋतुभिर्वर्धतु क्षयं दधातु नः सविता सूप्रजामिषम्।
स नः क्षपाभिरहभिश्च जीवन्तु प्रजावन्तं रयिमस्मे समिन्वतु।।

(*ṚV,* 4.53.7)

(with the year's seasons hath Sāvitrī, God, come high : may he prosper our home, give food and noble sons), may he send us opulence with progeny. Sāvitrī also produces day and night.

य इमे उभे अहनी पुर एत्यप्रयुच्जन् स्वाधीर्देवः सविता। (*ṚV* 5.82.8)

Therefore, he is connected with the east as well as the west. (10.139.1).

In *ṚV*, Savitṛ is described as the God who lights up and sustains the world. It is he who urges the priest to his sacrificial duty. He is all powerful and grants riches to the Gods. He blesses those who invite the Gods to the sacrifice. His sole object is to attend to the good of the world. It is said that the sacred waters flow in his service and the winds blow in limitless space.

विश्वस्य हि सृष्टये देव ऊर्द्धः प्र वाहवा पृथुपाणिः।
सिसति आपश्चिदस्य व्रत आ निमृगा अयं चिद् वातो रमते परिजमन्।

(*ṚV,* 2.38.2)

It is through his grace the whole world enjoys rest at night. It is said that all creatures are provided with nice dwellings by God Savitṛ. Indra, Mitra, Varuṇa, Aryamān and Rudra obey the laws laid down by Savitṛ and sing hymns in his praise.

न यस्येन्द्रा वरुणो न मित्रो व्रतमर्यमा न मिनन्तिसद्रः
नाशतयस्तमिदं स्वस्ति हुवे देवं सवितारं नमोमिः।। (*ṚV,* 2.38.9)

He protects both mortals and celestial Dames. It is through Savitṛ's favour that mankind attains bliss and wealth.

यः पार्थिवानि विममे स एतशो रजांसि देवः सविता महित्वना।
(*ṚV,* 5.91.3)

By meditating upon the excellent glory of the divine Savitṛ, our minds are illumined. The learned men worship Savitṛ in their sacred rites. He is the sustainer of the heaven and Lord of all creatures.

दिवे धर्त्ता भुवनस्य प्रजापतिः पिशङ्गं द्रापिं प्रतिमुञ्चते कविः।
विचक्षणः प्रथयन्नापृणुन्नुर्व जीजनव् सविता सुम्नमुक्थ्यम्।। (*ṚV,* 2.38.9)

He protects all living beings with his out stretched arms. He fills the earth and heaven and for his own delight sings a song. He guards each sacred law. He is mighty and great and with his own greatness fills the three domains, three realms and the three worlds. He has the ability to grant shelter and security for the virtuous persons. The enlightened person always concentrates on Savitṛ, who is the all knower creating God. He assumes all forms and brings forth good for the bipeds and quadrupeds.

देवस्य वयं सवितुः स्वीमनि श्रेष्ठे स्याम वसुनश्च दावने
या विश्वस्य द्विपदो चश्चतुष्पदो निवेशने प्रसवे चासि भूमनः।।
(*ṚV,* 6.71.2)

This supreme god Sāvitṛ is followed by all the other Gods. He has the capacity to measure out the earthly realms. Through the rays of the sun he goes in all the three shining spheres. He is awake at dawn and alert at night. He is verily Mitra as the lord of creation and generation. He is *Puṣan* going through his regulated paths.

शतं जीव शरदो वर्द्धमानः शतं हिमन्तात् ऋतम वसन्तान्।
शतं त इन्द्रो अग्निः सविता वृहस्पतिः शतायुषा हविषाहमेनम्।।

It is Savitṛ who causes men and animals to take birth and to die. Hence the poet wishes to enjoy Savitṛ's vivifying force.

उपायातं दाशुषे मर्त्याय रथेन वाममश्विना वहति।
युयुतमस्मदनिराममीवां दिवा नक्तं माध्वी चासीथा नः। (*ṚV,* 7.71.2)

It is the these two characteristic features of Savitṛ, *i.e.,* refulgence and vivifying force, that Gāyatrī has been closely connected.

As Gāyatrī is also regarded as luminary and as a protectress of *Prāṇa* or (vital force), Savitṛ is connected with Gāyatrī as described in *Taittiriya Saṁhitā* (6.5.71) *Maitrāyaṇai Saṁhitā* (1.11.10) and *Kauṣitaki Saṁhitā*.(2.87)

एष वै गायत्रो देवनां यत् सवितैष गायत्यै लोके गृह्यते यदाग्रयणो यदन्तर्यामपात्रेण सवित्राग्रयणाद् गृहणाति। (*Taittiriya Saṁhitā,* 6.5.71)

It has been said or pointed out that the essential distinction between the sun and Savitṛ did not continue longer and in *Brahmānic Upaniṣadic* and *Puraṇic* period, both are treated as identical. *BṛhU* (5.14.3) says that the fourth *Pāda* of Gāyatrī is the Sun, who shines having dispelled darkness. It means as shown else where the sun is also associated with Gāyatrī (*TS* 3.7.6.2). In this connection the analogy of Gāyatrī with Vāk is also significant as mentioned in *MS* (4.3.1).

Gāyatrī is regarded as Vāk having hundred syllables (1.4.1.3). *ChU* says that Gāyatrī is Vāk.

गायत्री वा इदं सर्वभूतं यदिदं किञ्च वाग् वै गायत्री वाग् वा इदं सर्वं भूतं गायत्री त्रायते वा। (*ChU* 3.12-1).

दूरे चित् सन्तमरुषाः इन्दमाच्यावयन्तु सख्याय विप्रम्।
यद् गायत्रीं वृहती मर्कमस्मै सौत्रामण्या दधृषन्त देवाः।। (*AV,* 3.3.2)

In the *Sautrāmaṇi* sacrifice, Gāyatrī along with Agni is asked to grant Indra power and life.

Savitru, Sāvitrī, Savitar and Savitā are the various names to identify the supreme solar deity who lights up and sustains the world. The other gods obey the laws laid down by Savitru. He protects all living beings with all his out-stretched golden arms. Savitṛ is closely connected with stimulation, sacrifices and wisdom. He is the most favourite god of the learned-worship of Sāvitrī through Gāyatrī hymn is considered beneficial for spiritual upliftment.

The supreme soul in his form is clearly stated as the first and foremost being of the golden Womb[2]. The sublime *Gāyatrī Mantra* has तत्सवितुर्वरेण्यं where Sāvitrī is none other than the supreme being in one of its embodiments.

It may be concluded that the divine effulgence of Savitrī is described as the auspicious light सुतेजाः भगः - (Light of all lights). It is nothing but *Parabrahman*. He alone destroys all ignorance. The invocation of तत्सवितुर्वरेण्यं is a prayer for the gracious inspiration, inner prompting of the mind and heart and soul which leads to the realisation of the divine light of Sāvitrī, which is beyond human perception. It can be realised only through meditation coupled with divine grace.

Gāyatrī and Agni

The seers of the vedic age used to worship various deities of nature always looking upon them as the total protector of the entire universe. They have not tried to give any scope for disparity or grades amongst the various deities and always considered the deities as the whole *Brahman* and the ultimate supreme reality. The seers (*Ṛsis*) submitted themselves entirely to God during *Yajña* with their mind to Him and prayed and got the world what it needed.

The hymns remind human beings that ऋत can be preserved or promoted only by a balanced relation between the earth and the heaven. Water is considered the common possession of earth and heaven. It is necessary for the growth of food grains. Food is the mainstay for existence on this earth.

अन्नाद् वै प्रजाः प्रजायन्ते या काश्च पृथिवी श्रिताः अथो अन्नेन वै जीवन्ती।

(*TS*)

It is through water that human beings propitiate and please Gods by performing sacrifice. A hymn says that water in the from of showers protects the heavenly abode (*ṚV* 1.164.51). This is made possible through sacrificial fires. Agni is the mediator who receives the sacrificial offering and satisfies the highest heavens by conveying the same to the Gods.

So, just as Agni is important for a sacrifice so is Gāyatrī.

गायत्री वा अग्निः गायत्रोऽग्निः अग्निर्वै गायत्री गायत्रमग्नेश्छन्दः।

(*ŚB*, 4.1.3.19)

Gāyatrī has close connection with Agni. Agni in Vedic literature is described as *Purohita* (one who is placed in front of the sacrifice).

The very lustre of Gāyatrī has been attributed to her association with Agni[3].

Agni is the mouth of Gāyatrī. (*JUB* 4.6.3.2, *Bṛh U* p.5.14.7). The *ṚV* (10.130.4) states that Agni is closely conjoined with Gāyatrī. अग्नेर्गायत्र्य-भवत् ...।

Prajāpati created Agni and Gāyatrī from his mouth.

प्रजापतिरकामयत प्रजायेयेति स मुखतस्त्रिवृतं निरमिमीत तमग्निदेर्वताऽन्वसृज्यत गायत्री। (*TS* 7.1.1.4)

By means of metres, namely, Gāyatrī, Triṣṭup and Jagatī. Agni bears the oblations to different Gods. (*TS* 2.2.48, *VS* 13.34, *MS* 1.6.1).

The *Brāhmaṇical* texts *KS, TS, MS, ŚB* and *JB*, state that Agni is Gāyatrī.

AB (3.13) says that Prajāpati allotted to the Gods the sacrifice and the metres in different portions.

He assigned the Gāyatrī metre to Agni and Vasus at the morning pressing. Vasus are regarded as *Prāṇa*. They are connected with the morning-pressing. So is Gāyatrī (*JB* 1.10), (*ChU* 3.16.1).

JUB (1.4.41-4) has the following legend. Prajāpati created Gods and Death. Gods were afraid of Death. They approached Prajāpati. Prajāpati asked them to bring the metres and enter in to them. The Vasus brought Gāyatrī. They entered into her and thus they were saved from death. There are eight Vasus, eight are the syllables of Gāyatrī (*TS* 3.8.9.7).

It is to be noted that Agni and Sun are often treated as identical[4], It is said in *ṚV* (5.37.1; 7.2.1) that, Agni united himself with the rays of the sun.

It is Agni who is known as Mitra in the morning, as Savitṛ he wanders through the sky and as Indra at noon.

स वरुणः सोऽयमग्निर्भवति, स मित्रो भवति प्रातरुद्यन्, स सविता भूत्वान्तरिक्षेण याति, स इन्द्र भूत्वा तपति मध्यतो दिवं तस्य देवस्य। (*AV*, 13.3.13)

When the sun sets he actually enters into Agni[5]. Men light Agni on earth, the gods light him in the heaven as *ṚV* says.

सजोषस्तवा दिवो नरो केतुमिन्धते यज्ञस्य मानुषो जनः सुस्मायुर्जुहे अध्वरे।
(*ṚV,* 6.2.3)

It is repeatedly said that Agni has a threefold personality[6]. This three-fold personality of Agni is generally explained as terrestrial, mid-regional and heavenly *i.e.,* as the fire, lightning and the Sun. Sometimes lightning is replaced by Vāyu or Indra. Agni is indeed, regarded as a force which causes even the sun to rise.

A common characteristic of Gāyatrī, Savitṛ and Agni is that they are all regarded as a bird. Agni is regarded as the eagle of the sky.

नवं नु स्तोममग्नये दिवः श्येनाय जीजनं वस्वः कुविद् धनानि नः।
(*ṚV,* 7.15.4)

He is the divine bird (Suparṇa). दिव्य सुपर्ण वायसं बृहन्त..। (*ṚV* 1.164.52). Savitṛ is also regarded as a Falcon. सुपर्णो अङ्गं सवितुर्गरुत्मान् पूर्वो जातः स उ अस्यानु धर्म...। (*ṚV,* 10.149.3)

The eagle that is referred to in the stories is Gāyatrī. Soma may be taken to mean then effulgence of Āditya. Āditya is *Parabrahman.* Gāyatrī is Agni. Gāyatrī as Agni brought the Soma. So it helped the performance of the sacrifice. If Soma is considered as a symbol for the effulgence of Āditya this episode of Gāyatrī bringing Soma may mean that through Gāyatrī alone we realise *Brahman*. If Soma is considered as an article of worship in a sacrifice, then the episode means Gāyatrī is the direct means for realisation and also the important means for the completion of the sacrifice (*Yajña*), which leads to realisation. These ideas are expressed in various ways in the vedic texts such as *Ṛk Saṁhitā, TS, AĀ* etc. The ideas and symbology are spread over the entire *Mantra* and *Brāhman* portion[7].

However, the main purpose of showing the connection between Sāvitrī on the one hand and Sāvitrī and Agni on the other is to emphasize that they combine in them a common factor-that of stimulating, vivifying and arousing. It is even suggested that Sāvitrī is the solar energy and the very principle of procreation[8].

Gāyatrī and Soma

The concept of *Soma* at the celestial level, is not different from that of the Sun or Agni. Indeed he is known to be both. Soma too is a shining divinity as described in *ṚV*.

प्र गायत्रेण गायत पवमानं विचर्षणिम्, इन्दु सहस्रयक्षसम् (9.60.I)

"Sing forth and loud with sacred song most active *Pavamāna, laud, Indu* who sees with thousand eyes.

पवस्वेन्दो वृषा सुतः कुधी नो यशसो जने, विश्वा अप द्विषो जहि।
(9.6I.18)

They, juice, O Pavamāna! sends its rays abroad like splendid skill, like lustre, all heaven's light, to see.

गिरस्त इन्दु ओजसा मर्मृज्यन्ते अपस्थुवः यामर्मदाय शुभ्यसे। (9.2.7)

Now whether thou be far away, or in the heaven, or on the earth, O Indra!, mighty-thoughted, harnessing thy Bays, come lofty with the lofty ones.

पुनानो देववीतय इन्द्रस्य याहि निष्कृतम्। द्युतानो वाजिभिर्यतः। (9.64.15)

Purified for the feast of Gods go thou to the Indra's special place, resplendent, guided by the strong.

यस्य वर्णं मधुश्चुतं हरिं हिन्वन्त्यद्रिभिः इन्दुमिन्द्राय पीतये। (9.65.8)

Whose coloured sap they drive with stones, the yellow meath-distilling juice, Indu for Indra, for his drink.

पवमानो व्यश्नवद्रश्मिभिर्वाजसा तमःदधत् स्तोत्रे सुवीर्यम्। (9.66.27)

May Pavamāna, best to win the booty, penetrate with rays, giving the singer her strength.

अस्मभ्यं त्वा वसुविदमभि वाणीरनूपत। गोभिष्टे वर्णमभिवासयामसि।
(9.104.4)

Voices have sung aloud to thee as finder out of wealth for us. We cloth the hue thou wearest with a robe of milk.

गोमन्न इन्दरे अश्ववत् सुतः सुदक्ष धन्व।
शुचिं ते वर्णमधि गोषु दीधरम्।

Flow to us, Indu, passing, strong, effused with wealth of kine and steeds. I will spread forth above the milk thy radiant hue.

आ रत्नधा योनिमुतस्य सीदस्युत्सो देव हिरण्ययः।
दुहान ऊर्ध्वदिव्यं मधुप्रिय प्रत्नं सधस्तमासदत्। (9.107.4)

Cleansing thee, Soma in thy stream, thou flowest in a watery robe, giver of wealth, thou sittest in the place of law, O God! a fountain made of gold.

त्रिधातुभिररुषीभिर्वयो दधे रोचमानो वचे दधे। पूर्वामनु प्रदिशं याति
चेकिंतत् सं रश्मिभिर्यतते दर्शतो रथो देव्यो दर्शतो रथः। (9.111.2)

That treasure of the panis thou discoveredst, thou with thy mother deckest thee in thine abode, with songs of worship in thine home. As't were from far, the hymn is heard, where holy songs resound in joy. He with the ruddy-hued, three-fold hath won life-power, he, glittering, hath won life-powers.

अया रुचा हरिण्या पुनानो विश्वा द्वे तरति स्वयुग्वभिः सुरो न
स्वयुग्वभिः धारा सुतस्य रोचते पुनानो अरुषो हरिः। (9.111.1)

With this his golden splendour purifying him, he with his own allies subdues all enemies as *Sura* with his own allies. Cleansing himself with stream of juice he shines forth yellow-hued and red, when with the praisers he encompasses all forms, with praisers having seven mouths.

Soma is also compared with the Sun as we found in *ṚV.*

अध्वर्युभिर्भरमाणा अयंसत वायो शुक्र अयंसत।
आ वां रथो नियुत्वान् वक्षदवसेऽभि प्रयांसि सुधितानि वीतये वायो हव्यानि
वीतये। (1.135.3)

Come thou with hundreds, come with thousands in thy team to this our solemn rite, to taste the sacred food, Vāyu to taste the offerings. This is thy seasonable share, that comes co-radiant with the Sun.

अचिक्रद्वृषा हरिर्महान् मित्रो न दर्शः। स सूर्येण रोचते। (9.2.6)

The twany bull hath bellowed, fair as mighty Mitra to behold. He shines together with the Sun.

परि यो रोदसी उभे सद्यो वाजेभिरर्षति। मदेषु सर्वधा असि। (9.18.6)

Who in a moment mightly floweth around these two world-haves. All bounteous art thou in course.

उभे सोमावयाकशन् मृगो न तक्तो अर्षसि सीदन्नुतस्य योनिना। (9.32.4)

O Soma! viewing heaven and earth, thou runnest like a darting deer. Set in the place of sacrifice.

अयं सूर्य इवपहगयं सरांसि धावति। सप्त प्रवत आ दिवम्। (9.54.1)

In some aspects he is like the Sun, runneth forward to the lakes like Seven currents flowing through the sky.

अयं विश्वानि तिष्ठति पुनानो भुवनोपरि। सोमो देवो न सूर्यः। (9.54.2)

He shining in his splendour, stands high over all things that cxist, Soma as good as Sūrya.

अभि प्रियाणी काव्या विश्वा चक्षाणे अर्षति। हरिस्तुञ्जान आयुधा। (957.2)

He flows beholding on his way all well beloved sacred lore, green tinted. brandishing his arms

पवमानो व्यश्नवद्रश्मिमिर्कजसातम्। दधत् स्त्रोत्रे सवीर्यम्। (9.66.27)

May Pavamāna best to win the booty, penetrate with rays, giving the singer hero strength.

त्वं सोम सुर एष स्तोकस्य साता तनूनाम्। वृणीमहे सख्याय वृणीमहे युज्याय। (9.66.18)

Soma, as Sura, brings us food, with offspring of our bodies we elect thee for our friendship, we elect thee for companionship.

पवमानो अति स्त्रिधोऽभ्यर्षति सुष्टुतिम्। सुरो न विश्वदर्शतः। (9.66.22)

Dcyond his enemies away to sweet praise Pavamāna flows, like Sūrya visible to all.

हिन्वन्ति सूरमुस्त्रयः पवमानं मधुश्चुतम्। अभि गिरो समस्वरन्। (9.67.2)

The glittering maids send *Sura* forth, they with their song have sung aloud to Pavamāna dropping meath.

मन्द्रस्य रूपं विविदुर्मनीषिणः श्येनो यदन्धो अभरत् परावतः।

तं मर्जयन्त सुवुधं नदीष्वां उशनतमंशुं परियन्तमृगियम्। (9.68.6)

The sages knew the from of him the gladdener, what time the falcon brought the plant from faraway.

सूर्यस्येव रश्मयो द्रावियत्नवो मत्सराय: प्रसूप: साकमीरते।
तन्तुं ततं परिसर्गास आशवो नेन्द्राद्देते पर्वते धाम किंचन।। (9.69.6)

Even as the beams of Sūrya, urging men to speed, that cheer and send to sleep, together rush they forth. These swift out pourings in long course of holy rites, no form save only Indra shows itself so pure.

व्रतानि पानो अमृतस्य चारुण
उभे नुचक्षा अनुपश्यते विशै।। (9.70.4)

He, while he is adroned by the ten skillful ones, that he too in the midst mothers may create, while he is watching over the lovely *Amṛta's* ways, looks on races as beholder of mankind.

त्वेषं रूपं कृणुते वर्णो अस्य स यचाशयत् समृता सेधति स्त्रिध:।
अप्सा याति स्वधया दैव्यै जनं स सुष्ठुती नसते स गोअग्रया।। (9.71.8)

He covering assumes a radiant the, where'ver he comes into the fight he drives the foe a far. The winner of the floods, with food he seeks the host of heaven, he comes to praises glorified with milk.

स नू पवस्व परिपार्थिवं रज: स्तोत्रे शिक्षन्नाधून्वते च सुक्रतो।
मा नो निर्मांग् वसुन: सादनस्पृशो रयिं पिशङ्ग बहुलं वसीमहि।। (9.72.8)

Over the earthly region flow thou on thy way, helping the praiser and the pourer, thou most wish. Let us not lack rich treasure reaching to our home, and may clothe ourselves in manifold bright wealth.

सहस्रमुकां पथिभिर्वयोविदध्वष्मभि: सरो अन्नं वि याति।
ऋजा चिद्रक्षस: सदासि पुनान इन्द्र ऋणुहि वि वाजान्।। (9.91.3)

Steer roaring into steer, this Pavamāna, this juice runs to the white milk of the milch-cow. Through thousand fine hairs goes the tuneful singers, like *Sura* by his fair and open pathways.

अधि यदस्मिन् वामिनीव शुभ: स्पर्धन्ते धिय: सूर्ये न विश:
अपो वृणान: पवते कवीयन् व्रजं न पशुवधनाय मन्म।। (9.94.1)

When beauties strive for him as for a charger, then strive the songs like Soldiers for the sunlight. Acting the sage, he flows enrobed in waters and songs as, there a stall that kine may prosper.

अन्तः पश्यन् बृजनेमावराण्या तिष्ठति वुषभो गोषु जानन्।
स मत्सरः पुत्सु वन्वन्नवातः सहस्ररेता अभि वाजमर्ष।। (9.96.7)

Some Pavamāna, like a river, hath stirred the wave of voice, our songs and praises. Beholding these inferior powers in cattle, he rates among them as a steer well-knowing.

अयं पूषा रयिभर्गः सोमः पुनानो अर्षति।
पतिविश्वस्य भूमनो व्यख्यद्रोदसी उभे। (9.101.7)

As *Puṣan,* Fortune, *Bhaga,* comes this Soma while they make him pure. He, lord of the multitude, hath looked upon the earth and heaven.

एते पूता विपश्चितः सोमासो दध्यशिरः,
सूर्यासो न दर्शतासो जिगत्नवोध्रुवा घृते। (9.101.12)

These Soma Juices, skilled in song, purified, blent with milk and curd, when moving and when firmly laid in oil, resemble lovely Suns.

स तू पवस्यू परिपार्थिवं रजो दिव्या च सोमधर्मभिः।
त्वां विप्रासो मतिभिर्विचण शुभ्रं हिन्वन्ति धीतिभिः।। (9.107.24)

Flow to the realm of earth, flow to the realm of heaven, O Soma, in thy righteous ways. Fair wit thou whom the sages, O Far-seeing one.

अया ऋचा हूरिण्या पुनानो निश्ना द्वेषंसि तरति स्वगुण्भिः सुरो न
स्वयुवभिः धारा सुतस्य रोचते पुनानो अरषो हरिः। (9.111.1)

With this his golden splendour purifying him, he with his own allies subdues all enemies, as Sūrya with his own allies. Clean sing himself with stream of juice he shines forth Yellow-hued and red. When with the praisers he encompasses all forms, with Praisers having seven mouths.

अग्मन्तवथानि पौस्ये द्वे जैत्राय हर्षयन्
वज्रश्च यदूवथो अनपचयुता समस्वनपच्युता।। (9.11.3)

He moves intelligent directed to the East. The very beauteous can rivals the beams of light the beautiful celestial car. He is regarded as Agni. There are soma hymns of *ṚV* which praises some as Agni.

यशस्य केतुः पवते स्वध्वरः सोमो देवानामुप याति निष्कृतिम्।
सहस्त्रधारं परि केशमर्षति वृषा पवित्रमत्येति एनम्।। (9.86.7)

Served with fair rites he flows, ensigh of sacrifice, Soma advances to the special place of Gods. He speeds with thousand currents to the reservoir, and passes through the filter bellowing as a bull.

ब्रह्मा देवानां पदवीः कवीनामृषिर्विप्राणां महिषो मृगाणाम्।
श्येनो गृध्राणां स्वधितिर्वपनां सोमः पवित्रमत्येति रेभन्।। (9.96.6)

Brahman of Gods, the leader of the poet, *Ṛsi* of sages, Bull of savage creatures, falcon amid the vultures, axe of forests, over the cleansing sieve goes Soma singing.

परिण्य सुवनो अधा इन्दुख्ये मदच्युतः
धारा च उध्वो अध्वरे भ्राजा नैति गव्ययुः।। (9.98.6)

Effused, this Indu hath flowed on, disting rapture, to the feece. He goes erect, as seeking kine in stream, with light, to sacrifice.

The close connection of Soma with the sunor Agni would indicate that Soma is endowed with the same invigorating and vivifying potentiality which Savitṛ Possesses.

Another common characteristic of these three divinities namely, Agni, Sun and Soma, is that they are endowed with and are protectors of *Prāṇa.* In *AV* same Soma is invoked as *Prāṇa* in similarity with the sun or Agni, *AV* identifies sun as *prāṇa*.

प्राणो विराट् प्राणो देष्ट्री प्राणे सर्व अपास्ते।
प्राणो ह सूर्यश्चद्रमाः प्राणमाहुः प्रजापतिम्। *AV* (11.4.12)

The sun causes the mortals to die, and it is he who also causes them to breathe.

यो मारयाति प्राणयति यरमात् प्राणा भुवनानि विस्वा तस्य देवस्य।
(*AV* 13.3.3)

Sun pervades the heaven and earth with breath.

यः प्राणेन द्यावापुथिवी तर्पयन्तपानेन समुद्रसय जठरं यः पिपर्ति तस्य देवस्य।
AV (13.3.4)

He himself is *Prāṇa* (*Praśna Upaniṣad* 1.5)

Similarly in the *Saṁhitā'a* of *AV* we come across the concept of *Prāṇa* in different content.

अपामग्निस्तनुभिः संविदानो य औषधींनामधिपा वभूव। स नो वर्ष वनुतां जातवेदाः प्रजाभ्यो अमृत दिवस्तरि। *AV* (4.15.10)

Agni is prayed to grant breath like Sun.

Agni is *Prāṇa.* अग्नेष्टे प्राणाममूतादायुष्मतो वन्वे जातवेदसः यथा न रिण्या अमृतः सर्जूरसस्तत् ते कृणोमि तदु ते समूध्यताम्।। *AV* (8.2.13)

Agni is invoked for breath, expiration, life and splendour etc.

अग्निर्माग्निनावतु प्राणायापानाचायूष वर्चस ओजसे तेजसे स्वभूतये स्वस्तये स्वाहा। *AV* (19.45.6)

In *Maitryupaniṣad* (6.33) he is indeed *Prāṇa*. *Prāṇa* is closely associated with Soma. The poet wishes that the honey mixed with Soma may bring to him Prana along with breath and splendour (*AV* 3.13.5).

AV (18.4.88) mentions that the breath of rivers has made the Soma-*vats* resound loudly, there, Soma, the bull of the prayers, purifies himself and thus purified, he enters in to the heart of Indra. It is prayed that Soma, with his powers may protect men's *Prāṇa Apāna, Āyu* (life) etc.

सोमो मा सोम्येनावतु प्राणायापानायायूषे वर्चस ओजसे तेजसे स्वसस्तये सुभूतयै स्वाहा। (19.45.8)

Soma, verily is *Prāṇa* (*SB* 7.3.12) *Praṇa* is the Sun (*AV* 11.4.12). It is the almighty *Brahman* (*BṛhU* 4.1.3). It however is Indu who produces the light in the Sun (*ṚV* 9.97.41). He gave splendour to the Sun to shine (*RV* 9.28.5, 37.4).

एष सूर्यमरोचयत् पवमानो विचर्षाणिः विश्वा धामनि विश्ववित्।
ṚV 9.28.5

पवमानो असेचयत् जामिभिः सूर्य सह। (9.37.4)

In this context we may study the two legends relating to Gāyatrī which occur in the Vedic and *Purāṇic* literature. They are 1. Gāyatrī bringing Soma from the heaven and 2. Sāvitrī bringing *Prāṇa* of her husband. The first legend[9] is in brief as follows :

Soma was in the heaven, and the Gods were on the earth. They wished that the Soma be available to them on the earth so that they might sacrifice with him. They produced two allusions. Suparṇi and Kadru. Once a dispute arose between the two on the point as to who of the two could see farthest. Suparṇi said 'On the far side of the ocean a white horse stands at a post'. Kadru said 'She sees it' and added 'Its tail is hanging and being tossed by the wind'. By 'ocean' Suparni meant the fire-altar, by 'white horse', she meant the fire burning on it, and by 'Post' (she meant) the sacrificial post. "Kadru said she sees it" and added 'Its tail is hanging and being tossed by the wind.' Suparṇi said "Let us now fly there and ascertain who the winner is" Kadru asked Suparṇi to fly out there and find out whether what she said was correct or not. Suparṇi did fly out whether what she said was correct or not, was right.

Kadru won and asked Suparṇi to fetch Soma from the heaven as a requital. Suparṇi brought forth the metres. Gods asked the metres to fetch Soma. Having become birds they flew up. Jagatī first flew up, but having gone only half the way she became weary, having laid aside her three syllables she returned and exhausted without getting Soma, she brought with her consecration (*Diksā*) and fervour (*tapas*). Then triṣtup flew up. She was able to go a little more than half the way but she also felt exhausted. She laid aside one syllable and came back bearing the sacrificial fee (*Dakisinā*). Seeing that these two metres failed in their mission, the Gods asked Gāyatrī to try her hand. She flew-up, grasped Soma with her foot and mouth, and together with the syllables left behind by Jagatī and Triṣtup returned to the earth.

An Assimilation

In the light of what has been said above, it seems most probable that the legend of the bringing of Soma by Gāyatrī is analogous to the bringing of the puranic force from the heaven to the earth. This accords very well with the later development of the Epic and *Puraṇic* version of the legend of Sāvitrī and Satyavān.

References

1. Swami Amritananda : *Ṛgvedic Suktas,* p. 11-13.
2. *Cakravarty G.N.* : *The concept of cosmic harmony in Ṛgveda,* p. 90.
3. *Tāṇḍ B,* 6.1.6.
4. Keith : *Religion and Philosophy of the Vedas and Upaniṣadas,* p. 156.
5. *AB,* (8.28)
6. *Nir*, (7.28)
7. Amritananda Swami : *Ṛgvedic Suktas,* p. 21-22.
8. Dange, A.A.; "*Sāvitrī and the Banyan*", Purāṇa Vol. No. 2, July, 1963, p. 260.
9. *The legend is given in detail in SB.* 3.6.2.2; *AB*. 3.25.26; *TB* 8.4.1-4.

4

Significance of Gāyatrī in Vedic Literature

Importance of *AUM* (*OM*) and Gāyatrī

OM or *AUM* is the most comprehensive, universal, non-personal, holy sound-symbol (*Logos*) and signifier (*Vācaka*) of the supreme infinite divine reality. This divine reality is of the nature of *Ananta-sat-cit-ānanda* (Absolute infinite Existence, Consciousness bliss). It manifests as the totality of existence, from the external-most physical to the internal-most spiritual on four cosmic planes. It is regarded highly auspicious in Indian religious and philosophical scriptures.

To help in spiritual practice (*Upāsanā*) A, U, M, the phonetic constituents of *om*, are identified with different types of cosmic triads, from the theistic to the philosophic and the mystic levels, for meditation purposes according to the need and development of the aspirant. By the mystic repetition of the *om*, one attunes oneself to the cosmic mind and is spiritually lifted up. By connecting oneself mentally to the cosmic reservoir through *Upāsanā,* one's mind becomes conducive for the flow of inspiration from the cosmic mind. Hence it is considered the holiest *Mantra* for *japa* and placed at the beginning of all other *mantras* used for *japa Śrimad BG* announces that it is uttered at the beginning of all *mantras* and it is also taken as *Mantras* by itself.

ॐ तत्सदिति, निर्देशो ब्राह्मणस्त्रिविधः स्मृतः
ब्राह्मणस्तेन वेदाश्च यज्ञाश्च विहिताः पुरा
तस्माद् ओ मित्युदाहृत्य यज्ञदानतपः कियाः
प्रवर्त्तन्ते विधानोक्ताः सततं ब्रह्मवादिनाम्।। (*Ch* 11.77.23-24)

'om' is the best of all *mantras.*

The *Sāmkhya* and the *Vedānta* philosophies interprete '*Om*' as the symbol of the supreme being which manifests itself in three stages of human experience *i.e.,* waking, dream and slumber and also exists above these three stages as *Turīya*. Thus '*Om*' symbolises the supreme divinity manifested in names and forms as well as the unmanifested *Brahman* which exists beyond the world of names and forms.

The *Gāyatrī-Mantra,* the greatest prayer *Mantra* incorporates all the ideas of the *om*-symbolism. It is a prayer to the supreme infinite divine reality for the enlightenment of the intelligence (*Dhī*) of all human beings, to enable them to realize the supreme truth. It is also known as the *Sāvitrī-Mantra*, since it is addressed to the divine person in the Sun (Savitā) who is considered as the visible symbolic representation of the supreme divinity. For, He destroys darkness and promotes life, and He is also identified with the inner self of man (*Isaupaniṣad* 15-16).

Sāvitrī signifies that which is related to Savitr (Savitā) which means the source or originator of the universe, as well as the sun. The *Sāvitrī-Mantra* is composed in the *Gāyatrī-Mantra*, and it being the best and most significant of *mantras* in that metre it has becomes famous as Gāyatrī. This *Mantra* occurs in the Vedas and is considered to be their very essence or even their mother (Gāyatrī Vedamāta). Later on Gāyatrī was associated with *Om*, which is also considered as the source of the Vedas. *Om* was prefixed to it along with the three *Vyāhṛtis*, which are utterances of the Divine creator representing the three cosmic planes, *Bhūḥ-Bhuvaḥ-Svaḥ* (*BṛhU* 14.1-8) and *ChU* (11.23.2-3), *Om* and the *Gāyatrī-Mantra* have acquired such great importance that they are often referred to as the Pranava and the Gāyatrī just as the *BG* is referred to as the Gitā[1]. In the *Vedas*, *Upaniṣ das*, the Gitā and the later literature, there are numerous references to the holiness, importance, and significance of the Pranava and the Gāyatrī. We shall give here a few of the important original quotations in translation from the *Upaniṣat* as the Gitā and the *Purāṇas* referring to Praṇava and the Gāyatrī. *Kaṭha Upaniṣat* (1.2.15-17) says

सर्वे वेदाः यत्पदमामनन्ति, तपांसि सर्वाणि च यद्वदन्ति
यदिच्छन्तो ब्रह्मचर्यं चरन्ति तत्ते पदं संग्रहेण ब्रवीमित्येतत्।

The Goal which all Vedas proclaim, which all austerities and meditations (*Tapāmsi*) seek, and desiring which the sages lead the life of *Brahmacarya*, is '*Om*'.

This immortal word is verily also the highest *Brahman*. Having understood this immortal word, whatever one desires, one gets that.

एतदालम्बनं श्रेष्ठम् एतदालम्बनं परम्
एतदालम्बनं ज्ञात्वा ब्रह्मलोके महीयते।। (1.2.17).

This support (*Oṁ* as a means of realization of *Brahman*) is the best, knowing this support (realizing the truth signified), one is exalted in the world of Brahmā.

The importance of *Oṁ* has been described in whole of the 4th section of *Prasna Upanisad.*[2]

"What is *Oṁ*, O Satyakāma! is verily the higher or transcendental *Brahman* and the relative or phenomenal creator-God Brahmā. Therefore the knower attains either of the two by this means."

"If one meditates upon only one of the three *mantras* of *Oṁ*, he comes back to this world very soon (after his death), being enlightened by that, स यद्येकमात्रभिध्यायीत स तेनैव सवेदितस्तर्णमेव जगत्यामभि-संपद्यते, तमृचो मनुष्यलोकमुपनयन्ते स तत्र तपसो बह्मचर्येण श्रद्धया सपत्नो महिमानमनुभवति।। V(3)

The *Ṛg* hymns lead him to the world of man, where he attains greatness in life, being endowed with austerity (*Tapasyā*), continence (*Brahmacarya*), and faith (*Śraddhā*)".

If again, one meditates upon two *mātrās*, one is united with the mind after death. He is led to the world of the moon (the presiding deity of the mind) in the intermediate region, of moon, and having enjoyed its grandeur world, he comes back again. अथ यदि दिमात्रेण मनसि सम्पद्यते, सोऽन्तरिक्षं यजुर्भिन्नीयते सोमलोकम्। (4).

"Again, he meditates upon the supreme puruṣa (*parameś- vara*) with the immortal world.

Om, constituted of all the three *mātrās*, becomes united with the effulgent sun. He is freed from all sins, as a snake is freed from its slough. He is led to the world of Brahmā by the *Sāma* chants. Then he beholds the supreme *Puruṣa* residing in the Heart, higher than this highest totality of *Jivas* (Brahmā or Hiraṇyagarbha). त्रिमात्रेणोमित्येननैवाक्षरेण परं पुरुषमभिध्यायीत से तेजसि सूर्ये सम्पन्नः। (5)

"Verily, with this *Om-kāra* (the a-*matra*) as the support, the knower attains what is peaceful, undecaying immortal, fearless and supreme (*Ātman Brahaman*)", (*Muṇḍaka Upaniṣat*).

"Taking as bow the mighty *Upaniṣadic* weapon, fix on it the arrow sharpened by constant meditation. And having drawn it to be full with the mind absorbed in its thought, penetrate and target, my dear, the immutable reality".

"Praṇava (the mystic word *Om*) is the bow, the soul within, the arrow, and *Brahman,* the target. One should hit that mark with an undistracted mind, and like the arrow, become one with it".

प्रणवो धनूः शरो ह्यात्मा ब्रह्म तल्लक्षमुच्यते।। (2.4.)

Where all the arteries meet like the spokes of a chariot-wheel in the hub-there within the psychic heart. He moves, becoming manifold. Meditate on that self as *Om,* Godspeed to you in crossing to the farther shore beyond all darkness.

ओमित्येवं ध्यायथ आत्मामं स्वस्ति वः पराय तमसः परस्तात्। (2.6.)

The whole of the *Māṇḍūkya Upaniṣad* is devoted to the delineation of the Spirituo-philosophical significance of *Om.* Though the *Upaniṣat* contains only twelve verses, it is considered so important that numerous commentaries are written on it. To briefly quote.

ओमित्यक्षरमिदं सर्वं...भूतं भव्यं भविष्यत् यदिति सर्वमोङ्कार एव।

All this cosmic universe is the eternal word *Om.* It's further explanation is this, the past, the present and the future, everything is just on. And whatever transcends the three divisions of time that too is just *Om.*

"For verily, everything is *Brahman.* And this self (*Ātman*) within is *Brahman.* The *Ātman* has four quarters-waking, dream and deep-sleep state of consciousness and the fourth one *i.e., Turīya* or *Samādhi,* the super-conscious state." This *Ātman* is to be identified with *Om,* when *Om* is considered as a single complete word. When *Om* is considered as a compound of parts, the aspects of the *Ātman* are to be identified with the parts, and the parts with the aspects.

The parts of *Om* are *A, U, M* to be identified with waking, dream and deep-sleep states of the *Ātman.* सोऽयमात्माऽध्यक्षरमोङ्कारोऽधिमात्रं पादा अंकार उकार मकार हति।

The immortal word *Om* in its partless aspect is the fourth (*Turīya*) the transcendental, devoid of phenomenality, the supreme bliss, and non-dual. Thus the word *Om* is verily the self (*Ātman*). He who knows this, with his self (*Jiva*) enters the self (*Ātman*). शिवोऽद्वैतमेवमोङ्कार आत्मैव संविशत्यात्मना आत्मानं य एवं वेद।

In *Taittiriya Upaniṣad* the significance of *om* is described in the whole of *Anuvāka* VIII in ch. I ओमिति ब्रह्म, ओमिति सर्वम्, ओमित्येत-दुनकृति ह स्म अप्यो श्रवयेत् आश्रावयन्ति। ओमिति सामानि गायन्ति। ओम् शोमिति शस्त्राणि शंसन्ति। ओमिति अध्वर्युः प्रतिगरं प्रतिगृणाति। ओमिति ब्रह्मा प्रस्तौति। ओमिति अग्निहोत्रमनुजानाति। ओमिति ब्राह्मणः प्रवक्षन्ताह ब्रह्मोपास्तवानित ब्रह्मोपासनेति।

BṛhU describes the ritualistic and meditational application of Gāyatrī.

According to *Śvetāśvatra Upaniṣat* (1.1.7) it is stated that "Making one's own body the lower piece of wood (Araṇi)[3] and the Praṇava the upper piece of wood and practising churning in the form of meditation, one should realise the inherent divine as one would find out something hidden like fire in the Araṇis.'

A few passages from *Maitri Upaniṣat* (also called *Maitreyi* or *Maitrāyaṇī Upaniṣat*) are quoted here.

"Those two, the spirit within and the Sun, go forth toward each other. One should reverence them with the word *Om,* with the mystic utterances (*Vyāhṛtis*) *Bhuḥ, Bhuvaḥ, Svaḥ* and with the Sāvitrī (Gāyatrī).

There are, assuredly, two forms of *Brahman,* the formed and the formless. Now, that which is the formed is unreal and that which is formless is real and that which is *Brahman,* is light. That light is the same as the Sun. Verily, that came to have *om* as its soul. He divided himself threefold. *Om* consists fo three *mātrās* (*A-U-M*). By means of these the whole world is woven as with warp and woof across him. Thus it has been said "one should absorb oneself meditating that the Sun is *Om*" (VI. 2.3).

ChU puts more importance on *Om.*

One should meditate on the syllable *Om,* the Udgitha, for one sings the Udgitha beginning with *Om,* ओमित्येतदरमूद्गीथमूपासीत, ओमिति हद्गयति। (1.1).

Now, that which is Udgitha is verily Praṇava and that which is praṇava for he moves along pronouncing *Om.* Prajāpati (the vedic lord of creation) brooded (made *Tapas* or meditated) on the worlds. From them, thus brooded on, issued forth the three-fold Veda and as their essence, (the mystic word) *Om.* Just as all the parts of the leaf are permeated by the ribs of the leaf, so are all words permeated by the *Om-kāra* is all this. 23. (11.2-3).

"Gāyatrī indeed is all this, whatever being exists. Speech indeed is Gāyatrī for speech indeed sings and removes fear of all that exists. Such is the greatness of this Gāyatrī. The supreme cosmic person is even greater than this. All this cosmic universe is a quarter of him, the other three quarters of Him constitute the immortal transcedent". (III.12.1 to 6).

According to the *Mahānārāyaṇa Upaniṣad* (14) "The one-syllabled om is *Brahman.* (For this *Mantra,* Agni is its deity). Its *Ṛsi* is also *Brahman.* Its metre is Gāyatrī. Its application is for the union with *Paramātman.*

आयातु वरदा देवी अक्षर ब्रह्मसम्मितम् गायत्रीच्छन्दसा माता इदं ब्रह्म जुषस्व नः।

May the boon conferring divine Gāyatrī come to us in order to instruct us about the imperishable *Brahman* who is determined by the *vedānta.* May Gāyatrī, the mother of metres, favour us with the supreme *Brahman.*

This is the Gāyatrī invocation used in the twilight devotion. The instruction on the supreme *Brahmopadesa* is mainly conveyed through Pranava and Gāyatrī. Here, therefore, a prayer is addressed to Gāyatrī, requesting her to visit the devotee and to favour him with the intuition of supreme *Brahman.* Sec. 34.I.

It is to be pointed out that in the *kenopaniṣat* it is stated that *Brahmavidyā* is acquired through the grace of the divine mother *Umā Haimavati.*

'O Gāyatrī, thou art the essence of strength, thou art patience or the subduing power. Though art the physical capacity. Thou art splendour. Thou art the abode of Gods and their names. Thou art the universe and its duration. Thou art all that exist and their span of life. Thou art the vanquisher of all that is hostile to us. Thou art the

Truth denoted by the Praṇava. I invoke Gāyatrī, I invoke Sāvitrī, I invoke Sarasvatī'.

ओजोऽसि सहोऽसि बलमसि भ्रजोऽसि देवानां धाम नामासि विश्वमसि विश्वाय: सर्वमसि सर्वायरभिभु: ओम् गायत्रीमावाहयामि सावित्रीमावाहयामि. सरस्वतीमावाहयामि।

'*Om* Earth, *Om* Sky, *Om* Heaven, *Om* middle region, *Om* place of birth, *Om* mansion of the blessed, *Om* abode of the Truth. *Om* may we meditate on the adorable light of that Divine generator who quickens our understanding. *Om,* it is the casual waters, light, Bliss, *Amborsia, Brahman,* and also the three worlds. All these are verily *Om*. (35-2).

The syllable Om added at the Gāyatrī head represents *Parabrahman* in the three aspects of Brahmā, Viṣṇu and Śiva responsible for the creation, protection and destruction of the universe respectively. *Āpaḥ* expresses the omnipresent existence which is also the *Jyotis* or self-luminous pure consciousness. The same reality is *rasa*-original bliss and *amṛtas* immortality. It is *Brahman* because it is not limited by time, space and casualty. The same reality is *bhūḥ* being *bhuvaḥ*-the substance of all that exists and *svaḥ,* the dissolver.

ओमापोज्यातीरसोमृतं ब्रह्म भूर्भुव: स्व:।

During *prānāyāma,* the praṇava with seven *Vyāhṛtis* measures the inhaling. Gāyatrī headed by praṇva limits the period of retention of breath and *Gāyatrīsiras* given here with praṇava spans the breathing out.

When a person performs the *prānāyāma* and concentrates his thoughts on this *Mantra*, the latent spiritual tendencies in the depth of his being are awakened and he becomes fit for communion with the supreme reality and eventually he realises the spiritual goal.

The *BG* describes that "confining all the sense, confining the mind in the heart, drawing up the *prāṇa-vāya* through the *Suṣumma* towards the head *sahasrāra,* and thus occupied in the practice of *yoga,* he who departs from the body uttering the one-syllabled *om* denoting *Brahman,* and meditating the supreme Goal. (viii. 12-13).

The *Vedas, Upaniṣadas, Smṛtis* and *Brāhmana* texts mention *Om* constantly. Therefore, let us glace at something in our *purāṇas* and holy scriptures.

The Lord says, *Praṇavah Sarva Vedeṣu*-प्रणवः सर्व वेदेषु'-(I am the *Om* in all the *Vedas*). (VII. 8).

पवित्रम् ओंङ्कारः-I am the holy word *Om* (1X.17).

गिरामस्ति एकम् ओंङ्कारम्-of words, I am the singly-syllabled word *Om* (X.25).

Om, Tat, Sat, this has been declared to be the triple designation of *Brahman,* Because they were made of the *Brāhmaṇas,* the *Vedas,* and the *Yajñas.* Therefore, uttering *Om* the secrets of sacrifice, gift, and austerity, as enjoined in the ordinances, is always begun led the followers of the *Vedas.* (XVII. 23-24).

Agni-Purāṇa stresses the greatness of *'AUM'* while describing the mode of reciting the *Gāyatrī Mantra.*

One who knows the syllable *AUM* is verily a *yogin* and the lord Hari. Hence one should practice the syllable *AUM,* that is the essence of all sacred syllables and giver of all the things.

> ओंकारं यो विजानाति स योगी सः हरिः पुमान्,
> ओंकारमभ्यसेस्मात् मन्त्रे सारन्तु सर्वदम्।। *Agni-Purāṇna* ch-2.51

The Praṇava is known to be the first in the application of all the sacred syllables. So the act which becomes complete with that, will not get completed with any other syllable.

> सर्वमन्त्रप्रयोगेषु प्रणवः प्रथमः स्मृतः
> तेन सम्परिपूर्णयत्तत् पूर्णा कस्मै नेतरम्।। 2

The one syllable is the supreme *Brahman,* and the *prāṇāyām* is the supreme penance. There is nothing greater than Sāvitrī. Truthfulness excels silence.

> एकाक्षरं परं ब्रह्म प्राणायमपरन्तपः।
> सावित्र्यास्तु परं नास्ति मौतात् सत्यं विशिष्यते।। 5

According to the *Vāyu-Purāṇa* the single syllabled om is the *Brahman* hidden in the cavity of the heart. This *Om* is the set of three Vedas, three worlds, three fires, three steps of Viṣṇu and *Ṛk, Sāman* and *Yajur Mantras.*

> ओमित्येकाक्षरं ब्रह्म गुहायां निहितं पदम्।
> ओमित्येतत्रयो वेदास्त्रयो लोकास्त्रयोऽग्नयः
> विष्णुकूमास्तयदस्तवे ते ऋक्सामाना यजुषि च।। *Vāp.* Ch.I. (6)

It should be known that in fact, it consists of four *mātrās*. The *yogin* who is in communion with these will attain the *sālukya* form of salvation.

मात्राश्चात्र चतस्रस्तु विज्ञेयाः परमार्थतः
तत्र युक्तश्च यो योगी तस्य सालोकयां ब्रजेत्।। 7

The letter 'A' should be known as phoneme. The letter 'w' is *Svarita*. The letter 'M' is the prolated syllable.

अकारस्त्वधरो ज्ञेयः उकारः स्वरितः स्मृतः
मकारस्तु प्लुतो ज्ञेयस्त्रिमात्र इति संज्ञितः।। 8

The letter 'A' is *Bhūrloka,* the letter 'U' is *Bhuvaḥloka* and the letter 'M' with its consonant part is *Svarloka.*

The *Omkāra* is a set of three worlds. Its head is the heaven. It is the entire universe. It is the region of Brahmā.

ॐकारस्तु त्रयो लोकाः शिरस्तस्य त्रिविष्टपम्।।10

The *Skanda-purāṇa*[4] analyses the syllable '*omkāra*' as representing Brahmā, Viṣṇu, and Rudra respectively.

The *Nārada-Purāṇa* glorifies *omkāra* and says in primeval time Brahmā uttered the words '*om*' and *'Atha'* and hence these sounds are considered auspicious on all occasions.

ओंकारश्चाथशब्दस्य द्वावेतौ ब्रह्मणः पुरा
कण्ठ भित्त्वा विनिर्यातौ तस्मान् माङ्गलिकवुभौ।।

(*Nārada-purāṇa.* 51.10)

According to the *Padma-Purāṇa* the practitioner is to utter the sound *AUM* first. Then the name of *Ṛsi, Chanda* and *Devatā.* Then *Gāyatrī-Mantras* should be invoked. This *purāṇa* further explains how are *Prāṇāyāms* to be exercised for the deity connected with each syllable.

Apāna remains at the *anus* and *Prāṇa* in the heart of a man. So having contracted the *anus* one should get it united with *Prāṇa.* Then doing *kumbhaka* exercise with *puraka* and thus practising the *Prāṇāyām,* a *Brahmāṇa* should matter the Gāyatrī hymn.

Gāyatrī, according to *Manu* is the essence of the whole of Veda as the creator milked the three lines of *Gāyatrī-Mantras* from the three Vedas respectively that is *ṚV, YV* and *SV.* Along with them the three *Mahāvyāhṛtis Bhūh, Bhuvah,* and *Svaḥ* have also been derived from the three Vedas[5].

Bhaviṣya-purāṇa states

अकारश्च उकारश्च मकारं च प्रजापतिः
वेदत्रयामु निरुध्य भूर्भुवःस्वरितीति च (1.4.14)
त्रिभ्य एव तु वेदेभ्यः पादं पादममूद्वहन्।।
नदित्युयोऽस्यां सावित्र्याः परमेष्ठी प्रजापतिः।। (15)

एतदक्षरमेतां च जपन्व्याहृति पूर्विकाम्।
ओंकारपूर्विकास्तिस्त महाव्याहुतयोऽन्यथा।
त्रिपदा चैव सावित्री विज्ञेयं ब्रह्मणो मुखं।। (19)

There are three great unmultilating *Vyāhṛtis* which are preceded by the syllable *Om.* The three-footed Sāvitrī (Gāyatrī) should be known as the face of Lord Brahmā.

In the present times, the greatness of *Om* can be seen by its use. Every nation in today's times has used the omnipresent *Om.*

The tree of *Sanātana Dharma*/the Eternal wisdom, whose glory is spread through its branches - *Jains, Śikhs, Buddhists, Christians, Muslims, Jews* and every other religion had used or sought shelter in the *Om* in some form or the other.

The *Buddhist Māntrās* is "*Om manipadme Hum*" the *Jain's Māntrās* is "*Om Arihantaya nama*". In the holy scriptures it is stated, "*Ek Om karsat Nam*" Even our *Muslim* literateurs use a word similar to *Om* "*Amen*'! *Christians* and *Jain's* also use a similar word "*Amen*".

In this way, all religions have been fortunate in improving them- selves through the help of the word *Om.*

Gāyatrī and *Vyāhṛtis*

Gāyatrī can also be studied along with *Vyāhṛtis, Pruṇava* and *Brahman-Vyahṛtis* are भूः भुवः and स्वः. These form a part of Gāyatrī in its extended form.

The universe is identified with *Vyāhṛtis.* They are the limbs of Praṇava ओं भूः भूवः स्वः. The extended Gāyatri is ओं भूर्भुवः स्वः तत्सवितुर्वरेण्यं भर्गो देवस्य धीमहि धियो योनः प्रचोदयात्। Therefore it is said that *Brahman* should be worshipped (Meditated upon) with the prayer तत्सवितुः etc. The three worlds भूः etc. were created by uttering the *Vyāhṛtis* भूः भुवः स्वः by *Brahman.* Therefore it is said that *Brahman* should be worshipped by uttering Gāyatrī with *Vyāhṛtis.* So the *Maitri Upaniṣat* (VI. 6) says, अथाव्याहृतं वा इदमासीत् स सत्यं प्रजापति स्तपस्तप्त-वानुव्याहरद् भूर्भुवस्स्वरित्यैषैवास्य प्रजापतेः स्थविरुथा तनुर्या.....भूर्भुवः स्वरित्युपासीतानेनाहि प्रजापतिर्विश्वा विश्वचक्षुरिवोपासितो भवतीत्येवा हयाहैषा वेः....तस्मादेषोपासीत।

In the beginning there were no *Vyāhṛtis.* The supreme being who is the creator (Prajāpati) and who is the embodiment of truth performed *tapas* and in the end uttered *Bhūḥ, Bhuvaḥ* and *Svaḥ.* This is the gross form of the world which is his body. The world of Āditya gross is his head, Mid-region is his navel, Prithvi in his feet, Āditya in his eyes through which he sees everything. Therefore *Brahman* should be worshipped with *Vyāhṛtis.* This *Brahman* is in the form of Prajāpati in whom reside all the worlds, with eyes which can see everything is to be worshipped. (With Sāvitrī metre and with *Vyāhṛtis*).

Brahman that is described as above is of the nature of light as stated in the *Vedas. Maitryupaniṣad* (VI-V) says that अथ य एषोऽन्तरे हत्पुष्कर एवाश्रितमन्नमत्ति। स एषोऽनर्दिवि श्रितः सौरः कालाख्योऽदृश्यः सर्वभूतान्यन्नमत्तीति। कः पुष्करः किमयो वेति इदं वाव तत्पुष्करं योऽयमाकाशोऽसे माश्रितस्ते। दिश श्वतस्त्रः उपदिशो दलसंस्था आसन्। अर्वाग् विचरत एतौ प्राणादित्या एता उपासितोमित्यक्षरेण। व्याहृतिभिः सावित्र्या चेति।

One who resides in the heart-lotus and eats food is Fire, Time and Sun. The all-Pervading Sky itself is this lotus. Four cardinal directions and four directions in between are its eight lotus petals. *Ātman* and Āditya (*Brahman*) are facing each other in this. One should meditate on this using *Vyāhṛtis Bhūḥ Bhuvaḥ Svaḥ Prāṇava* (*Om*) and the *Mantra* तत्सवितुर्वरेण्यं भर्गो देवस्य धीमहि, which is Sāvitrī in Gāyatrī metre.

The *śrutis* have sung the praise of the Praṇava and Gāyatrī as the direct instruments for the realisation of the eternal cosmic spirit in as much as they are composed of the *Vyāhṛtis* and hence pervade all the worlds symbolised by these mystic letters. This is contained in *TUp* and *Śri Śankara* attaches great importance to it. अनन्तरं व्याहृत्यात्मनो ब्रह्मणः अन्तरुपासनं स्वाराज्य फलं प्रस्तूयते। (1-5)

It is also said in *TU* that the supreme being dwells in the inner heaven of the heart. He is *manomaya,* the quint essence of mind and spirit, *Amṛita,* immortal and Hiranmaya, the being of golden effulgence. The seeker who contemplates this being within him becomes there by established in the Agni known as *Bhūḥ,* in the rays called *Bhuvaḥ,* in the Āditya termed *Svaḥ* and in the *Brahman* denominated by the supreme particle, *Mahaḥ.* He attains *Sāyujya,* identity with the supreme self. He becomes the lord of mind. He gains mastery over all forms of speech, over all senses like sight and hearing and over all types of *Vijñāna,* Knowledge informed by truth. Above all, he becomes one with and indistinguishable from the *Brahmān* himself, in as much as he is established firmly in the *Brahmān* whose body is all space, who is the informing spirit of all things, who is the thrill of all life, who is the bliss of all mind, who is the inexhaustible fountain of peace and who, above all, is the very spirit of immortality.

The *Vyāhṛti Upāsanā* is *TU* (1-5) given as follows :

The question may arise regarding the *Vyāhṛtis* of *Gāyatrī-Mantras.* The *ChU* and *TU* etc. mention three *Vyāhṛtis.* But later on the three *Vyāhrtis* were raised to seven[6]

पुराकल्पसमुत्पन्ना भूर्भुवः स्वः सनातनाः
महाव्याहृतयस्तिस्रः सर्वाः शुभनिभर्हणाः।। *Kurma Purāṇa* 54-55

According to *MNU,* by sub-dividing *Suvaḥ* into *Suvaḥ, Mahaḥ, Janaḥ, Tapaḥ,* and *Satyam* corresponding to the seven higher worlds. These are used in the *Mantras* of the *Sandhyā-Vandana* and other rituals.

The seven *Vyāhṛtis* denote the seven worlds created by Brahma by uttering them in the beginning. The first three of them are called *Mahāvyāhṛtis Praṇava* is added to each of them to point out that each *Vyāhṛti* independently also stands for the supreme. After the seven *Vyāhṛtis* the *Gāyatrī-mantra* follow them headed by another Prāṇava which again implies that the supreme alone is denoted by the *Gāyatrī-Mantras*. This is succeeded by Gāyatrī *siras* bracketed by the Praṇavas in the beginning and in the end. Gāyatrī coming in the middle is the fundamental element and the rest are auxiliaries thereof.

The *Vyāhṛtis* have a mystical significance and describe effulgent *Brahmān* as well as Prāṇava and Gāyatrī. Gāyatrī and Praṇava may be described as means for reaching *Brahmān*.

In various *Upaniṣadas* the glory of the *Vyāhṛtis,* Prāṇava and Gāyatrī is extolled.

Identity of Praṇava and *Brahman*

There are *upaniṣadic* texts which state the identity of Prāṇava and *Brahmān. Brahmān* that is light has become fire and light (*BṛhU* 1.ii 2). Similarly Praṇava with the *Vyāhṛtis* has become the three worlds which are the bases of Agni, Vāyu and Āditya in the form of light. Gāyatrī which is Sāvitrī (*Mantra* used to praise Savitṛ) praises Praṇava as *Brahmana.* These are discussed in *Maitryuponiṣad.* From this we conclude that Gāyatrī with *Vyāhṛtis* and Praṇava with *Vyāhṛtis* are but two names of *Brahman,* that is light. उपासीत औमित्येतदक्षरेण व्याहृतिभि: सावित्र्या चेति–worship *Brahmān* using *Om* (*AUM*), *Vyāhṛtis* and Sāvitrī. This *Brahman* is nothing but *Om*. (*Maitreyī Upaniṣad* III: 62-10 III. 6-25).

It is said in (*BṛhU*-1.ii-3) that *Brahman* includes the three, Agni, Vāyu and Āditya. In *Maitri upaniṣad,* it is said that Praṇava becomes three letters *A.U.M.* It is these three letters which form the warp and woof the universe. So, Āditya, who has manifested this universe, should be worshipped as the embodiment of Praṇava द्वे वाव ब्रह्मणा रूपे मूर्त्तचामूर्त्त चाथ तन्मर्त्ते तदसत्यं यदमूर्त्ते तत्सत्यं तद्ब्रह्म, तज्ज्योति:, यज्ज्योति: स आदित्य:। स वा एष ओमित्येतद् आत्माभवत्। ओमिति तिस्त्रो मात्रा एताभि: सर्वमिदमोतम् प्रोतं, आत्मानं युञ्जीतेति। *Maitri-upaniṣat* (VI-3)

In the manifested form Praṇava has three aspects. Those are also called as the limbs of *Brahman.* The aspects as per the considerations of gender, illumination, lordship, face, knowledge, worlds, time, energy, nourishing aspect, consciousness, and vitality, are common to *Brahman* and Praṇava. So *Brahman* should be worshipped as Praṇava; both *Brahman* and Praṇava are spoken of as having three limbs in the following way. अथान्यत्राप्युक्तं स्वनवत्येषास्य तनूर्य्या ओमिति (अ,उ,म), अथ स्त्री, पुं, नपुंसक इति लिङ्गवत्येषा–triad of genders. अथ अग्निः वायुः, आदित्य इति–भास्वत्येषा–triad of illuminations. अथ ब्रह्मारुद्रो–विष्णुरिति–अधिपतिवत्येषा–Lordship with respect to the universe. अथ गार्हपत्यो–दाक्षिणाऽहवनीय इति मुखवत्येषा–Agni is the face of *Om*. It is three types. अथ ऋग्यजुः सामेति–विज्ञानवत्येषा-Consciousness or knowledge embodied in the three Vedas. अथ भूः भुवः स्वः इति लोकवत्येषा-three worlds. अथ भूत भव्यं भविष्यदिति कालावत्येषा–Valour or strength (Präna, Agni, Surya). अथ अन्नमाप श्चन्द्रमा इति–...आप्यायनवत्येषा– nourishment (Food, water and moon). अथ बुद्धिर्मनोऽहंकार इति–चेतनवत्येषा–Sentinence, (*Buddhi,* mind, and ego) अथ प्राणोऽपानो व्यान इति–प्राणवत्येषा–Vitality (*Prāṇa, Apāna* and *Vyāna*). इत्यत ओमित्युत्केनैताः प्रस्तुता अर्यिता अर्पिता भवन्तीत्येवं ब्रह्म यदोमित्येतदक्षरमिति–*Maitrī upaniṣat*-(VI-5).

Om (*AUM*) is *Brahman.* When we utter *Om,* we are taking all the above triads.

The *Taittiriya upaniṣad* says (1-8) :

ओमिति ब्रह्म, ओमिति सर्वम्, ओमित्येतदनुकृति ह स्म वा अप्यो श्रावयेत् आश्रावयन्ति। ओमिति सामानि गायन्ति। ओम् शोमिति शस्त्राणि शंसन्ति। ओमिति अध्वर्युः प्रतिगरं प्रतिगृणाति। ओमिति ब्रह्मा प्रस्तौति। ओमिति अग्निहोत्रमनुजानाति। ओमिति ब्राह्मणः प्रवक्षन्वाह ब्रह्मोपास्तवानित ब्रह्मोपासनेति।

ओं is *Brahman. AUM* is all this universe. *AUM* is the reply to a question in a sacrifice indicating acceptance (अनुकरणम्). The *samans* are chanted beginning with *AUM. Adhvaryu* does *Pratigara* every action by uttering *AUM, Brahman* utters *AUM* to indicate his consent. Agnigotra is started with the utterance of *AUM,* after uttering *AUM* study of the Vedas is permitted. One who starts by saying *AUM.* May I attain *Brahman.*

In this connection we can cite the *ChU* (1-4-5) also in support स य एतदेव विद्वानध्वरं प्रणौत्यतदेवाक्षरं स्वरममृतमभयं प्रविशति तत्प्रविश्य सदमुता देवास्तदमृतो भवति। This Praṇava confers fearlessness. It confers immortality. Gods also attained immortality and fearlessness by taking recourse to meditating on Praṇava. The process is as follows, as per *Mundaka Upaniṣat* (11-2-4).

प्रणवो धनुः शरोह्यात्मा ब्रह्मतल्लक्ष्यमुच्यते अप्रमत्तेन वेद्धव्यं शरवत् तन्मयो भवेत्।

'Praṇava is the bow. Soul is the arrow. *Brahman* is the target. One should be alert and hit it. Like the arrow one should be one with the target. So Praṇava is the means for the arrows hitting the target'.

Again, *Praśna Upaniṣat* (v-6) says,

तिस्रो मात्रा मृत्युमत्यः प्रयुक्ता, अन्योन्यसक्ता अनतिप्रयुक्ताः, क्रियासु वाह्या-ऽभ्यन्तरमध्यमासु, सम्यक् प्रयुक्तासु न कम्पते ज्ञः।

The three *matras A,U,M* should never be separated. They should be chanted together. Otherwise they will cause death. In the three courses of action external, internal or middle one should use the three *mātrās* together maintaining harmony. Then the man would be firm and free from fear. Again,

ऋग्भिरेतं यजुर्भिरन्तरिक्षं सामभिर्यत्तत्कवयो वेदयन्ते। तमों कारेणै वायतनेनन्वेति विद्वान् यत्तच्द्धान्तमजरममृतमभयं परं चेति। (5-7)

The wise one knows that this world is attainable by *Ṛ-Mantras* the middle region by *Yajus* (*mantras*) and the Āditya loka by *Sāma* the wise (one) harmonising all this as *AUM* attains that which is peace, immortality, free from decay, and is the transcendental truth.

The Praṇava with the *Vyāhṛtis* and the Gāyatrī pervade the worlds indicated by the letters *A.U.M* and becomes the means for realising *Brahman.* Gāyatrī is eulogised as the potent principle that sings as well as protects, even so the Praṇava represented by *Omkāra* has also been similarly eulogised.

ओमित्येतदक्षरमुद्गीथमुपासीत। ओमिति ह्युद्गादति। *ChU*-(1.1.1)

You must meditate on *AUM* as Udgitha (Song chanted in *Sām Veda*). *Brahman* is chanted as word *Om* which is also the song sent up to the *Brahman* and should be contemplated with inwardness of soul. *Om* sings of the cosmic principle called the *Brahman* and thus gives him its musical praise. Indeed, the all-pervasive *Brahman* himself abides in this Udgitha, song lifted up to the all-high. That which is called Praṇava in *ṚV,* is called Udgitha in *SV.*

The Udgitha is Praṇava and Praṇava is Udgitha. And Āditya himself is Udgitha and Praṇava too. The supreme being who dwells in the heart is in the same form there as Āditya or the *Brahman* who is other wise known as Pranava or Udgitha. अथ खलु उद्गीथः स प्रणवो यः प्रणवः स उद्गीथ इत्यसौ वा आदित्य एव प्रणव ओमिति ह्येष स्वरत्रेति–

Therefore one should meditate on *Brahman* with the help of *Om* and Gāyatrī.

Regarding the definition of the word Praṇava, the *Śiva-purāna* engages in several etymoligies of the term.

प्र हि प्रकुतिजातस्य संसारस्य महोदधिः।
नवम् नावम् वरम् इति प्रणवम् वै विदुर वुधः। *Siva-Purāna* (1.17.4)

Praṇava is the best of boats (*nava*) to cross the ocean, *i.e.,* the *Samsara* evolved out of the *Prakrti.*

प्र प्रपञ्च न नास्ति युस्माकं प्रणवं विदुः। (1.77.4)

Praṇava means that there is no (*n*) diffusiveness (*pra*) for you (*va*).

प्रकर्षेण नयेद् युष्मान् मोक्ष वः प्रणवं विदुः। (17-5)

Praṇava is so called because it is ideal (*pra*) guide (*na*) to *moksa* for you (*va*).

स्वजपकान् योगिनां स्वमन्त्रपुजकस्य च, सर्वकर्मक्षयंकुत्वा दिव्यज्ञानं तु नूतनं।
तमेव मायारहितं नूतनं परिचक्षते प्रकर्षेण महात्मातां नवं शुद्धस्वरपकम्।

(1.17.6-8)

Praṇava is the ideal way to eliminate all *karma* of those who recite and worship it, deliver them from *Māyā,* and provide them with new (*nāva*) purified personality.

Elsewhere, it is said to be the *Prāṇa* of all living beings, all the way from Brahmā down to immobile objects.

प्राणः प्रणव एवायम् तस्मात् प्रणवः ईरितः। (6.3.14)

This shows that Gāyatrī and Praṇava are on the same plane in so far as their greatness and strength are concerned.

Āditya and *Brahman*

तत्सवितुर्वरेण्यमित्यसौ वा आदित्यः सविता स वा एवं प्रवरणीयः आत्मकामेनेत्याहुः ब्रह्मवादिनः। (*Maitryupaniṣat* VI-6)

The glory of Savitṛ who is none other than Āditya in the highest region is to be worshipped by one who wants to realise *Ātman*. This is the statement of *Brahmavādins* (Knowers of *Brahman*).

Again, the Same *upaniṣatas* continues. भर्गोदेवस्य धीमहीति सविता वै देवस्ततो योऽस्य भर्गाख्यस्तं चिन्तयामीत्याहुर्ब्रह्मवादिनः। May we know the Bharga (glory) of that Savitṛ and meditate on it. It is further *Brahmā- vādins* say धियो यो नः प्रचोदयात् इति बुद्धयो वै धियः योनः प्रचोदयादिति, बुद्धयो वै धियस्ता योऽस्माकं प्रचोदयादित्याहर्ब्रह्मवादिनः (*Maitryupaniṣat* 6-7) May that Savitṛ inspire our intellects.

This light known as Bharga of Savitṛ can be realised only through meditation. We may accept *Chāndogya's* statement in this connection.

अथ यदतः परोदिवो ज्योतिर्दीप्यते विश्वतः पृष्ठेषु सर्वतः तद्यदिदमस्मिन्नन्तः पुरुषे ज्योतिः (*ChU.* 111-13-7)

There is this great light in the world beyond *Dyuloka* (heaven). The same light shines in the lotus of the heart of *Jiva.* This light is spoken of as the Bharga of Savitṛ. In other words this is the supreme light of the supreme being. It has been discussed in the *Brahma Sūtras* under the *Sūtras* ज्योतिश्चरणाभिधानात्। (1.1.25) and छन्दोविधानात् ज्योतिः चेन्न। (1.1.26).

Dhīmahī indicates both knowing and meditating. Sāyaṇa says, परब्रह्मात्मकं तेजः ध्येयतया मनसा धारयामः।

'Let us meditate on the effulgence of *Para-Brahman*'. In statements like शाधि यां देवतामुपास्ये (*ChU.*IV.2.2), तं पश्यते निष्फलं ध्यायमानः। In *Māndukya Upaniṣat* (111.1-8), verbal roots like उपास्, विद्, ध्यै are used in the sense of meditating or knowing. We find in *Ṛk-Saṁhitā* (V. 81-1) युञ्जते मन उत युञ्जते धियो विप्रा विप्रस्य वृहतो विपश्चितः। वि होत्रा दधे वयुनाविदेक इन्मही देवस्य सवितुः परिष्टुतिः।

Wise sages concentrating their minds meditate on Savitṛ.

So far we have discussed the concealed and expressed forms of Gāyatrī. Now we may discuss its all-pervasive nature.

Vāk (word, speech) is at the root of all our knowledge and worldly transactions. It is all pervasive in its influence. So the *ChU* says that Gāyatrī is Vāk, and Vāk pervades everything and therefore Gāyatrī pervades everything. गायत्री वा इदं सर्वभूतं यदिदं किं च वाग्वै गायत्री वाग्वा इदं सर्वं भूतं गायत्री त्रयते च। (*ChU.* III. 12.1)

Everything in the universe is revealed to us by Vāk. Vāk illumines even world's existence. So Vāk is called Gāyatrī. Again we get in the *ChU.* (III. 12-2) या वै सा गायत्रीयं वावसा सेचं पुथिव्यस्यां हीदं सर्वं भूतं प्रतिष्ठितमेतामेव नातिशीयते। Gāyatrī sings the existence of everything and protects them as Vāk. Similarly Gāyatrī is identified Pṛthivi (earth) and Pṛthivi protects and supports everything.

Again *Chāndogya* says (III. 12-3) या वै सा पुथिवीयं वाव सा यदिदमस्मान् पुरुषे शरीरमस्मिन् प्राणाः प्रतिष्ठिताः एतदेव नातिशीयन्ते। The principle behind earth also becomes in effect the body of a being. All beings are established in the earth and all *prānas* are established in the body. They do not cross their limits.

The principle behind the body is Gāyatrī. This is the heart-lotus of a being. *Prāna* does not cross the limits.

Such Gāyatrī having four *Pādas* and of six types is described in *Ṛk-Samhitā* as follows :

> सैषा चतुष्पदा षड्विधा गायत्री तदेतदृचाभ्यनूक्तं।
> एतावानस्य महिमानो ज्यायाश्च पुरुषः।
> पादोऽस्य विश्वा भूतानि त्रिपादस्यामृतं दिवि। (*ṚV* X-903)

'This is the description of the glory of *Puruṣa.* एतावान् refers to past, present and future, conscious and inert being in the world. Manifestation as world is only one-forth of his glory. The rest remains in him as effulgence free from destruction'.

Śri Śankara states that this is the description of *Brahman* called Gāyatrī.

> तावानस्य गायत्र्याख्यस्य ब्रह्मणः समस्तस्य महिमा विभूतिविस्तारः।

The beings, knowledge in the three Vedas, earth, body, heart and the *Prāṇa* are just one *Pāda* of Gāyatrī or of *Puruṣa* identified with Gāyatrī. The remaining three *Pādas* refer to immortality, and not to this mortal world. The descriptions given by *Chāndogya* and *Bṛhadāranyaka* are different. But this is not going to effect the all pervasiveness of Gāyatri preached there in. According to *Brhadāranyaka,* it was said earlier that the three worlds, the three *Vedas,* and the *Prāṇas* constituted the three *Pādas* of Gāyatrī. These ideas are also discussed in the *Mandūkya Karikā* and are scattered over the *Ṛk Saṁhitā.*

Significance of the Name Gāyatrī

The term Gāyatrī denotes a particular metre in which a very large number of vedic hymns are composed. Of all these hymns the most outstanding one is at *ṚV* (3.62.10) of which the seer is Visvāmitra. Hence the *mantra* is known by the name of Gāyatrī or Savitṛ.[7] Its importance can easily be apprehended as the Lord identified himself with the *mantra* as गायत्री छन्दसामहम्[8].

The derivation of the word Gāyatrī has been traditionally from the root *gai* and *trai,* and is mainly attributed to the saviour nature of the *mantra.*

JB (1.III) states that यद् गायन्तं त्रायत तद गायत्रस्य गावत्रत्वम्। *Nir* (1.3.3) declares that गायत्री गायतेः स्तुतिकर्मणः।

Gāyatrī Puraścaraṇa Padhati of *Śankar Sūri* (P.1) declares that-गायन्तम् जपादिकर्तारं त्रायत इति गायत्री।

The *Brāhmanic* literature explains the word Gāyatrī as per its postulation of the sequential stages of the creation of the universe. Thus *ŚB* (6.1.1.8-5) describing the creation says, when Prajāpati created the earth, she tought herself to be quite perfect, and out of delight she sang because she sang, she is called Gāyatrī.

According to the *Brahdāranyaka Upaniṣat,* Gāyatri is so called because it saves the Gāya (*Prāṇa*) of the invoker. सा ह्येषा गायांस्तते, प्राणा वै गायास्तत्रे प्राणास्तते तद् यद् गायांस्तत्रे तस्माद् गायत्री। (5.14.4).

Śankar clarified it further by adding the Gāyatrī saves the Gāya or life of the ivoker from falling into the hell.

माणवकस्य गायन् प्राणान् त्रायते नरकादिपतनात्। Again, according to Śankar, other functionaries like speech etc. Are also included in the category of *Prāṇa* or Gāya as they also produce sound (and the very derivation of the word Gāya may be traced to the root i.e., to sing). Sankar writes प्राणा वागादयो वै शब्दकरणात्।

The *ChU* (3.12.1-2) derives the word Gāyatrī as गायति च त्रायते च to which Śankar further clarifies गानान् त्राणात् च गायत्र्या गायत्रीत्वम्, which means Gāyatrī has the quality of singing and saving. The whole concept has been attired in appropriately expressive words and versified in the following manner by Bharadvāja[9].

प्राणा गया इति प्रोक्तस्तायते तानथापि वा।
गायत्रीति भवोन्ताम केवलं त्रायतीति वा।

Vyāsa advocates the view as गायत्री प्रोच्चते यस्मात् गायन्तं त्रायते यतः।

The great *mantra* Gāyatrī is also famous by the appellation of Sāvitrī as it expresses the lord Savitā who is the progenitor of the world. The name Sāvitrī signifies the generating potential as clarified by Bharadvāja.

सवितृ प्रकाशकरणात् सावित्यभिधा भवेत्।
जगतः प्रसवित्रीति हेतुनानेन वापि च।

Gāyatrī is also famous in the name of Sarasvatī as it remains on the tongue of the invoker as has been put by Bhardavāja-

व्यानशे प्राणिजग्धासु सदावाग्सवर्तनात्
सारस्वतीति नान्मा च समाख्याता महर्षिभिः।

In fact the attribution of the three names is due to the timing of meditation of Gāyatrī. It is called Gāyatrī if it is meditated in the morning and is called Sāvitrī when meditated in the mid-day. The same if meditated in the evening is called Sarasvatī; Yājnyavalkya says :

गायत्री नाम पूर्वाह्णे सावित्री मध्यमे दिने।
सरस्वती च सायाह्णे सैव सन्ध्या त्रिषु स्मृता।

Gāyatrī is also famous in the name of *sandhyā* as it is invoked during the meeting moments of two phases of time like dawn and twilight mid-day and mid-night. Says Bharadwāja,

तस्मादित्यं सदोपास्या निशादिवसयोर्द्विजैः।
गायत्री सन्धिवेलायां सैव सन्ध्येति कीर्तिताः।।

and again says,

सा सन्ध्या सैब गायत्री द्विधाभूता व्यवस्थिता।

The *Agni-Purāṇa* explains in same manner as she protects the devotees or disciples and their wives from the cycles of re-birth, she is called Gāyatrī. Since its essence serves to illumine the sun and forms the light in the universe, it is known as Sāvitrī. As it first came as a word or in the form of speech; so it is called Sarasvatī.

गायांच्छिष्यान् यतस्त्रायते भार्य्या प्राणांस्तथैव च।
प्रकाशनातमा सवितुर्वाग्रूपा सा सरस्वती।। (216.1-2)

According to *PadP* and *SkP* as she was caused to enter the mouth and come out from the anus of the cow, she was named Gāyatrī.

प्रविष्टा गोमुस्बे यस्मादपानेन विनिर्गता।
गायत्रींन्नाम ते पत्नी तस्मादेषा भविष्यति।। *SkP* (VI. 70)

Interpretation of the *Mantra*

After discussing the greatness of Gāyatrī from different angles the various significant words in the *Gāyatrī-Mantra* need a description. They are therefore described in the following pages.

Tat

In interpreting this *Mantra* (*ṚV.* III. 62.10) two different grammatical relations are suggested for the word '*Tat*'. Some take it as the epithet of the word 'Sāvituḥ' and others have considered it as the attribute of 'Bhargaḥ'. Despite this divergence, both the interpretations amount to the same thing.

If '*Tat' is related to* Sāvituh, then since the noun substantive 'Savituh' is in genetive singular, '*Tat*' would come to have the singular meaning '*Tasya*'. The relation of the words would thus be '*Tasya Devasya Savituḥ-Bhargaḥ*' etc.. 'The radiance of that supreme deity *Savita* or *'Tasya'* by itself would mean *Brahmanaḥ i.e.,* of the *Brahman*'-for the term '*Tat*' itself denotes the *Brahman.*

ओं तत्सदिति निर्देशो ब्रह्मणः त्रिविधो स्मृतः।
ब्राह्मणास्तेन वेदाश्च यज्ञाश्च विहिताः पुरा।। (*Gitā* 17.23)

For interpreting the colophon at the end of every *adhyāya* or chapter of the *BG* Śri Ramānuja says तत् शब्दो हि ब्रह्मवाचि प्रसिद्धः। It is well known that the term "*Tat*" itself means the *Brahman*". Śri

Śankarācārya, in the same context comments तत् इति ब्रह्मभिधानमुचार्य्य (or having mentioned the designation of the *Brahman*) by the usage of the term "*Tat*".

Again, there are several passages of the *Upaniṣadas,* where the term "*Tat*" is used as the equivalent of the term '*Brahman*'. Among these the most famous passage is तत् त्वमसि *Svetaketu.* सर्वं तत् सत्यं च आत्माऽतत्वमासि श्वेतकेतो-*ChU* (VI. 3.7). Here as all interpretations agree, '*Tat*' is the *Brahman,* and '*tvam*' means the individual soul. Hence, the *mantra* '*Tat-tvam-asi*' means 'Thou art that' and thus it identifies the *Jiva* with the *Brahman* or the individual with the supreme soul.

Everywhere the term '*Tat*' denotes the supreme being, the *Brahman* who is all-knowing, who is of true will and who is the cause of the cosmos. In the *ChU* the passage तज्जलानिति....(III. 14.1) has been called the तद् क्रतुमय passage, that is to say, the section dealing with sacrifices to the *Brahman.*

The *Taittiriya* texts ओं तत् ब्रह्म, ओं तत् वायुः and तत् तद् आत्मा also express the same truth, namely, that '*Tat*' means the *Brahman.*

Hence, in the text of the *Gāyatrī-Mantra* too, since the term '*Tat*' is synonymous with the *Brahman,* it has been used as the attribute of *Savitā,* the *Parabrahman.* So '*Tat Savituḥ*' should be understood, as '*Tasya Savituḥ*', belonging to that *Savitā,* the *Brahman.* This is one view.

The Second view is that the term '*Tat*' is the epithet describing 'Bhargaḥ'. Bhatta Bhaskara, commenting on the *Gāyatrī-Mantra* which is quoted in the *TU* and *Āraṇyaka Upaniṣad,* says that the *Mantra* has been interpreted in the section सम् पश्यामि..of the *TU.* Then he proceeds to the interpretation of the text of the *Gayatri-Mantra.* There is a slight difference between the *Āraṇyaka* and *Saṁhitā* interpretations. In the first case the commentator considers the term '*Tat*' as an epithet of the term Bhargaḥ-

ततस्य सुपां सुलुक् इति षष्ठ्या लुक्। तस्य सवितुः वेवस्यानादि गुणयुक्तस्य। (*TS.* 1.5.6) and describes this as the radiance of Savitā, the creator of the cosmos, which is known to and is to be worshipped by all the worlds. But in the interpretation of the *TS* passage, he expresses the view that '*Tat*' should be related to 'Savituḥ' and so should be understood as '*Tasya Savituḥ*' of the *Brahman,* namely Savitā.

In the texts like *Mundaka Upaniṣad Jyotiṣām-Jyotiḥ,*" the *Brahman* is identified with light itself. The whole discussion thus imports that the same supreme principle is denoted by two different names. Hence, if the term '*Tat*' is related to 'Savituḥ', it would mean '*Tasya Jagatprerakasya Savituḥ*', (belonging to that Savitā who is the creator of the universe). But if it is related to the term 'Bhargaḥ' then it would mean '*Jagat-prasiddham-Jyotiḥ*' (that is known to the whole universe[10]).

Agni-Purāna also states that

अग्नौ प्रास्ताऽऽहुतिः सम्यगादित्यमुपतिष्ठते।
आदित्याज्जायते वृष्टिः वृष्टरन्नं ततः प्रजाः।। (83.11)

Libations of clarified butter cast into the fire are carried to the Sun God (Āditya) who creates the rain-clouds. The Rain causes the stalks of food grains (*annam*) to shoot out and man is the offspring of food.

Savituḥ

What the term *Savitṛ* denotes has been described in the foregoing discussions and it has been shown that the *Parabrahman* Himself is termed 'Savitṛ'.

One way in which 'Savitṛ' has been explained is that Āditya Himself is Sāvitṛ, as he is the generator of the rains which bring content and joy to all the worlds.

सूते सकलजननिवृति हेतो-वृष्टिः।

Another derivation is '*Sauti-sakala-sreyansi*',

देवस्य सवितुर्वयं वाजयन्तः पुरन्ध्या भगस्य यतिमीमहे।
देवं नरः सवितारं विप्रा यज्ञो सुवृतिभिः नमस्यन्ति धियोषिताः।।
(*ṚV* 62.11.12)

He confers all blessings on devotees. This brings out the significance of the term Savitṛ in yet another way[11].

A third one could be उद्यन्तमस्तंयन्तमादित्यमभिध्यायन् कुर्वन् ब्राह्मणः विद्वान् सकलं भद्रमश्नुते–one who meditates on the rising and setting Suns will achieve all auspiciousness.

सविता सर्वभूतानां सर्वभावान् प्रसूयते। सवनात् प्रेरणाच्चैव सविता तेनचोच्यते। (Yogi Yājñavalkya). One who is responsible for the creation of beings and the universe and one who is the source of all transactions and inspires beings, he is Savitā.

Thus the term 'Savitṛ' can be interpreted in diverse ways in accordance with diverse derivations.

Vareṇyam

The *ṚV Saṁhitā* shows how Savitā is '*Vareṇya*', the Being fit to be aspired after and sought, fit to be pursued and chosen, fit to be attained.

Savitṛ, the creator embraces and wears in his own being the configurations of all the worlds. He procreates all species of creatures, biped and quadruped or other, and confers upon them all things auspicious. He also makes all creatures instinctive with consciousness. Hence he is *Vareṇya.*

विश्वा रूपाणि प्रति मुञ्चते कविः प्रसावीद्भद्रं द्विपदे चतुष्पदे।
वि नाकमख्यत्सविता वरेण्योऽनुप्रयाणमुषसो वि राजति।। (*ṚV* v.81.2)

The description corresponds closely to the eulogy contained in *upaniṣadic* utterances like "*Tasya bhāsa-Sarvam-idam-vibhāti*". It is by His light that all this (universe) is illumined." The *upaniṣads* also declare that Savitṛ Himself is the lord of all the affairs of the universe.

उतेशिषे प्रसवस्य त्वमेक इदुत पूषा भवसि देव यामभिः।
उतेदं विश्वं भुवनं वि राजसिश्यावास्वस्ते सवितः स्तोममानशे।
(*ṚV.* v.81.5)

Other *Upaniṣadic* utterances like "*Devaya Savitre satya prasavaya*" describes the nature of Savitṛ more elaborately (*BṛhU* 6.5.9.). Savitṛ, who inspires consciousness in all creatures, at first composed his mind and willed to give birth to truth. Then he spread the radiance of Agni over all cosmos. It is for this reason that the *Sruti*-text enjoins, यञ्जते उत मन यञ्जते धियो विप्र विप्रस्य बृहतो विपश्चित। Bent is the mind and fixed indeed are the intellectual powers of that person who having observed well and widely is the knower of reality. In other words, in seeking to attain the supreme being who is the cause of the universe the *Mantra* declares that this cause is Savitṛ, manifesting himself as the divine light.

It is also declared in *Agni-Purāṇa* that the word वरेण्यं shows how Savitṛ is revered in the highest degree as the whole universal spirit or highest of all lights and she is the most adored of all existences. It is also described that the root '*Vr*' of the term *Vareṇyam* may also mean 'to cover it'. It necessarily signifies that which envelops or lies behind the states of waking, sleeping, dreaming and hence a being who is changeless, eternal and absolutely pure, the perfect knowledge and the infinite reality.

वरेण्यं सर्वतेजोभ्यः श्रेष्ठं वै परमं पदम्।
स्वर्गापवर्गकामैर्वा वरणीयं सदैव हि।।

वृणोतेर्वराणार्थत्वाज्जाग्रत्स्वप्नादिवर्जितम्।
नित्यं शुद्धमेवमेकं सत्यं तद्धि महीश्वरम्।। (*AP* ch. 83.3-4)

Swami Amritānanda in *ṚV Sūktas* opines that पुरुषार्थकामिभिर्वरणीयं श्रेष्ठो वा। He is to be worshipped by all those who desire to get the *Puruṣārthas* fulfilled. Savitṛ is revered in, because it is through him that all blessings sought after are obtained by his grace alone and because he, in the form of light, is the most sacred being. He is the soul of the universe. He is truth. He is the abode of enjoyment, bliss and peace. Hence the abode of object fit to be heard of, borne in mind and meditated upon is this divine light.

सत्यात्मप्राणारामं मनसः आनन्दं शान्तिसमृद्धममृतम्।।

Bhargaḥ

The *Upaniṣads* have described it as "this supreme light." Here "the light of all lights" is itself named Bharga. This Bharga is that supernatural light of the *Parabrahman,* which is destructive of all ignorance.

The prayer enshrined in the Gāyatrī asks for that gracious inspiration, that inner prompting of the mind and heart and soul which leads through meditation, to the realisation of the transcendental light of Savitā. It is beyond human perception and cannot be attained by the mere pouring over or recitation of the Vedas for the realisation of the nature of the transcendental light of the supreme spirit, the contemplation and meditation of Gāyatrī, accompanied by its recitation, is the right way.

Śri Śankarācārya explains this fact in his introduction to the passage on Gāyatrī in his commentary on the *Chāndogya*. The *Brahman* is not perceptible to the senses of sight and so on. He is not something in this gross, empirical, phenomenal world. Writing in this strain, the great commentator concludes that the description of the supreme soul is possible only in negative terms. He is not this, not this...realisation of him is non-material, hence formless, essence is therefore, possible only through spiritual meditation. And for such meditation, the right means is this sublime *Gāyatrī-Mantra*.

'Bharga' denotes the supernatural light of Savitṛ which is worthy of quest, pursuit and attainment. The *Maitri Upaniṣad* (VI. 7) explains the significance of this term.

1. *Bhāḥ* means radiant ray. Āditya's light has been called 'Bharga' because its movement is in the form of such rays and because his all-pervasiveness is due to this movement of the rays. भाभिः किरणैरधिष्ठानधर्मैरस्य गतिर्गमनम्।
2. The *Brahmavādins* hold the view that it is Rudra who is called Bharga in as much as he dissolves the universe. भर्जयति जगत् संहरतीति रुद्रो भर्ग इति।
3. Another interpretation seeks to reveal the mystic significance of all the three letters, '*Bha*', '*ra*' and '*ga*' harmonised in the word Bharga.
   - (*i*) '*Bhā*' stands for 'bhāsayati', it signifies that Savitṛ illumines all the worlds by his unparalleled radiance.
   - (*ii*) '*Ra*' stands for 'ranjayati' it signifies that Savitṛ delights all the worlds and makes them happy by his *Sat-Citānanda* nature (or by virtue of his being Existence-consciousness-bliss).
   - (*iii*) '*Ga*' denotes both '*gachanti*' and '*āganchanti*', it signifies that it is in the *Parabrahman* that all existences, whether in the state of dreamless sleep or at the time of waking whether from sleep or the manifest state, from whom all existences emerge.

भ इति भासयतीमान् लोकान्। र इति रञ्जयतीपानि भूतानि।
ग इति गच्छन्त्यस्मिन्नागच्छन्त्यस्मादिमाः प्रजास्तस्माद् भरगत्वाद् भर्गः।
(*Maitryupaniṣat* 6-7)

'Bharga' is also interpreted as 'radiance' or 'food' or 'wealth' as found in the *Agni-Purāṇa.* The word Bharga occurring in the middle of the *Mantra* represents the supreme light, the essence of the *Parabrahman.* The root '*Bha*' means to shine and *bhrasja* (to cook or ripen).

तज्ज्योतिः चरमं ब्रह्म भर्गस्तेजो यतः स्मृतम्।
भा दीप्ताविति रूपं हि भ्रस्ज पाकेऽथ तत्स्मृतम्।।
औषधादिकं पचति भ्राजृ दीप्तौ तथा भवेत्।
भर्गः स्याद् भ्राजत इति बहुलं च्छन्द ईरितम्।। (*Agni-Purāṇa* 83 2.3)

Devasya

The term *Devasya* (*Deva*) refers to Savitṛ. It is said that the word *Deva* is derived as follows :

दीव्यते क्रीडते यस्माद्रोचते द्योतते दिवि।
तस्माद्देव इति प्रोक्तः स्तूयते सर्वदेवतैः।।

He sports, the world are entertained. He illumines, so he is *deva* and is praised by gods[12]".

In other words, this attribute is an appropriate description of Savitṛ, because he delights eternally manifesting his joy in sport (the sport of creation, maintenance and dissolution of the cosmos) or indeed, because He is joy itself.

The *Śrutis* have declared that this being who is joy itself has *Moda* and *Pramoda* for his two fortnights. दीव्यति नन्दतीति देवः। In other words, he manifests his bliss in enjoyment and more enjoyment in the two fortnights, of the month. That is to say, eternal joy, revealed in eternal sport and enjoyments, is the nature of the *Parabrahman.* It is this unique characteristic of Savitṛ that is denoted by the term *Deva.*

Dhīmahi

'*Dhīmahi*' has been explained as 'Let us contemplate or meditate upon' or 'Let us bear in mind (मनसा धारयामः।)

In other words, the term *Dhīmahi* signifies that we should ever bear the image of Savitṛ in mind as the one object fit to be contemplated and meditated upon.

Brahman cannot be expressed by speech or thought of the mind. By meditation we develop intuition, and this intuition leads us straight into *Brahman.* This is not a mental transaction and comes only when the mind does not function as mind. Pure mind and *Ātman* are one and same as *Śri Ramkrisna* says so the word '*Dhīmahi*' used in the *Gāyatrī Mantra* suggests that our meditation leads to spiritual intuition and illumination[13].

The *Taittiriya Upaniṣad* commends as the means of realisation that kind of spiritual meditation and communion in which the seeker endeavours to cross all the limitations of the worlds of opposites and, having realised the *Brahman,* himself to become one with and indistinguishable from the *Brahman.* न कश्चन वसतौ प्रत्याचक्षीत। तद् व्रतं बलमिति विद्युति। यश इति पशुषु। ज्योतिरिति नक्षत्रेषु....। अहं विश्वं भुवनमभ्यभवाम् सुवर्ण्ण ज्योतिः (*TS* ch. 10).

The mortal becomes immortal by virtue of this meditation instinct with the knowledge of the *Brahman.* As Āditya shines in the heaven, so does he shine with the divine radiance of the *Brahman.*

The *Agni-Purāna* states that the word *Dhīmahi* in the text may be also derived from the root '*dhā*' to hold, and accordingly the *Mantra* may be interpreted to mean "may we make a full comprehension of the god who is the creator of seven regions known as the *Bhūḥ, Bhuvaḥ* etc." The word '*Naḥ*' is the possessive plural form of the personal pronoun 'I' and the word Bharga means divinity or divine essence.

दधातेर्वा धीमहीति मनसा धारयेमहि।
नोऽस्माकं यश्च भर्गश्च सर्वेषां प्राणिनां धियः।। (*AP* 83.12).

Dhiyaḥ

In order to attain the sense of identity with the *Brahman,* two things are indispensable–Firstly, the knowledge that the self and the *Brahman* are indeed one and secondly, the act of meditation through which alone the sense of union can be achieved. Gāyatrī embodies the prayer that Savitṛ may inspire in the seeker, that *Dhī* gives him both these requisites of self realisation. *Dhiī* here means both discriminating sense, the power of the intellect, illumined with the light of the soul, and the power of action assuming the form of spiritual meditation and leading to realisation, to the sense of oneness with the *Brahman.* Prajñā or knowledge is necessary because only through it *avidyā* or ignorance can be destroyed. And this *prajñā* can be attained only through the *karma* of *upāsanā* or through the act of seeking the *Brahman* through contemplation. Thus there is no inconsistency between the two interpretations of the term *Dhī* given above. On the contrary, the two hold together, as knowledge and action are complementary and interdependent.

Right action, right knowledge, and right praise are all one. If not their identity, is described in the *TU* in the passage–

> विज्ञानं ब्रह्मेति व्यजानात्। विज्ञानाद् दैव खल्विमानि भूतानि जायन्ते
> विज्ञानेन जातानि जीवन्ति। विज्ञानं प्रयत्यभिसंविशतीति तद्विज्ञाय:।
>
> (*TS.* ch-5)

Knowledge assumes the from of sacrifice. It is also assumes the form of all other righteous acts. All the Gods pursue and adore knowledge, which itself is the *Brahman.* The *Ātman* who is informed with and charged with *Vijñāna* or knowledge is the *Brahman* himself. But in order to attain that state of realisation in which the *Brahman* is seen as *Ānandamaya,* bliss itself, not merely *Vijñānamaya* or knowledge, the act of meditation instinct with the knowledge of the *Brahman* is required.

So it is that in the Gāyatrī the term *Dhī* compounded of all the three elements *Jñāna, Karma* and *Dhyāna,* action and communication have been employed to emphasize the importance of that spiritual meditation. The prayer embodied in the Gāyatrī is-'May Savitṛ inspire us and prompt us into this act of meditation[14]'.

Yaḥ

One interpretation of the term '*Yaḥ*' is expressed in "*Yaḥ-Savitā Sūryaḥ*". The significance is may he who is the Sūrya known as Savitā inspire us! Alternatively य इति लिङ्गव्यत्यय: यद्भर्गो धिय: प्रचोदयात् तत् ध्यायेम इति समन्वय:–says Sayanācārya. From this interpretation we must meditate on that Bharga or that divine radiance of Āditya which inspires us into the act of meditation filled with knowledge.

It is also suggested that the term *Yah* undergoing a change of gender, indicates the *Brahman* directly-यच्छब्दनिर्दिष्टस्यात्मनः स्वरुपभूतं परम्ब्रह्म तत्सवितुरित्यादिपदे निर्दिश्यते। The term *Yaḥ* points to that *Ātman* whose essential nature is *Parabrahman* described by such term as Savituḥ. By this comment Śri Śankarācārya has interpreted *Yah* as signifying the *Parabrahman* himself.

Naḥ

Naḥ means 'to us'. The use of this term apparently suggests that the *Brahman* and the *Jivas* are different entities. Some hold that, although in reality there is no difference between the individual soul and the supreme soul, this mistaken sense of difference is born in the individual owing to his ignorance springing from his physical nature. So the commentators say, the prayer uttered in the Gāyatrī differentiating between the individual and the supreme, asks to us who are different from thy, grant thou that sense and will which is the means to their pursuit and attainment.

Pracodayāt

Pracodayāt is interpreted as *prerayet.* The significance of this term is 'may Savitṛ inspire in us the right sense which prompts us to right action'. In other words, the prayer here uttered is that Savitā may grant us the power to realise the nature and virtue of his divine radiance by the performance of the right action, inspired by the right knowledge.

Gāyatrī is a unique *prayer.* It is of extraordinary significance. To understand that without the grace of god, it is impossible to attain the fruit of knowledge. God says to Arjuna in the Gitā-

मया प्रसन्नेन तवार्जुनेदं, रूपं परं दर्शितमात्मयोगात्।
तेजोमयं विश्वमनन्तमाद्यं, यन्मे त्वदन्येन नदृष्टपूर्वम्। (*Gitā* 11.47)

"O Arjuna, it is I, who, being pleased with thee revealed to this transcendental form by my power of *yoga.*" Thus the god himself makes clear to Arjuna that it is by his grace that Arjuna was able to see the god's cosmic form. The *Kaṭhopaniṣad* (11.25) also states :

नायामात्मा प्रवचनेन लभ्यो न मेधया न बहुना श्रुतेन।
यमेवैष वृणुते तेन लभ्यस्तस्यैष आत्मा विवृणुते तनूं स्वाम्॥

"This *Ātman* is not attainable by learning or the power of intellect. He is to be attained neither by hearing the *Srutis* a great deal, nor by means of sweet-speech. He is attainable only by him, whom this *Ātman* himself chooses. To such a person *Ātman* fully reveals his form." Here again it becomes clear that it is only the god's chosen ones that receive his grace and it is only by his grace that they can gain him. The *Mantra* of the *ṚV Saṁhitā* (1.189.1) also prays to god for his own gracious guidance in order to attain him. Even so, here in the *Gāyatrī-Mantra,* although the means to the attainment of Savitā's Bharga are first stated to be the individual's own endeavour through meditation, inspired by knowledge. It is finally stressed that the most important means to the realisation of the *Brahman* is his own grace.

It has already been discussed about the importance of *AUM, Vyāhṛtis,* Praṇava and their identification with Gāyatrī.

Many *Sruti* texts declare that, just as the *Parabrahman* who is the *Paramjyotih* has taken the forms of Agni, Vāyu and Āditya, even so Pranava compounded of *Vyāhṛtis* or mystic words manifests itself in the three worlds, *Bhuḥ, Bhuvaḥ,* and *Svaḥ* which are the abodes of Agni, Vāyu and Āditya. It is for this reason that the *Brahman* should be contemplated and worshipped by means of the prayerful *Mantra* '*Tat Savituḥ*----dedicated to him in torn from and designation of Savitā'.

Two points deserve to be noted in these descriptions. Firstly, it is declared that all the three-worlds, the earth, the sky, and the heaven were all created by the utterance of the mystic particles *Bhūḥ, Bhuva* and *Svaḥ.* Secondly, it is enjoined upon us that, for this very reason, the pursuit of the *Brahman* should be made by means of the same mystic particles *Bhuḥ, Bhuvaḥ* and *Svaḥ.*

If this sublime image in first formed in the seeker's mind, then the procedure for the realisation of the *Brahman* can be easily grasped. The *ṚV Mantra* says "*Tat Savituḥ Vareṇyam..iti asau.. Ādityah.. Savitā...ahu..Brahmavādinah*". At the first step, it is here pointed out, to realise that the object to be worshipped is the radiant light of Savitā. He who is after self-realisation must at the outset understand the nature and form of Savitā and then set about his task of attaining him.

The second step is indicated in the *Mantra* "*Bhargo-Devasya-dhīmahi-iti-Savitā-vai-Devah...iti-ahuh-Brahmavādinah.*" *Savitā* himself is the *Parabrahman.* Therefore, let us endeavour to realise his Bharga, his ineffable effulgence. Concentrating on that let us contemplate him and attain him.

The *Brahmavādins,* the knowers of the *Brahman,* have declared, the *Maitri Upaniṣad* goes on to explain, that the final step is to pray Savitā for His own grace and guidance. May *Savitā* grant us the power to know Him! May He grant us the spiritual consciousness to realise Him! For only by the grace of the supreme Lord we can succeed in the endeavour to know him and attain him. This is the interpretation of the *ṚV* texts given by the *Maitri Upaniṣad.*

An Assimilation

It is true that there are several other poetic meters. But it is only through the *Gāyatrī*-metre that realisation of the supreme is possible. That it is only Gāyatrī, of all metres, which has this power is proved by its prominent place *i.e.,* ceremony of sacrifice which is the means to the knowledge of the divine reality. Hence, the most important instrument for the attainment of the knowledge of the *Brahman* is Gāyatrī.

The importance of Gāyatrī for supreme realisation is revealed by three factors. It was Gāyatri who brought and delivered to the gods the Soma-juice, one of the principal accessories to sacrifice. Secondly Gāyatrī pervades over all other metres and embraces them all in her own being. And, finally, she pervades the atmosphere and presides over sacrificial acts during all the three auspicious periods prescribed for such duties. It is for these reasons that Gāyatrī has such a conspicuous place in the performance of fire-sacrifice.

Moreover, Gāyatrī is the mother of the *Brahmanas.* The knowledge of the nature of the *Brahman* depends on Gāyatrī. Hence, Gāyatrī alone is the supreme instrument for the realisation of the fundamental nature of the light divine called the *Prabrahman.*

References

1. Swami Mudhyananda, *Om Gāyatri and Sandhya* p. 20.
2. *Prasna Upanisad* v. (2-5), 7.
3. *For the purposes of rituals, fire is kindled by rubbing two pieces of holy wood or short sticks called Araṇis.*
4. *SkP.* 11.66-70.
5. *Manu Smṛti* (2.76) Ed. Narayan Ram Acanya.
6. *Mahānārāyaṇa Upaniṣat; Gāyatrī Upaniṣat, KP.* 54-55, etc.
7. *GB* 1.1.13, *SkP, Āvantya Khanda, Revā Khanda,* 200.3f; *AP.* 216.2f J. Gonda, "*The Indian Mantra*" oriens, Vol. 16, 1963; Ram Sharma Vasistha, "*Gāyatrī Mantra*" (*Hindi*), *Sasvatavani,* 2(12), Dec. 1962; KS. Hetresh Chandra Chattopadhyaya, "*Gāyatrī Mantrakā Ṛsi Visvāmitra ya Jamadagni* (*Hindi*), *Visva Jyoti,* Vol. 21, June-July, 1972, 196.
8. *Bhagavata Gita* 10.35.
9. *Bharadvāja Smṛti* quoted in *Gāyatrī Artha Samgraha,* p. 139.
10. Joshi M.N : *Gāyatrī in ṚV.* p.100-102; Amritananda Swami, *Rgvedic Suktas,* p. 55.
11. Joshi M.N : *Gayatri In RV.* p.103; Amritananda Swami, *Rgvedic Suktas*, p. 57.
12. Swami Amritānanda–*Ṛgvedic Suktas,* p. 61.
13. *Ibid.*
14. Joshi, M.N. Gāyatrī in ṚV. p. 109-110.

5

Origin and Birth of Gāyatrī in the *Purāṇas*

The exaggerated exaltation of sacrifice and the predominance of the priestly class prepared the ground for *Upaniṣadic* speculation and the rise of religious reformations like *Buddhism* and *Jainism*. As a result there was a decline of *Vedism*. But from very early times, there existed in India, side by side with the *vedic* religion, various popular faiths and beliefs. Due to the sweeping ascendency of *vedic* tradition these popular ways of life were restricted to the respective tribes among which they had originated. The decline of *vedic* way of life afforded them an opportunity to assert themselves under the changed social environs. It would seem that propagondist of Brahmanism encouraged these popular traditions and assimilated them to meet the challenge posed by the heterdox movements. Now, *Brahmanism* engaged itself in onerous task of remodelling and assimilating the indigenous beliefs and religious practices, growth and changes are reflected in the two epics the *Rāmāyaṇa* and the *Mahābhārata*, and is well-known as *Hinduism*. Hopkins rightly observes that the epic period marks a change in *Brahmanism* through this new faith has its root in the *Vedas* and the *Brāhmaṇas*, yet the indigenous belief and religious practice of the environment were remoulding the old faith unconsciously and were causing new interpretation and inspiration.[1]

The epics are the result of the greatest efforts made to conserve in a collected form all the ancient beliefs and traditions of the country. In these works an attempt has been made to present a complete embodiment of the ideals to be found in the social organization and religion of the Indian people. Hence if we want to trace the development of Indian mythology from its dim beginning to its perfect maturity through all its multiform intermediate phases, we cannot have a better source than the two epics[2].

The salient feature of the epic mythology is the emergence of Brahmā, Viṣṇu and Śiva as the three supreme gods. In both the epics, the older gods like Indra, Varuṇa, Soma etc. occupy subordinate position, while some goddesses like Lakṣmi, Sarasvatī and Durgā attain comparatively more exalted stature. Thus Gāyatrī, who in the Vedas as a metre and whose divinity was hinted at only in the later vedic texts, becomes a fullfledged divinity in the *Purāṇas*.

However, the concept of Gāyatrī has been described in details in some of the *Purāṇas* like *Agni-Purāṇa, Brahmavaivarta-Purāṇa, Brahmāṇḍa Purāṇa, Garuḍa-Purāṇa, Kurma-Purāṇa, Linga-Purāṇa, Matsya-Purāṇa, Padma-Purāṇa, Skanda-Purāṇa, Viṣṇu-Purāṇa, Vāyu-Purāṇa, Vasāha-Purāṇa and Devī-Bhāgavat Purāṇa* etc.

Origin of Gāyatrī

The vedic texts do not furnish us with the legends regarding the Origin of the Gāyatrī but the Epic-*Purāṇic* texts are prolific in this respect. It is pointed out that Gāyatrī is not treated as a mother-goddess in the vedic literature but in the *Purāṇic* literature her procreative nature becomes manifested along with *Brahmā*.

Epithets and attributes associated with them help much to bring about the characteristic features of a deity. So, there are a number of epithets and attributes of the goddess Gāyatrī in *Mahābhārata* and *Purāṇas* which throw ample light on the concept of the goddess. The evolution of Gāyatrī from the position of a mere metre to that of a mother goddess will be explained in the following context.

The *Purāṇas* have recorded a curious legend regarding the origin of Gāyatrī. Anthropomorphizing these two (Gāyatrī and Sāvitrī) by stating that Gāyatrī and Sāvitrī are different from each other and both being associated with Brahmā, the Prajāpati of *vedic* and *Brāhmaṇic* period.

Brahmavaivarta Purāṇa

It is said that with a view to creating the universe *Brahmā* put semen in Sāvitrī. She bore the foetus for hundred divine years and later gave birth to the four Vedas and a variety of other lores.

ब्रह्मा विश्वं विनिर्माय सावित्र्या वरयोषिति,
चकार वीर्य्याधानं च कामूक्यां कामुको यथा
सा दिव्यं शतवर्षं च धृत्वा गर्भं सुदुःसहम्।
BrahmavaivartaP, Brahmākhanda (ch. 8.1-2)

She is called the mother of the *Vedas* (Vedamātā) and she presides over them[3]. Gāyatrī is also regarded as one of the five *Prakṛtis*[4] and included among five forms of *Devi*[5]. Only after association with Śiva group, Gāyatri is regarded as the mother of gods or the mother of the world.[6]

Matsya Purāṇa

According to the *Matsya-Purāṇa,* Lord Brahmā after creating his ten mind-born sons (*Manas-putras*) like Marichi, Atri, Angiras, Pulastya, Pulaha, Kratu, Pracetas, Vasiṣṭha, Bhṛgu and Nārada was not quite satisfied with the work of his creation. He set about devising some plan which would carry on the work of creation and would relieve him of the task. With this view he began to invoke Gāyatrī.

Purāṇas mention three wives of Brahmā-Sarasvatī, Sāvitrī and Gāyatrī. But three are according to *Matsya-purāṇa,* one and the same person. This *purāṇa* mentions that Brahmā created from his own effulgence, a woman, who became famous under the names of Satarupā, Sāvitrī, Gāyatrī and Brahmanī. At the first sight mistakenly he took her for his daughter.

शतरूपा च सा ख्याता सावित्री च निगद्यते।।

सरस्वत्यथ गायत्री ब्रह्माणी च परन्तप।
ततः स्वदेहसम्भूता मात्मजाप्रियकल्पवत्।। *MP*-III.30-31

Afterwards, the creator, seeing that form of exquisite beauty, was fired with love and repeatedly uttered, 'what an enchanting form'.

At this the mind-born sons of Brahmā *i.e.* Vasiṣtha and others taking Sāvitrī for their sister, began to express their feelings of seething indignation and contempt to the attitude of their father (Lord Brahma) but he was so much absorbed in the least. Brahmā continued uttering "Oh! What an enchanting form"?

Brahmā fixed his gaze on Gāyatrī (*i.e.* also called here Sāvitrī) and could not distract himself from her. As she was circumambulating him, Brahmā continuously turned his head in her direction. He felt shy because his mindborn sons were standing close by. He therefore, created four heads and each pointed to a direction in order to see her undisturbed, without having to turn his head each time in course of her circumambulations. Seeing Brahmā in such a condition, Gāyatrī also called Satarupā went to the heaven with the mind-born sons of the creator and as she was travelling towards the heaven, Brahmā put on a fifth head right on top which afterwards, he covered with his long matted hair. After this, Brahmā lost his powers that he had acquired by practicing ascesticism, owing to not controlling his mind and falling into the snares of cupid. Then Brahmā dispersed his sons, after directing them to carry on the work of creation. The sons of Brahmā in obedience to his instructions set themselves to complete the work of creation and afterwards they took leave of Brahmā with salutations.

Brahmā fired with passion in her company married Satarupā (literarily one with hundred or many forms) and began to pass his days in enjoyment inside a lotus. He enjoyed the company of her for hundred years and after a long time Manu was born to them.

यावदब्दशतं दिव्यं यथान्यः प्राकृतो जनः।
ततः कालेन महता तस्याः पुत्रोऽभवन् मनुः।। *MP* (3.45)

In another context *i.e.* in the 4th ch. of *Matsya-Purāṇa,* it is also stated that as Lord Brahmā is the governor of the *Vedas,* so is the goddess Gāyatrī of the *Brahmaṇas* (the sacred text *i.e.* the *Vedas*). She is the better half of the Lord, and that is why she appeared from his body.

अन्यच्च सर्ववेदानामधिषिठता चतुर्मुखः
गायत्री ब्रह्मणस्तद् वद् अङ्गभूता निगद्यते।। *MP* (4.16).2.13 p. 3

Skanda Purāṇa

According to legend of *SkP*, Brahmā was performing a sacrifice at Hatakesvara. In the sacrifice tradition, *yajamāna* or sacrificer's wife was to be with him. So, Brahmā sent Nārada for Sāvitrī. Nārada desired to play mischief and wanted to create a quarrel between Sāvitrī and Brahmā, so he told Sāvitrī to go to the sacrificial place at her leisure, along with other female deities (the wives of the gods).

As time glided along, and the proper time was elapsing, Brahmā asked Indra to bring some other maidens.

Indra saw a *Gopa-Kanyā* or a cowherd girl with a *jar* of butter milk on her head, and called her. He caused her to enter the mouth of a cow and pulled her through her anus.[7] Thus he purified her, gave her birth and brought her to the place of sacrifice. Viṣṇu told Brahmā to marry the maiden forth-with as she was now purified.

As she was caused to enter the mouth and come out from the anus of the cow *i.e.* go she was named Gāyatrī.[8] The account comes also at another place in *Skanda-Purāṇa.*[9]

When the sacrifice of Brahmā was about to start at Hatakesvara, the wives of gods assembled to witness the ritual of establishing the branch of the *Audumbara* tree (*Audumbirī*)[10], Sāvitrī comes along, she cursed the *Brāhmaṇas* saying that they would not get a dwelling place, and that the *Nāgara Brāhmaṇa* will not attain the fruits of worship.

The goddesses took resort to the *Audumbirī* who assured them that would be respected in sixty eight families.[11]

According to another account in *Skanda Purāṇa*, Sāvitrī came to the sacrificial *Pandal* of Brahmā at Hatakesvara, after learning about the marriage of Brahmā and Gāyatrī.

She cursed them and all other gods and said "I shall go to such a place where even the name of the voluptuous one, Brahmā would not be heard. Saying this she went away and placed her left foot on the side of the mountain, and with the right one she climbed up to the top. It is said that even now the left step of Sāvitrī is visible at Hatakesvara. One who worships this foot-print of Sāvitrī gets all his desires fulfilled. Her worship is enjoined on the full-moon day.

In the same context earlier we note that Sāvitrī curses the cowherd-maiden Gāyatrī, saying that she is a censured cowherdess (*i.e.* Vigarhitā ābhirī) of character like a prostitute (*Veśyevanaṣṭa caritrā*) and having many husbands, (*bahubhartṛkā*).[12]

Sāvitrī also curses Gāyatrī by saying that none shall worship her, and if a women worships Gāyatrī, she would be inviting sorrow and will be issueless.[13] She would also be termed as one having five husbands.[14]

Padma Purāṇa

Regarding the origin of the goddess Gāyatrī the same account also occurs in *Padma-Purāṇa, (Srṣṭikhanda* ch. 17).

Once Brahmā went to *Puṣkara* to perform a sacrifice. Śiva, Viṣṇu and all other gods and hermits came there. Everything was ready for the sacrifice according to convention. But Sāvitrī had not yet arrived. So an *adhvaryu* was sent to bring her. Sāvitrī said to him "I have not finished dressing, and there are so many things to be done here. Moreover, *Lakṣmī, Bhavānī, Gangā, Svāhā, Indraṇī* and other celestial women, wives of *Ṛsis*, none of them have arrived yet. How can I enter the hall as the only woman?"

The *adhvarya* returned and reported that it was not convenient for Sāvitrī to come just then as she had so much work to do. Brahmā became angry and said to Indra "Lord Sakra, it is up to you to bring me a wife from wherever you like, but it must be done instantly." Hearing the order of Brahmā, Indra selected Gāyatrī who was a good-natured damsel of a cowherd's family and brought her to the sacrificial dias. With the blessings of the hermits and gods, Brahmā held her hand and acknowledged her as his wife.

Sāvitrī dressed well, adorned herself with ornaments and reached the sacrificial hall. She saw the marriage scene and became furious. Trembling with anger Sāvitrī said, "oh Brahmā, how is that you have committed this sin? Have you not married me with fire as witness? I am your wife, Are you ashamed of this?" The three godheads shivered with fear. Sāvitrī cursed everybody.

The curse given to *Brahamā* was that no-body should worship him or on any other time except in the month of Kārtika in a year. She cursed Indra that enemies would enter the world of gods and would make Indra their captive. Sāvitrī cried out that Viṣṇu would take the birth of man by the curse of Bhṛgu. She cursed Śiva that he would lose his manliness. She cursed the *Brāhmins* that they would be wandering about from temple to temple and from *tirtha* to *tirtha* merely for gain.

Uttering these words of curse Sāvitrī left the sacrificial hall. Then Gāyatrī rose up and looking at everybody, declared same remissions of the curses-those who worship Brahmā will be blessed with the pleasure of wife and children and wealth and they will be united with Brahmā at the end of their life.

सर्वयज्ञतपोदानं तीर्थवेदेषु यत् फलं
तत् फलं कोटिगुणितं लभेतैतत्प्रतिष्ठया।। *PadP, 17.225*

पौर्णमास्युपवासं वै कृत्वा भक्त्या नराधिपः
अनेन विधिना यस्तु विरञ्चिम्पूजयेन्नरः। *Ibid.,* 226

कार्त्तिकमासि देवस्य रथयात्रा प्रकीर्तिता,
यां कृत्वा मानवा भक्त्या संयाति ब्रह्मलोकताम्।।

Even if Indra is taken captive, he will be made free by his sons and will become the king of heaven again, Viṣṇu will rescue his wife and kill the enemy.

Though Gāyatrī is depicted as *saptani* of Sāvitrī in *Padma-Purāṇa*. But in another context it is stated that after leaving the sacrificial place, Sāvitrī returned on the request of Narāyaṇa with Lakṣmi.

The *Brahmā* along with Gāyatrī fell on her feet and begged for forgiveness.[16] Having firmly and respectfully embraced her at the throat, Sāvitrī consoled Gāyatrī. "My husband is honourable", Sāvitrī said; "I have resorted to his right side" with these advice, she stayed happily at the sacrifice.

Birth of *Gāyatrī*

The *Purāṇas* have presented difference of opinion regarding the birth of Gayatri :

Mahābhārata

The most popular *Savitryupākhyāna* in the *Mahābhārata* (*Vana-Parvan*, ch. 290, 293) has narrated the birth of Gāyatrī as follows :

In the country of Madra, famous in the *Purāṇas*, there was a king named Aśvapati. His wife was Mālati. Though the couple grew old they were childless. At last they worshipped goddess Sāvitrī, who is the sovereign deity of the *Mantra*.

The king offered ten thousand oblations to the fire, recited *Mantras* in honour of Sāvitrī and ate temperately at the sixth hour. And he passed eighteen years practising such vows, as such goddess Sāvitrī was pleased with him. Issuing herself with great delight in embodied form, from the Agnihotra (sacrificial fire), a conversation ensued between the goddess and the king.

Aśvapati said "it is with the desire of attaining virtue that I have been engaged in this task. O goddess, may many sons be born to me worthy of my race. I ask for this boon. The twice-born ones have assured me that great merit lies in having off-springs." Sāvitrī replied "in having already learnt your intention I had spoken to the lord, the Grandsire (*Brahmā*) about your sons. Though the favour was granted by the self-creator, there shall speedily be born to you on earth a daughter a daughter of great energy, I tell you on the command of the Grandsire."[16]

After that Mālati conceived and delivered a daughter whom they named as Sāvitrī, who later was bestowed to Satyavāna as his wife.

Liṅga Purāṇa

According to *Liṅga-Purāṇa,* Gāyatrī is called Māheśvarī as she is said to be born from the mouth of Śiva Maheśvara. Further she is said to be the daughter of Brahmā, being the source of creation is the form of cow.[17]

Vāyu Purāṇa

The *Vāyu-Purāṇa*, while describing her as the '*Prakrti Gau*' presents as follows :

The lord of the chief of the *Devas,* Brahma was meditating on the four-footed great goddess Māheśvarī with a desire to have sons. Then realising by his *yogic* meditation that she was the supreme goddess, Brahmā who deserves obeisance from all the world, sought refuge in her. Having meditated on the Gāyatrī pertaining to Rudra, god Brahmā, became self controlled.

ब्रह्मा लोकनमस्कार्यः प्रपद्यतां महेश्वरीम्।
गायत्रीन्तु ततो रौद्री ध्यात्वा ब्रह्म सूयन्त्रितः।। *Vāyu-Purāṇa* 23.11

After performing the *Japa* of Rudra Gāyatrī the vedic lore that was given to him and the great goddess bowed to by the people of *Rudra-loka*, he resorted to the great lord (Rudra) with his mind fixed on him in meditation.

इत्येतां वैदिकी विद्या रौद्रीं गायत्रीमर्पिताम्।
जपित्वा तु महादेवीं रुद्रलोक-नमस्कृताम्।। *Ibid.*, 12

This venerable goddess is the mother of the self-born god. She has four-faces. She is the origin of the universe. She is glorified as *prakṛti*, the cow whom the meditators of the reality call *prakṛti* and *pradhāna*. This onborn goddess is red, white and black complexion. She is beautiful in form and creator of the universe. However, Gāyatrī is the Universal formed cow.

सैषा भगवती देवी तत्प्रसूतिः स्वयम्भूवः
चतुर्मुखी जगद्योनिः प्रकृतिर्गौ प्रकीर्तिता।।

अजामेतां लोहितां शुक्लकृष्णां
विश्वं सम्प्रसृजमानां सुरूपाम्।
अजोऽहं बुद्धिमान्विश्वरूपां गायत्रीं
गां विस्वरूपां हि बुद्ध।। *Ibid.*, 50.51

Due to the grace of the lord Maheśvara the lord of *Devas* possessed white limbs and white blood. The Gāyatrī called Brahmā Gāyatrī was of white complexion. When lord next became *lohita* (red) the *Kalpa* too was known as *lohita* through the colour assumed by Maheśvara. Then Gāyatrī, the cow was glorified as endowed with red flesh, bones, blood, milk, eyes and udder.

Viṣṇu-Purāṇa

Viṣṇu-Purāṇa mentioned that, when everything sets in, the awful *Rakṣas* named *Mandehās* attempt to devour the sun. A fierce battle takes place between the *Asura* and sun. At this time the holy water consecrated with the *Gāyatrī-Mantra,* and offered to the sun by the *Brāhmaṇas* destroys the *Raksases*.[18] The same story also occurs in *Vāyu-Purāṇa*.[19]

सूर्यं हि ग्रसमानमां सन्ध्याकाले हि रक्षसाम्
प्रजापतिनियचोगेन शापरतेषां दुरात्मनाम्।
अक्षयत्वञ्च देहरय प्रापिता मरणं तथा। -162

तिस्रः कीटास्तु विख्याता मन्देहा-नाम राक्षसाः
प्रार्थयन्ति सहस्रांशुमुदयनित दिने दिने। -163

अथ सूर्यस्य तेषाञ्च युद्धमासीद् सुदारूणम्
ततो ब्रह्मा च देवाश्च ब्राह्मणाश्चैव सत्तमाः। -164

ओंकारब्रह्म-संयुक्तं गायत्र्या ह्यभिमन्त्रितम्
तेन दह्यति ते दैत्या वज्रभुतेन वारिणा। -165

Padma-Purāṇa

Padma-Purāṇa describes her as she is born in the family of Samkhyāyana. It is further said that she is known to have the three worlds as her feet. She remains in the womb of the earth.

उपनयने नियोगः स्यात्सांख्यायन-गोत्रजा
त्रैलोक्यचरणाज्ञेया पृथिवी-कुक्षि-संस्थिता। (*PadP.* 46-40)

Garuḍa-Purāṇa

Garuḍa-Purāṇa describes her as she is born in the race of Kātyāyana. It is also stated that she has flame and is stationed in the heart of Viṣṇu. She is known as having the three worlds for her feet and is placed in the belly of the earth.

ब्रह्मशीर्षा रुद्रशिखा विष्णोर्हृदय-संस्थिता।
विनियोगैक-नयना कात्यायन-सगोत्रजा। (*Garuḍa P.* 1-2)

त्रैलोकयचरणा ज्ञेया पृथिवी-कुक्षि-संस्थिता। (*Ibid.*, 3)

Kālikā-Purāṇa

According to *Kālikā-Purāṇa* the place of Sāvitrī is in the orb of the sun, *Sūrya Maṇḍala,* where she sits in the *Padmāsanā* pose.[20]

Varāha-Purāṇa

According to *Varāha-Purāna,* Brahmā created the world, was engaged in mediting on Gāyatrī, the *māyā* of the supreme being, within water which was flowing from Viṣṇu's feet.[21]

Once there was a valiant king named *Sindhudvipa*, a manifestation of Varuṇa. He was performing severe penance in the forest with a view to begetting a son who would kill Indra.

With this determination first he stood in constant penance emaciating his body. In his former birth, he was the son of Tvaṣṭā and he was killed by foam. Being immune against the attack of any weapon, he was dissolved in it. Then he was born in Brahmā's line as the valiant *Sindhudvipa* and he performed penance always thinking of his enemity with Indra. After a long time, the auspicious river Vetravati assumed a beautiful human form and went to the place where the king was engaged in his austerities.

Seeing her in that beautiful form, the king's mind was disturbed and he asked who she was. "I am the wife of Varuṇa, the lord of waters and my name is Vetrāvati. I came here loving you responded"– Vetravati The king enjoyed her heartily.

To Vetravati was born immediately a son named Vetrāsura who was resplendent like the dozen sons, mighty and brilliant and he became the king of *prāgjyotisa*. In due course he became a powerful and courageous youth, much lucky, and he conquered the whole world consisting of seven islands and then going up the Meru mountain, conquered Indra, then Agni and then Yama. Indra, when vanquished went to Agni, Agni when vanquished went to Yama, then to Varuṇa, Indra, Vāyu and Kuvera. Finally went to Śiva. The *asura* was chasing them all with his club, and so he too came to *Śivaloka.* Śiva knowing that he could not be easily killed, took the gods to Brahmā worshipped by *Siddhas* and others.

There Brahmā having created the world was engaged in meditating on Gāyatrī, (the *māyā* of the supreme being). Within the water which was flowing from Viṣṇu's feet.

At this *Devas* cried aloud "O Brahmā! protect all of us *Devas* and contemplate on *Māyā* by whose prowess there will be no *asuras* or *rākṣasas.*" Then appeared there out of the water the great goddess, a maiden wearing garlands and crown, clad in white cloth, with eight hands and each holding a divine weapon (disc, conch, mace, rope and sword) on a lion.[22]

She fought with the *asuras* with great agility for a thousand divine years and with various divine weapons. Finally the demon Vetrāsura was killed (by her in battle) and there was then a great shout of joy in the ranks of *Devas*.

Then Brahmā said she should be worshipped with all concentration of mind on navami tithi. On this day a man or woman fasts taking only some flour. He or she gets all desires accomplished.

About the creation of Gāyatrī we have the following account, (*ŚB* 1.7.2.11) from the heart of the divine *AUM-KĀRA* was produced the sound *vaṣat*.[23] By the side was seen the goddess Gāyatrī, the very excellence of the *Mantra* of twenty-four syllables, three feet of eight letters each. She has six sides (*ṣat kukṣih-Sk. P* V. 2.52.9). She is endowed with five heads.

षट्कुक्षिः सा त्रिपाच्च पञ्चशीर्षोपलक्षिता
समीपवर्त्तिनी देवी पार्श्वे तस्य व्यवस्थिता।

Gāyatrī metre was of melodius voice. She also became famous as Sāvitrī.

गायत्री मधुरा भाषा सावित्री लोकविश्रुता। *Sk.P.* V.2. 52.8-10

Skanda-Purāṇa

According to *Sk.P* once Nārada saw a girl in the *Sveta-dvipa* and asked who she was. Immediately he forgot all his learning. After that he surrendered to her. In her body he saw a divine man, in her chest another and in the heart he saw more. Now the girl of the *Sveta-dvipa* said "I am the mother of all the *Vedas* and you do not know me? Hence I have taken all the *Vedas* from you."

हृदयात्तस्य देवस्य वषट्कारः समुत्थितः
छन्दसा। प्रवरा देवी चतुर्विंशाक्षरा परा। *Sk.P.* V.2.58.6-13

The three persons those Nārada saw in the body of Vedamātā were the *Vedas ṚV, YV* and *SV* respectively. Vedamāta said "In my body reside the three *Vedas* and the three fires, (1) Gārhpatya, (2) Āhavaniya and (3) Daksināgni respectively."

Sāvitrī is established at the non perishing fig. tree (*Akṣayavata*) at Prayāga. A similar accounts occur in *Varāha-Purāṇa* where *ṚV* is called to be Nārāyaṇa, *YV* to be Brahmā and *SV* to be Rudra.

Brahmavaivarta-Purāṇa

In the *Brahmavaivarta-Purāṇa,* Sāvitrī has been mentioned as the wife of Brahmā and when the latter enjoyed her company the *Vedas, Śāstras,* year, month, day, night, sunlight and dawn etc. came in to existence.[24] It is also stated that Gāyatrī is born from the tip of Kṛṣṇa's tongue.[25]

An Assimilation

As we can observe, though the legend illustrating the origin of Gāyatrī is nearly similar in the *Skanda-purāṇa* and the *Padma-purāṇa*, the account is more appealing in the *Padma-purāṇa* due to its vivid and coherent description.

On general observations, we happen to see that there are many allegorical descriptions in the *purāṇas.* The marriage between Brahmā and Sarasvatī/Gāyatrī/Śatrupā though allegorical, has been mentioned several times in some of the *Purāṇas.*

According to *Matsya-purāṇa,* Sarasvatī was born as his daughter but when he looked at her, he was fired by her peerless beauty and praised her for it incessantly, "oh! what an enchanting form."

From this *Purāṇa*, it is not clear as to how Brahmā, in spite of the unwillingness of Sarasvatī, won her as his wife. But the *Bhagavāta-purāṇa* clarifies this point to some extent. It says that Sarasvatī was quite devoid of passion, when Brahmā fell under the irresistible influence of love. He had to win over the heart of his daughter.[26]

Besides this, it is said that Brahmā has produced all the *Vedas* and *Śāstras* from his mouth. Sarasvatī is the supreme goddess of learning and represents all sorts of sciences and *vidyās.* To connote this, she is given a book and a jar (*Kamanḍalu*) in her hands in the *Purāṇas*. All knowledge or learning developed from the Vedas are reckoned to represent the mouths of Brahmā. Sarasvatī as the goddess of learning is the daughter of Brahmā, because as Vāk she took her birth from them. The romance between Brahmā and Sarasvatī represents pure and sacred learning. Since this episode between the two, proved unaesthetic, the idea to depict the father as husband of his own daughter was dropped later on.

The account of Brahmās incestuous connection with his daughter has been refuted by the *Matsya-purāṇa* (IV. 78, 10)

अन्यच्च सर्ववेदानामधिष्ठिता चतुर्मुखः
गायत्री ब्रह्मणस्तद्वदङ्गभूता निगद्यते।।
विरञ्चिर्यत्र भगवांस्तत्र देवी सरस्वती।।
भारती यत्र यत्रैव तत्र तत्र प्रजापतिः।।
वेदराशिः रमृतो ब्रह्मा सावित्री तदधिष्ठिता।। (*Matsya-purāna* 4.6-9)

References

1. E.W. Hopkins, *The Religions of India*, p. 348.
2. M. Winternitz, *A History of Indian Literature,* Vol. E, p. 446.
3. *Brahmavaivarta-Purāṇa,* Anandashram Sanskrit Series, Poona, *Brahmakhanda,* Ch. 23.-50

   वेदाधिष्ठातृदेवी च वेदशास्त्रस्वरूपिणीम्
   वेदे बीजस्वरूपा च भजे त्वां वेदमातरम्।।50
4. *Bṛhad Upaniṣad*, DBP, 9.1.1., 4.4
5. *When Primordial nature (Mula prakrit) incarnated or manifested in the form of Viṣṇu the desire for creation raised its head in him. And at ones, the Devi female-aspects in Viṣṇu manifested in five forms like Durgā, Lakṣmi, Sarasvatī, Sāvitrī and Rādhā. These five forms are designated as panca Devis-Vetam mani, (Puranic encyclopaedia, M.L.B.D.)*
6. *Kālikā Purāṇa*, 23.15
7. गोवक्त्रेण प्रवश्याथ यूह्येनाकर्षयत्ततः Sk.P. VI. 181. 62.
8. प्रविष्टा गोमुखे यस्मादपायेन विनिर्गता,
   गायत्री नाम ते पत्नी तस्मादेषा भविष्यति।। Sk.P. VI. 70.
9. *SkP*. VI. (188.56-83.189.1.ff).
10. Audumburi is to be first planted on the main support of the Sacrifical Pandal, in the beginning of the Vedic Sacrifice, *ŚB*. III.6.1.188.
11. *SkP*. VI. 189. 15.
12. (a) प्रभुक्ता बहुभिः पूवे तथा गोपकुमारिकाह,
    एषा प्राप्ता सूपपाद्या वेश्याजनशताधिका।। *SkP.* 192.42.

    (b) एतत् पुर्न महहुःखं यदाभीरी विगर्हि ता
    वेश्येव नष्टचरित्रा त्वयेषा बहुभतृका।। *Ibid*. 54.
13. करिष्यति च या नारी पूजा यस्या अपि क्वचित्,
    सा भविष्यति दुःखाद्या वन्ध्या दौर्भाग्यसंयुता।। *Ibid*. 61.

14. पापिष्ठा नष्टचरित्रा यथैवा पञ्चभर्तृका।
15. पादयोः पतितादेवी गायत्री ब्रह्मचोदिता।
    कृतवत्यपरा धत्ते क्षम देवि नमोस्तुते।। *Padma P.* ch. 16-69
16. *The Mahābhārata, Vana Parvan* 292.17-18
    प्रसादाच्चैव तस्मात्तेस्वयं भुविहिताद्धुवि,
    कन्यातेजस्विनी सौम्यक्षिप्रमेव भविष्यति।।17।।
    उत्तरं चनतेकिंचिद् व्याहर्त्तव्यं कथञ्चन।
    पितामह निसर्गेण तुष्टाह्येवं ब्रवीमिते।।18।।
17. *Liṅga Purāṇa* 1.18.5-7, Venkatesvar Prees, Bombay.
18. *VP.* 9.1-5
19. *VaP.* Ch. 23, 50
20. *Kālikā P.* 23. 18-19
21. तत्र ब्रह्मा जगत्स्त्रष्टा विष्णुपादोद्भवे जले।
    नियमेन च संयुक्ताजपनन्तार्जले शुभे।। *Varāha P.* 23.20
22. शुक्लाम्बरवरा कन्या स्त्रीकिरीटोज्ज्वलानना।
    अष्टाभिर्वाहुभिर्युक्तादिव्यप्रहरणोद्यता।।
    चक्रं शङ्खं गदां पाशं खड्गं धण्टां तथा धनू
    धारयन्ती तथा चान्यान् जग्धतृणाजलाद्वहिः।।
    निश्चक्राम महायोगा सिंहवाहनवेगिता।। *Vardha P.* 23.25-27
23. *ŚB.* 1.7.2.11, 1.4.1.2
    The both 'Oṁ' and 'Vaṣat' are believed in the Vedic tradition to be the males of the verse female. The utterance 'Vasat' is used at the actual offering, where the sound 'Him' is said to be male.
24. *BrhP.* 1.8, 9.
25. आविर्बभूव तत्पश्चात्कृष्णस्य रसनाग्रतः। *BrVaiP.* 4.1
26. *BhaP.* 111. 12.28

6

Forms, Appearances and Iconographical Features of Gāyatrī

A very significant part of *Hindu*-religion is the worship of goddesses in various forms each of which celebrates a specific aspect of feminine energy and power. Each is associated with her own mythology and history and they are received in terms of specific roles and appearance.

Forms of Gāyatrī

The vedic and *purāṇic* literature describe the three fold nature of Gāyatrī. This three fold connection of Gāyatrī with the three pressing and three *Trirātra* rites has probably given rise in the post vedic period to the concept of three Gāyatrīs belonging to the three junctions of the Sun – the morning, the mid-day and the evening. However the forms of Gāyatrī can be classified into two aspects, (*i*) Form of Gāyatrī as a meter and (*ii*) Form of Gāyatrī as a deity.

Form of Gāyatrī as a Meter

Forms of Gāyatrī as a meter is found in several *mahāpurāṇas*. They are as follows :

Agni-Purāṇa

The *Agni-purāṇa* provides more details about the structure of Gāyatrī meter. It says that in the tradition of the *Mantras* (*Chando-dhikāre*) the metre known as the divine (*devī*) Gāyatrī consists of a single syllable. The *āsuri* (demonic) Gāyatrī consists of fifteen syllables while she pertains Prajāpati as her ruling deity, she has eight syllables[1].

The *Yajurvedins* have the Gāyatrī meter of six syllables. The followers of *SV* Gāyatrī is of twelve syllables and for the *Ṛgvedins* it is of eight syllables and further for the *Sāmavedins* two syllables may be more[2].

Besides the *Agni-purāṇa* names various other metres such as Uṣnik, Anuṣṭup, Bṛhati, Paṅkti, Triṣṭup and Jagati as Prajāpatya Gāyatrī or Brahmā - Gāyatrī[3]. When there is necessity of supplying a letter to complete the foot, that type of Gāyatrī metre is called Vasu type of Gāyatrī.

पाद आपादपूरणे गायत्रे वासवः स्मृतः ।

Matsya-purāṇa

According to *Matsya-purāṇa* while describing the chariot of the Sun that moves about in the heaven everyday; the various parts of the sun as well as of his chariot denote the various parts of the year. However, the vedic metres are the seven horses, that like the air swiftly glide with the chariot.

गायत्री चैव त्रिष्टुप्च जगत्यनुष्टुप्चैव च।
पङ्क्तिश्च बृहती चैव उष्णिगेव तु स्मुतौ।। *Matsya-purāṇa* 125-47

Garuḍa-purāṇa

According to the account of *Garuḍa-purāṇa,* she is said to be of three feet having eight letters in each or having four feet having six letters in each. It is said that in the *Japa,* silent muttering of the three feet Gāyatrī should be used and that of the four words for the purposes of adoration.

त्रिपदाऽष्टाक्षरा ज्ञेया चतुष्पादा षडक्षरा।
जप्या च त्रिपदा प्रोक्ता ऊच्चैश्च चतुष्पदा।। *GP* 15.4

Gāyatrī is of three *Pādas* (3×8 syllables) and is identical with Brahmā, Viṣṇu and Maheśvara. The *Japa* shall be started only after knowing the *Viniyoga* (application), *Ṛsi* (Sage) and the *chandas* (metre).

त्रिपदा या च गायत्री ब्रह्म-विष्णु-महेश्वरी।
विनियोगमृषिंछन्दो ज्ञात्वा तु जपमारभेत्।। *Ibid.,* 15.25

The fourth *Pāda* (last group of six syllables) is mentioned to be the essence beyond all *Rajas.* The sage of the fourth *Pāda* is "*Nirmala*". The *chandas* is divine "Gāyatrī" and the deity is *Paramātmā*[4].

Vāyu-purāṇa

Vāyu-purāṇa mentions that when medicinal herbs declined, the lord is worshipped by the *devas,* the chief of whom Prajāpati is who seeks fruits eagerly desired by them. He is worshipped by offering *puroḍāsa* in three *Kapālas* (pots known as *Ambaka*). Hence he is called *Tryambaka.* The vedic metres Gāyatrī, Triṣṭubh, and Jagati are remembered by the term *Tryambaka.* They are the sources of the origin of sacrifice[5]. It is remembered as *Tri-kapāla* as the *purodāsa* offering consecrated for achieving three means by repetition of those three metrical verses united into one and through their efficiency.

ताभिरेकत्व-भूताभिस्त्रिविधाभिः स्ववीर्यतः।
त्रिसाधन-पुरोडाश-स्त्रिकपालः स वै स्मृतः।। (*Vāyu-purāṇa* 31.48)

Brahmāṇda-purāṇa

Describes that

गायत्रीं च ऋचं त्रिवृत्स्तोमरथंतरे।
अग्निष्टोमं च यज्ञानां निर्ममे प्रथमान्मुखात्।।
यजुंषि त्रैष्टुभं छन्दः स्तोमं पञ्चदशं तथा।
बृहत्साम तथोक्तं च दक्षिणात्सोऽसृजन्मुखात्।।

Brahmānḍa-purāṇa 2.8.50-51

The *vedic* metres Gāyatrī, Triṣṭup, and Jagati are remembered by the term *Tryambaka.*

गायत्री चैव त्रिष्टुब्च जगती चैव याः स्मुता।
त्र्यंवका नामतः प्रेम्णा योनयस्ता वनस्पतेः।। *Ibid.,* 2.13.145

युगाक्षकोटी ते तस्य अर्थकामावुभौ स्मुतौ।
सप्ताश्वरुपाश्छदांसि बृहतो वामतो धुरम्।। *Ibid.,* 2.2.71

गायत्री चैव त्रिष्टुप्च ह्यनुष्टुब्जगती तथा।
पंक्तिश्च बृहती चैव ह्युष्णिक्यैव तु स्मुता।। *Ibid.,* 2.2.72

Padma-purāṇa

According to *Padma-purāṇa,* the form of this *Gāyatrī-Mantra,* consists of eight syllables. Elsewhere, also in *Srṣṭi-Khanda,* Gāyatrī herself refers to her *mantra* form and calls herself as the Vedamātā and aṣṭākṣarā-

"विशेषात् पुष्करे स्नात्वा मां जप्त्वा वेदमातरम्। (V. 17.278)
ओंकारेण त्रिमात्रेण अर्धेन न विशेषतः
पूज्याः सर्वे न संदेहो जप्त्वा मां शिरसा सह",
"अष्टाक्षरा स्थिता चाहम्" – (285 c).

माताऽहं सर्ववेदानां पदैः सवैरलंकृता।
जप्तवा मां परमां सिद्धि यास्यन्ति द्विजस्तमा।। (286)

The word form of Gāyatrī is not only limited to the *Gāyatrī-mantra* alone, but also includes all the letters. (अक्षराणि च सर्वाणि) and the seven fold speech (वाणी सप्तविधा तथा) in the form of the Vedas, and the seven notes of the *Gamut.* Like *Gāyatrī* as the *saptavidhā Vani* (as mentioned in this stuti of *Padma-purāna*) Sarasvati has also been mentioned as *Sapta-Svasā* (having seven sisters) in the *ṚV* (6.61.10) and Sāyaṇa explains it as "(सप्त स्वसा गायत्र्यादीनि सप्त छन्दांसि)" and in the *Brahmavaivarta-purāṇa,* Sarasvatī also has been spoken of as सर्वसङ्गीतसंधानतालकारणरुपिणी (11.1.34)[6].

Form of Gāyatrī as a Deity

The form of Gāyatrī as a deity is highlighted in some of the purāṇas. This can be analysed as follows.

Agni - Purāṇa

The *Agni-purāṇa* explains the three forms of Gāyatrī *i.e.* Gāyatrī, Sāvitrī and Sarasvatī in *Gāyatrī-mantra* as follows. As she protects the devotees or disciples and their wives from the cycles of re-birth, she is called Gāyatrī[7]. Since its essence serves to illuminc the Sun (Savitā) and forms the light in the universe, it is known as Sāvitrī[8]. As it first came as a word or in the form of speech she is called Sarasvatī.

Padma-Purāṇa

Padma-purāṇa says that, Gāyatrī is known as Gāyatrī in the morning in the eastern direction. She is known as Sāvitrī at noon in mid-sky, and she is known as Sarasvatī in the evening in the west[9].

Gāyatrī is portrayed as Jayā, Vijayā, Puṣṭi (nourishment), Tuṣti (satisfaction), forgiveness and pity. "जया च विजया चैव पुष्वि त्वं.." She is also depicted as Ambā, Kamalā, the mother of all gods Brahmāṇī and Durgā.

अम्बा च कमला माता ब्रह्माणि ब्रह्मचारिणी।
जननी सर्वदेवानां गायत्री परमांगना।।

(*Padma-purāṇa. Sṛṣṭikhanda,* 328)

In *Padma-purāṇa* it is also stated that Gāyatrī having many forms, a universal form, having charming eyes moves with Brahmā.

बहुरुपा विश्वरुपा सुनेत्रह्मचारिणी।
सुरुपा त्वं विशालाक्षी भक्तानां परिरक्षिणी।। (*Padma-Purāna,* 17-320)

Devī-Bhāgavat-Purāṇa

Devī-Bhāgavat also describes the three-fold naute of Gāyatrī. The world mother Gāyatrī is the prime force and infinite. She is omnipresent. According to *trisandhyā,* Gāyatrī is known by three names. She is known as Gāyatrī in the morning. Gāyatrī is known as Sāvitrī in the mid-day and she is known as Sarasvatī in the evening pressing. She is also known as Brāhmī, Vaiṣnavī and Raudrī respectively.

Gāyatrī is the mother of seven *Ṛsis.* She is also known as Māyā. She is sprung from eyes and hands, tears and prespiration of Śiva and Śivā, Gāyatrī in the form of Bhagavati in the world or *bhurloka* and Bhagavati in the *Pātala* and Mandākini in the heaven. (*ŚB* 12.4.12). So she is known as Sthānatrayanivāsinī.

Gāyatri in this world is the all enduring Pṛthvi (earth) and the power of wind (*Vāyu Śakti*) in the middle space or *bhuvarloka.* She is the ocean of *Tejas* in the heaven (*Svarloka*), great *siddhi* or fulfilment in the *Maharloka, Jana* in the *Janaloka* and *Tapasvini* in the *Taparloka.* She is known by truth in the *Satyalokam.* Gāyatrī is known as Kamalā in *Viṣṇuloka* and she is the *Śakti* of Viṣṇu. She is Gāyatrī in the *Brahmaloka* and is associated with Prajāpti Brahmā. The other half of Hara as Gauri in the *Rudraloka.* She is also known as *Sāmyavasthā Prakṛti.* She is *Parā, Paramā* and *Kriyā. Śakti* is also known as Trisaktida[10] and the *Mulādhārā.*

Liṅga-purāṇa

The *Liṅga-purāṇa* states that even as *Brahmā* desirous of a son was meditating, a boy of great splendour, wearing yellow robes, appeared before him. On seeing him *Brahmā* endowed with meditation mentally and he saw the excellent cow of the great lord. In her universal form it had come out of his mouth. It had four feet, four faces, four hands, four udders, four eyes, four horns, four teeth and four mouths.

The cow was goddess herself who had faces all round and who possessed thirty-two qualities. On seeing the great goddess in the form of cow, the great Lord who is worshipped by all *devas* said again repeating the words "O great goddess, symbol of intellect, and memory come on, come on." She joined her palms in reverence to the Lord and stood there. Then lord of the *devas* spoke to her, "O goddess enveloping the universe by your *yogic* power you should keep it under your control. You will be Umā for the welfare of the *Brāhmins-* and for the attainment of their liberation." By practising meditation Brahmā realised that she was the great goddess and accept her the preceptor of the worlds.

In *Viśvarupakalpa,* Brahmā said "when I assumed universal form Gāyatri, the sustainer of the worlds also assumed the universal form."

These four sons of the different colours are allowed to use Gayatri. Man's aim of life will be four-fold. All living beings will come under four groups and four stages of life. The feet of *Dharma* will be four. Since Gāyatrī was seen as four-footed and the worlds are also four, the animals shall also be four-footed. Their udders too will be four. Since the great goddess was seen as biped in course of rites, Gāyatrī the creator of the worlds is also of the same nature. Hence all human beings are biped, endowed with two breasts. Since the great goddess, the unborn deity of great strength, was seen as supporting all living beings, therefore, the subjects will have all kinds of them.

In chapter twenty-three of *Liṅga-Purana* lord Śiva in the form of Brahmā said Gāyatrī, the goddess of *devas,* born of me had white limbs, white colour, white blood. She was known as Brahmāni.

When the next *kalpa* known as *lohita,* as a result of my colour, Gāyatrī glorified as a cow, born with red flesh, red bone, red blood, red milk, red eyes and red udders was known as Brahmāṇī and similarly named Brahmāni. She was yellow in body, yellow in blood and yellow in colour and also was black in body, black in blood, black in colour and named Brahmāṇī.

Appearances of Gāyatrī

The descriptions about the appearance of Gāyatrī in different purāṇas differ to each other as mentioned below :

Agni-purāṇa

According to *Agni-purāṇa* the goddess adored in the three worlds, should be contemplated as possessed of a white complexion and seated on a full blown lotus flower and carrying a rosary.

अक्षसूत्रधरा देवी पद्मासनगता शुभा। *Skp.* 215

In another context it is stated that the colour which mark the body of the goddess are yellow, blue, brown, emerald, flame-colour (golden), lightning colour, yellowish black and blood red. Her five faces[11] have the colour of :

(*i*) Crystal pearl (*Muktā*)

(*ii*) Coral red (*Vidruma*)

(*iii*) Gold (*Hema*)

(*iv*) Blue sapphire (*Nilamani*)

(*v*) White (*Sphatika*)

The description of the physical appearance of the goddess also occurs in various ways as it stated, गौरी चतुर्मुखी ब्राह्मी अक्षमाला सुरान्विता । The four-faced Brāhmi (the female energy of Brahmā) is represented as of fair complexion, riding a swan and as carrying a rosary with different vessels such as *Surā* and *Kuṇḍa* in the left hand.

Padma-purāṇa

According to the *Padma-purāṇa* exquisite beauty of the various parts of her body is described in a very pictguresque style.

She represented as of the fairest colour and resemble the moon. She has large arms, delicated like interiors of plantain trees,

श्वेता त्वं श्वेतरूपासि शशाङ्केन समानता।
विभ्रती विपुलैर्वाहु कदलीगर्भकोमलै।। *Pad P.* 16.6

She holds deer's horn and an extremely clean lotus in her hand. She has put on a silken garment and the upper garment is red.

एणश्रुगंकरे गुह्य पंकजञ्च सुनिर्मलम्
वसानावसने क्षौमे रक्तेनोत्तरवाससा।। (*Ibid.*, 16.7)

She is adorned with a necklace, brilliant like the moon-rays round her neck. She is well beautiful with ears having divine ear rings.

राशिरश्मि प्रकाशेनहारेणोरासिराजिता
दिव्यकुण्डलपुर्णाभ्यां कर्णाभ्यां सुविभुषिता।। (*Ibid.*, 16.8)

She looks charming with a hair-band having an extremely pure crown. Her arms are like the hoods of serpents adorn the heaven.

भुजगा भोग सद्धशौभुजौ ते भूषणन्दिवः
स्तनौ ते रुचिरौ देवि वर्तुलौ समचुचुकौ।। - 20

She is also beautiful with charming and circular breasts.

The triple fold on the belly is proud of the division with the extremely fair hips and loins. Her navel has a circular shape which is deep and indicates auspiciousness. Her couple of thighs is very beautiful and round. She has good knees and legs.

जघनेनातिशुभ्रेण त्रिवली भंगदर्पिता
सुमध्यवर्तिनी नाभिर्गभीरा शुभदर्शिनी - 21
विस्तीर्णजघनी देवी सुश्रेणीच वरानने
सुजातवृतोरुयुगा सुजानुचरण तथा - 22

Garuḍa-purāṇa

Garuḍa-purāṇa describes that Gāyatrī is crimson - coloured. Sāvitrī is white hued and Sarasvatī is dark-blue. This forms the trio of the joints of time *trisandhyā i.e.* morning, noon, and evening.

रक्ता भवति गायत्री सावित्री शुक्लवर्णिका।
कृष्णा सरस्वती ज्ञेया सन्ध्यात्रयमुदाहृतम्।। (*Gp. 15*)

Garuḍ-purāṇa describes that the colour which mark the body of the goddess are the sapphire colour, the colour of fire, yellow, deep black twany, white, lightning colour, silvery white, dark, crimson, dark blue, white grey, ruby colour, conch colour, grey red as wine, sun colour similar to the colour of the moon and white as the lusture of the conch-shell[12].

Skanda-purāṇa

In *Skanda-purāṇa,* Gāyatrī is known as Gāyatrī in the morning in the eastern direction. She is known as Sāvitrī at noon in mid-sky, and she is known as Sarasvatī in the evening in the west[13]. The three Gāyatrī also known as Brāhmi, Māhesvarī and Vaiṣnavī respectively. According to *SkP* she is a young girl between ten and twelve years of age. She has red complexion like the morning sun.

She is said to be lustrous like the sun and wearing red garment, and she is decorated by red sandal paste. She has three heads and four hands. In her hands she respectively bearing a *pāśa,* a goad, a rosary and *Kamanḍalu* and rosary (*akṣamālā*) in upper two hands.

In the lower two hands, in some cases are shown in the *abhaya* and *Varadā* poses and the left hand just rests on her left thigh, mounts on a swan, is associated with Brahmā and the *ṚV.* She follows the track of the sun and connected with *Bhūloka,* the overall description contemplated her as *bālā* having red wearing at the morning or dawn twilight[14]. The physical description of Gāyatrī given in the Skp. is nearly similar to that in GRU. (pg. 28 of this book)

The appearance of *Sāvitrī* as mentioned in *SkP* that *Sāvitrī* should be contemplated as a young woman with full breasts, wearing white sacred thread. She has white complexion like moon and conch white clothes. She is decorated with white clothes, garland and white paste. Her two hands bear a trident and a *damaru,* Sāvitrī mounts on a bull. She is associated with Rudra and the *YV,* she follows the path of the sun and represents the *Bhuvaḥ loka*[15].

Sarasvatī is the old women with black complexion. She is decorated with black dress, black garland and black paste or she is decorated with *anulepana.* She would be contemplated as a woman having four hands; Three hands respectively bearing a conch, a disc and a club. Her fourth hand is shown in *abhaya* pose. She mounts on a Garuda. She is connected with Visnu and the *SV.* Sarasvati also follows the path of the Sun and represents *Svarloka*[16].

Brahmā is also one of the pose of mother goddess Gāyatrī or one of the seven little mothers[17]. She is related with Brahmā. On the other hand, she, the *Śakti* of Brahmā is conveyance dawn by swans, with rosary and water pot *Kamanḍalu,* Brahmā, carries no ordinary weapon. So Brāhmi takes this *Kamanḍalu* and makes a weapon of that.

We have found no instances of the word Brāhmi or Brahmānī in the vedic and epic literature. But *Purāṇic* literature defines her as a *bālā* of about sixteen years in age and she is connected with morning pressing in eastern direction[18].

According to *Devi Māhātmya,* Māhesvarī is understood to be one of the seven little mothers, the second in order of appearance. Māheśvarī is related to Maheśvara Śiva. She sailed forth and mounted upon a bull. On her two hands, she bears a trident, *trisula* and *damaru.* She is having great serpents for bracelets, adorned with the moon's crescent. She is ornate by the *biśesaṇā* of *candare- khāvibhuṣ aṇā.* Because Śiva is known as candraśekhar. The only information added in subsequent instances of this epithet is that the *triśūla* is Māheśvarī's preferred implement in battle. In the *Mahābhārata,* Maheśvaṛa is used as a name of Śiva. So Māheśvarī is Śiva's *Śakti.*

In the vedic literature, there are no use of Māheśvarī. But according to *Purāṇic* literature Māheśvari is another form of the Gāyatrī, who is associated with mid-day pressing.

Liṅga-purāṇa

According to *Liṅga-purāṇa,* Gāyatrī is called Māheśvarī as she is said to be born form the mouth of Śiva, Maheśvara[19].

She is said to be having four feet, four faces, four hands, four breasts, four eyes, four horns, four jaws having thirty two qualities and also facing all quarters. Further she is said to be the daughter of Brahmā, being the source of creation in the form of the cow[20].

According to *Purāṇic* literature, Vaiṣnavī is an old woman. The complexion of Vaiṣnavī is black. So she is compared with evening darkness. She is *Śakti* of lord Viṣṇu[21].

Gāyatrī is known as Ajapā mentioned in this connection and the Ajapā Gāyatrī is specially suited for the *Yogis*. By the very contemplation of this one, it is said that a man gets rid of sins.

अजपा नाम गायत्री योगिनाम् मोक्षदायिनी
अस्याः संकल्पमात्रेण नरः पापैः प्रमुच्यते।। *SkP.* IV. 14.58

Devī Bhāgavat-Purāṇa

Devī Bhāgavat-purāṇa also describes that Gāyatrī or Brāhmi is connected with morning pressing. She is a young *bālā.*

She has red complexion. Gāyatrī or Brāhmī mounts on a swan. She is associated with Brahmā and known as Brahmāṇī in the *Brahmaloka*[12].

Vaiṣṇavī is connected with mid-day pressings and she is a young woman with fully developed breasts. She has white complexion. She is riding on a Garuḍa. Vaiṣṇavī or Sāvitrī is seen as manifesting *YV* in the middle space, that is, *antarikṣam.* यजुर्वेदं पठन्ती च अन्तरिक्षे विराजते। Vaiṣṇavī is related with lord Viṣṇu and is known as Viṣṇu lokanivasini.

रुद्रलोकं गत्वा त्वं हि विष्णुलोकनिवासिनी
त्वमेव ब्रह्मणो लोकेऽमर्त्यानुग्रहकारिणी।

But in other *Purāṇas* like *SK* and Garuḍa etc., Sāvitrī and Vaiṣṇavī are different forms of Gāyatrī and they are different from each other by nature.

According to *SkP Revākhanḍa,* Sāvitrī is related with Rudra and *YV* and Vaiṣṇavī is related with lord Viṣṇu. But in *Devī Bhāgvata,* both Sāvitrī and Viṣṇavī are the same form of Gāyatrī. Both are related with Viṣṇu and Rudra.

Devī Bhāgavata describes the physical appearance of goddess Gāyatrī in the 8th chapter. Indra saw her on the ninth lunar day of the month of *Chaitra* (*i.e.* parts of March and April), within a great mass of light, a *virgin* form in full youth.

Her body is like that of ten million rising suns and the colour was rosy red like a full blown *Javā* flower. On her forehead was shining the digit of the moon. Her breasts were full and veiled under her cloth. She looked very beautiful. She was holding noose and a goad in her two hands and her two hands are in the *abhaya* and *baradā* pose. (*DB* 12.8.53).

Her body was decked with various ornaments and it looked auspicious and exceedingly lovely and comparable to none. She was like a *Kalpavṛkṣa.* She was three eyed and the braid of her hair was encircled with *mālati* garlands. She was praised on her four sides by the four Vedas.

The brilliancy of her teeth shed lusture on the ground as if ornamented with lustrous *ruby.* Her face looked smiling. Her clothing was red and her body was decorated with red sandal paste of white complexion.

The third form of Gāyatrī is known as Sarasvati and also Raudrī by name. Sarasvatī is connected with evening pressing and she is an old woman with black complexion कृष्णा सरस्वती ज्ञेया. She is described as riding on a bull. Sarasvati is seen manifesting *SV* everywhere in the *Rudraloka.* She is compared with evening darkness.

SkP denotes Sarasvati as the *Śakti* of Viṣṇu and it follows the path of the sun and represents *Svrloka.* But Raudrī is related with Rudra and she represents *Shuvaḥ loka.*

The accounts mentioned above, show that in course of time, various Gāyatrī *i.e.* verse in the metre of that name began to be enjoined by different sects, Gāyatrī meter has twenty-four syllables. It has said that each and every syllable has one deity. So the Gāyatrī meter is the total strength of twenty-four syllables.

In *Padma-purāṇa,* the first letter belongs to the Agni, the second to the Vayu, the third to the sun, the fourth one to the sky, the fifth to the Yama, the sixth one belongs to the Varuṇa, the seventh to the Bṛhaṣpati, the eight one to the prajanya, the ninth to the Indra, the tenth to the Gandharvas, the eleventh belongs to the Puṣam, the twelfth to the Mitra, the thirteenth belongs to the Tvaṣṭṛ, the fourteenth to the Vasus, the fifteenth one belongs to the Maruts, the sixteenth to Soma, the seventeenth to the Angiras, eighteenth to the Viśvedevās, the nineteenth to the Aśvinas and twentieth to the Prajāpati, the twenty-first letter known to be full of all god the twenty-second belongs to the Rudra, the twenty-third belongs to the Brahmā and the twenty-fourth to the Viṣṇu[23].

In *Liṅga-purana* also the twenty-four forms of *Gāyatrī-Mantra* are invoked to the concerned deity[24].

GRU also describes the twenty-four forms of Gāyatrī. They are as following :

1. Agni Gāyatri (प्रथममाग्नेयं स्वरूपम्)
2. Prajāpati (द्वितीयं प्राजापत्यम्)
3. Soumya (तृतीयं सौम्यं स्वरूपम्)
4. Isāna (चतुर्थमीशानं स्वरूपम्)
5. Āditya (पञ्चममादित्यं स्वरूपम्)
6. Gārhapatya (षष्ठं गार्हपत्यं स्वरूपम्)
7. Maitra (सप्तमं मैत्रं स्वरूपम्)
8. Bhagadaivatam (अष्टमं भगदैवतं स्वरूपम्)
9. Āryaman (नवममार्यमणं स्वरूपम्)
10. Savitṛ (दशमं सावित्रं स्वरूपम्)
11. Tvāṣṭr (एकादशं त्वाष्ट्रं स्वरूपम्)
12. Puṣan (द्वादशं पौष्णं स्वरूपम्)
13. Indra Agni (त्रयोदशमैनद्रां स्वरूपम्)
14. Vāyu (चतुर्दशं वायवं स्वरूपम्)
15. Vāmadeva (पञ्चदशं वामदेवं स्वरूपम्)
16. Mitra-Varuṅa (षाडशं मैत्रावरुणं स्वरूपम्)
17. Bhrātṛvyam (सप्तदशं भ्रातृव्यं स्वरूपम्)
18. Viṣṇu (अष्टादशं वैष्णवं स्वरूपम्)

19. Vāmana (एकोनविंश वामनं स्वरूपम्)
20. Viśva deva (विंशं वैश्वदेवं स्वरूपम्)
21. Rudra (एकविंश रौद्रं स्वरूपम्)
22. Kuvera (द्वाविंशं कौवेरं स्वरूपम्)
23. Aśvina (त्रयोविंशम् आश्विनं स्वरूपम्)
24. Brahmā (चतुर्विंशं ब्राह्मं स्वरूपम्)

As a sample only one of the form (स्वरूप) of Gāyatrī can be observed here. In the *SkP* the Rudra Gāyatrī, is described as youthful deity with lusture sprouting from her body. She is as bright as pure crystals. Rudra Gāyatri is endowed with Triṣṭup meter. The seer or *Ṛsi* of Rudra-Gāyatrī is Kāśyapa. She has the form of *YV.* It has three letters. She is mounted on the bull. This Gāyatrī is enjoined at the mid-day *Sandhyā*[25]. Gāyatri is said to assume a different name as the desire of the devotee is concerned.

Śiva Gāyatrī is one such illustration. Śiva, it is said took bath in the river Sarasvatī born of *Plakṣa, Plakṣaja* and muttered in the water himself, the Drupada Gāyatrī[26]. This Drupada-Gāyatrī originated here probably was later called Śiva-Gāyatrī.

Iconography of Sāvitrī / Sarasvatī / Gāyatrī

A sure proof of the existence of the cult of a god is found in the iconography where he is produced in art, for the urge to reproduce a god iconically springs from a desire to worship him. Hence the study of a deity is incomplete without the study of its iconography.

The study of images, their formation, transmission and transformation in their various cultures and civilisations and of their intrinsic meaning constitutes a fundamental aspect of research in the history of art tradition. Iconography is a descriptive discipline which deals with the study of images meant for worship. As the study of iconography, is almost conditioned by a study of religion, so the study of religion cannot proceed to any extent without the study of iconography. Particularly in India image worship forms the very pivot of the popular religion. The data for the study of this subject have been provided by the literary as well as archaeological sources[27].

Besides the Sanskrit works specially dealing with the iconography of deities, there are certain other vedic and post-vedic texts which refer to the iconographical features of the deity. Their descriptions also shed welcome light on his form and character.

Among the *Purānas,* the *Agni-Purāṇa, Padma-Purāṇa, MP* and the *Viṣṇudharmottara* deal with this prominently. *Agni-Purāṇa* describing the image of Brahmā lays down that the images of Sarasvatī and Sāvitrī should be respectively at the left and right sides of *Brahmā's* image, "*ajya sthāli : Sarasvatī Savitrī Vamadakṣine*"[28].

Like the *Agni-Purāṇa,* the *Matsya-Purāṇa* also maintains the same formula. It prescribes how the image of Sarasvatī and Sāvitrī should be made with Brahmā. It goes on saying that Brahmāṇī (Sarasvatī as either wife or daughter) should be made like Brahmā (*Brahmāsadrsi*[29]).

As to the image of Brahmā, it says that it should be made of four heads and there should be a water-vessel (*Kamanḍalu*) in one of his hands. He should be made riding a swan or seated on a lotus[30]. The image should have a site for oblations of ghee and the four Vedas. However to itself, there should be the image of Sāvitrī and to the right that of Sarasvatī.

वामपार्श्वेऽथ सावित्री दक्षिणे य सरस्वतीम्
अग्रे च ऋषयस्तद्वत् कार्याः पितामह-पदै।। *Matsya P.* (144-45)

In the iconographical representation in the Padma-Purāṇa Gāyatrī has been mentioned as seated on the left side of Brahmā and Sāvitrī on his right in all the temples of Brahmā but specially in *Puṣkara* as mentioned in *Padma-Purāṇa* V.29.81 refers to this fact that Sāvitrī says to Gāyatrī, सर्वकार्येत्वहं....नारदपुष्करैः। ब्रह्मस्थानानि..... वाम-पक्षमुपाश्रिता ।

Like the *AP,* the *MP,* the *PadP,* the *Viṣṇudharmottra Purāṇa* also mentioned that *Brahmā* has been pictured as sitting in the lotus posture (*Padmāsanā*) and has Sāvitrī placed in his left lap.

Identification of Gāyatrī with Other Gods

In *Hindu* religious life Gāyatrī as a metre holds a unique place. In vedic, *Śrauta,* and *Gṛhya* literature, Gāyatrī as a divinity does not play an important role. But in *Purāṇic* literature, Gāyatrī is herself regarded as a *devī* or goddess.

Purāṇa denotes Gāyatrī as Vedamātā or Devamātā or creator of *Veda* and *Devas.*

Gāyatrī is also regarded as one of the five *Prakṛtis.* When primordial nature (*mula-prakṛti*) incarnated or manifested in the form or Viṣṇu, the desires for creating raised its head in him and at once the *Devī,* female aspects in Viṣṇu manifested in five forms (*Panca Devi*) like Durgā, Lakṣmi, Sarasvatī, Sāvitrī and Rādhā[31].

In the Mahābhārata Anuśāsanaparvan, it is stated that Gāyatrī is the sum and substance of all the Vedas Gāyatrī is Brahmā; Gāyatrī is almighy god.

सर्ववेदादधृतः सारा मन्त्रोऽयं समुदाहृतः
ब्रह्मादिदेवा गायत्री परमात्मा समीरिता।

Agni-Purāṇa says that *Gāyatrī-Mantra* is associated with Sāvitrī who has been invoked as the supreme god, the creator and preserver of the universe. All other gods like Viṣṇu, Śiva, Śakti, Agni, Sun, Fire and Rudra makes no difference as quoted in *Agni-Purāṇa.*

It is also stated that one may read 'Śiva' or 'Śakti' or 'Agni' in the palace of light (Sūrya).[32] And since the term Viṣṇu has been described in the Vedas and other holy scriptures as synonymous with the sun, the fire or the Rudra, it makes no essential difference, whichever of these epithets has been used.

When the divine-self manifests as the sun or Viṣṇu, it produces the libations of clarified butter. When the self-same god manifests as the "light", Parjanya (the god of rain), Vāyu (the wind), Āditya (the sun) it grows and nourishes the cereals and vegetables by giving rise to heat and moisture.

महदाद्यं सूयते हि स्वयंज्योतिर्हरिः प्रभुः
गर्जन्यों वायुरादित्याः शीतोष्णाद्यैश्च पातयेत्–10

Libations of clarified butter cast into the fire are carried to the sun who creates the rain clouds and rain causes the stalks of food gains (*Annam*) to shoot out and main is the off-spring of food.

अग्नौ प्रास्ताऽऽहुतिः सम्यगादित्यमुपतिष्ठते।
आदित्याज्जायते वृष्टिः वृष्टरन्नं ततः प्रजाः।। (*AP* III.II)

Relationship between Gāyatrī/Sāvitrī with Brahmā

The concept of *Brahmā* in *puranic* literature is identical with the concept of Prajapati (*Śatapatha Brahmana* (11.16.1) in *Bṛhad Upniṣat*) (1.4.10) at *Ch Upaniṣat* (1.7.5). This might have led to the relationship of Gāyatrī and Brahmā in the *Purānas.*

In the *Mahābhārata,* in the most popular *Savitryupakhyāna* (*Vana-Parvan*) it is narrated that when king Aśvapati worshipped Sāvitrī for a child. Sāvitrī was pleased with him. Aśvapati then wanted many sons be born to him, worthy of his race. But Savitri, as wife of Brahma replied "O King having already learnt your intention I had spoken to the lord about your sons. Through the favour granted by the self-creator, there shall speedily be born to you on earth a daughter of great energy."

Chapter thirty-four of the *Sabhā-Parvan,* makes it clear that Sāvitrī shines in the palace of Brahmā.

According to the legend of *SkP,* Viṣṇu told Brahmā to marry the purified Gāyatrī at the Hatakesvara sacrifice and Brahmā married her. Another legend is that Gāyatrī herself said to Nārada "the three men, that Nārada saw were the three *Vedas i.e. RV., YV* and the *Sāmaveda*". She said "in body are the three Vedas and the three fires Gārhapatya, Āhavanīya, and Dakṣināgni."

A similar account occurs in *Varādh-Purāṇa* where the *ṚV* is said to be Nārāyaṇa, *YV* to be Brahmā and *SV* to be Rudra-so in this way the three persons whom Nārada saw were respectively Nārāyaṇa, Brahmā and Rudra.

While describing the relationship between Sāvitrī and Gāyatrī with Brahmā, *PadP* gives a detailed story supporting them as husband and wife.

Brahmā ordered Sakra to bring a wife and Indra selected Gāyarī who was a good-natured damsel of a cowherds family and brought her to Brahmā. Brahmā held her hand and acknowledged her as wife. The same story was also found in *Skanda-purāṇa.*

Gāyatrī herself granted a boon to Brahmā that those men who with devotion worship Brahmā, will have garments, grains, wives, happiness and riches. In addition they will have happiness intact in their house and will have sons and grandsons. Having enjoyed happiness for a long time, they will, eventually, attain salvation.

ब्रह्माणं पूजयिष्यन्ति नरा भक्ति-समन्विताः
तेषां वस्त्रे धनंधान्यं दाराः सौख्यं धनानि च।।
अविच्छिन्नं तथा सौख्यं गृहे वै पुत्र-पौत्रकम्।
भुत्कवा सौसुचिरं कालमेते मौक्ष्यं गामिष्यति।।

(*PadP, Srṣṭikhanḍa,* 17.221-222)

The chariot-procession of Lord is prescribed to be undertaken in the month of Kārtika. Undertaking this procession with devotion men reach Brahma's world. Playing on a number of musical instruments men should take out, along the road, the procession of Brahmā, with Sāvitrī, on the full-moon day of Kārtika.

कार्तिकमासे राजेंद्र पौर्णमास्यां चतुर्मुखम्।
मार्गेण ब्रह्मणा सार्द्ध सावित्र्या च परन्तपः।। (*PadP* Ch. 17-229)

The chariot of Brahmā should be moved by *Brāhmaṇs* learned in the four *Vedas*. The chariot is not to be moved by a *śudra* desiring his welfare and no wiseman, but the *bhojaka,* is to mount on the chariot. Gāyatrī should be placed to Brahmā's right.

ब्रह्मणो दाक्षिणेपार्श्व गायत्रीं स्थापयेन्नृपः।। (*Ibid.* 240)

According to the *GP,* Gāyatrī is said to be seated in the region of Brahmā[33]. In other place it is said that she has Brahmā at the head, Rudra at the top of the hair.

ब्रह्मशीर्षा रुद्रशिखा विष्णोर्हृदयाश्रिता।। *GP* 1.35.2

According to *Matsya-Purāṇa,* Brahmā and Gāyatrī are insepara ble. As sun-shines or light never lives devoid of its shadow, so does Brahmā ever live apart from Gāyatrī.

विरञ्चिर्यत्र भगवांस्तत्र देवी सरस्वती।
भारती यत्र यत्रैव तत्र तत्र प्रजापतिः।। *MP.* 111.7

In another context it is also stated that as Lord Brahmā is the governor of the *Vedas,* so is the goddess Gāyatrī of *Brāhmaṇa's.* She is the better half of the Lord and that is why she appeared from his body.

अन्यच्च सर्ववेदानामधिष्ठिता चतुर्मखः
गायत्री ब्रह्मणस्तद्वदङ्ग भूता निगद्यते।। *MP,* Ch. 3.16

In the *Brahmavaivata-Purāṇa,* Sāvitrī has been mentioned as the wife of Brahmā, and when the latter enjoyed her company the *Vedas, śāstras,* year, month, day, night, sunlight and dawn etc. came in to existence.

Relationship between Gāyatrī with Sāvitri

In vedic literature Gāyatrī is closely connected with Sāvitṛ. According to Vedic records, Sāvitrī itself is the creator of the universe. Sāvitṛ is the almighty god before whom the water bend themselves and the wind rests. (*RV.* 2.38.2).

It is with these characteristic features of Savitṛ, there is refulgence and vivifying force that Gāyatrī has been closely connected with Savitṛ.

But in *Purāṇas,* Gāyatrī has no close contact with Savitṛ. *SkP* has state that Gāyatrī and Sāvitrī are different from each other as we find in some contexts. Sāvitrī curses the cowherd- maiden Gāyatrī saying that she is a censured cowherdess, of no character like a prostitute, and having many husbands.

प्रभुका बहुभिः पूर्वैः तथा गोपकुमारिका।
एषा प्राप्ता सुपापाद्या वेश्याजनशताधिका।। 42(*SkP*)

Sāvitrī also curses Gāyatrī by saying that none shall worship her. If a woman worships Gāyatrī, she would be inviting sorrow and will be issueless." She would also be termed as "One having five husbands".

पापिष्ठा नष्टचारित्रा यथैषा पंचभतृका।

The same story is described in *PadP.* In some contexts we find Sāvitrī and Gāyatrī have no conflict but they are separate from each other.

Gāyatrī is depicted as *saptani* of Sāvitrī in *PadP.* In another context it is stated that after leaving the sacrificial place, Sāvitrī returned on the request of Nārāyaṇa with Lakṣmi and Pārvati with Siva. Then Brahmā, the grandsire of all the worlds with Gāyatrī said these words to her "This goddess Gāyatrī is your servant, and I am obedient to you. O you beautiful lady, order what I should do for you."

एवमेतत्करिष्यामि तव निर्देशकारिका।। (43-71)

Then Brahmā along with Gāyatrī fell on her feet and begged for forgiveness.

पादयोः पतिता देवी गायत्री ब्रह्मचोदिता।
कृतवत्यपराधते क्षम देवि तमोऽस्तुते।। (*PadP* 17.43.69)

Having firmly and respectfully embraced her at the throat, Sāvitrī consoled Gāyatrī. "This my husband is honourable", Sāvitrī said: "I have resorted to his right side and you should come to his left."

भवत्या च मया चैव स्थातव्यं च न संशयः
पुष्करे ब्रह्मणः पार्श्वे वामं च त्वं समाश्रय।। (*Ibid.* 76)

Then Gāyatrī told her that,

तवैवाज्ञा मया कार्या त्वं में प्राणसमा सखी।
अहं ते त्वनुजा देवी सदा मां पातुमर्हति।। (*Ibid.* 80)

It is said that Gāyatrī is known as Gāyatrī in the morning in the eastern direction, as Savitri at noon in mid-sky, and as Sarasvatī in the evening in the west.

The *Matsya-Purāṇa* mentions-that Brahma created from his own effulgences, women who became famous under the manes, Śatarupā, Sāvitrī, Gāyatrī and Brahmaṇī.

शतरूपा च सा ख्याता सावित्री च निगद्यते
सरस्वत्यथ गायत्री ब्रह्माणी च परन्तप।। *MP.* Ch. 3.31

Obviously, Sāvitrī and Gāyatrī are one and the same person. Sāvitrī is just another name of Gāyatrī in the context that follows :

In the *GP* they are not separate from each other. This *Purāṇa* mentions that invoking at the period of conjunction the twelve names of the goddess such as Gāyatrī, Sāvitrī, Sarasvatī, Sankṛti, Brhamaṇī, Kausiki, Sadhi, Sarvārtha Sadhini, Sahasrakṣi, with her each of her own *Mantra Bhuḥ, Bhubaḥ, Svaḥ,* destroys all sins.

> गायत्र्यै नमः सावित्र्यै सरस्वत्यै नमो नमः
> वेदमात्रे च सांस्कृत्यै ब्रह्माणयै कौशिक्यै क्रमात् 4
> साक्ष्यै सर्वार्थसाधिन्यै सहस्राक्ष्यै च भूर्भुवः।। 5 (*GP* Ch. 26.4-5)

Gāyatrī is known as Sāvitrī because she is *Sāvitra tej Sadrusi* or equal in lustrr to the sun. In *Puranic* is literature the place of Gāyatrī is in the orb of the sun, Sūrya *manḍala madhystā*, where she sits in the *Padmāsanā* pose.

As far as modern science is concerned the sun-god Savitṛ is the protector of vital force. And as far as shown earlier, Gāyatrī is also regarded as a luminary and as a protectress of vital force *Prāṇa.* So Gāyatrī should be worshipped with the three pressing of a day. On this back- ground we may study the legend of Savitryopākhyāna[34] that Sāvitrī brought *Prāṇa* for her husband.

The legend in brief is as follows-Aśvapati was the king of Madra. He was childless. His wife practised penance and worshipped the goddess Sāvitrī. Through Sāvitrīs favour they got a daughter. She was named Sāvitrī. When the princess became young (or of marriageable age) she was so lustrous that no man asked for her hand. King Aśvapati was worried. He asked his daughter to find a suitable husband, for the youthfulness of his daughter was fast passing. Sāvitrī wandered for long in search of a prospective husband.

One day she met Satyavān, son of Dyumatsen, the king of Śalvas. He had been thrown out of his kingdom by his enemies and he had also become blind. The royal family was accordingly leading a life of poverty and austerity in a jungle. Sāvitrī chose the young prince as her husband and told her father about it. In the mean time Narada arrived there and predicated that the prince had a very short life (*alpayu*) and would die within a year of her marriage. However, Sāvitrī stood by her decision and married Satyavāna.

Satyavāna used to go to the forest to gather fruits and fuel wood for their sustenance. On the fatal day, Śavitrī accompanied him. After the day's hard-work Satyavāna felt giddy and had terrible headache. Śavitrī understood that the time had come. Just at that moment, Yama the Lord of death arrived there and took away the vital breath of Satyavāna.

Śavitrī followed him and by means of her profound and persuasive arguments, pleased Yama. Yama released the life force of Satyavān and by his blessing Dyumatsena also regained his eye sight and lost kingdom. Here Yama may be regarded as representing the Sun-god, who is identified with the vital-force, and Śavitrī herself is regarded as the protectress of vital force.

According to *Savitryupaniṣat,* both Sāvitrī and Savitṛ are identical and both are regarded as a couple, the creator couble of this world[35].

So according to vedic and *puranic* literature Gāyatrī herself is closely connected with both the Brahmā and Savitṛ.

An Assimilation

The over-all description of the three-fold nature and physical appearance of Gāyatrī denotes that she is manifesting the three Vedas in the three worlds in the form of Gayatri, Sāvitrī and Sarasvatī or Brahmā, Viṣṇu and Rudra.

References

1. छन्दोधिकारे गायत्री देवी चैकाक्षरी भवेत्
   पञ्चदाशाक्षरी सा स्यात् प्रजापत्यष्टवार्णिका। AP, 30.1
2. यजुषां षड्वर्णा गायत्री साम्नां स्याद् द्वादशाक्षरा
   ऋचामष्टादशार्णा स्यात् साम्नां वर्द्धेत च द्वयम्। *Ibid.*, 2
3. उष्णिगनुष्टुब् बृहती पङ्क्तिस्त्रिष्टुब् जगत्यपि।
   तानि गेयानि क्रमशो गायत्रौ ब्रह्म एव ताः। *Ibid.*, 3
4. तुरीस्थ पदस्यापि ऋषि निर्मल एव च
   छन्दस्तु देवी गायत्री परमात्मा च देवता। *Ibid.*, 3 *GP.* 15.16
5. गायत्री चैव त्रिष्टुण्च जगती चैव या स्मृता
   त्र्यम्बका नामतः प्रोक्ता योनयः सवनन्तथा। *VāP*-31.47
6. रुद्रकृताः गायत्री स्तुति, Sri Ananda Swarupa Gupta, Vol-VII. No-1-Jan, 1965; PURĀṆA-VASANTA-PAMCAMI-Number, All India Kasiraj Trust, Fort, Ramnagar, Vārāṇāsi.
7. AP-83.1
8. ततः स्मृतेयं गायत्री सावित्री ततो यतः।
   प्रकाशनात् सा सवितुः वाग् रूपत्वात् सरस्वती।। AP- 83.2
9. *SkP Āvantya Khanḍa, Revā Khanḍa,* 200.7

10. *DBP* 12.4.16, She is known as Trisaktidā because she is the mulādhāra of icchāśakti, kriya Śakti an jñāna Śakti and she gives that three Śakti to the generation.

11. पीतः श्यामश्च कपिलो मरकतोऽग्नि-सन्निभः
रूक्म-विद्युद्-धूम-कृष्ण-रक्त-गौरेन्द्रनीलभाः।
स्फटिक-स्वर्ण-पाण्ड्वाभाः पद्मरागोऽखिलद्युति।
हेम-धुम्र-रक्त-नील-कृष्ण-सुवर्णभाः।। *AP.* 215, Anandashrama Sanskrit Series, Poona, 1957

12. इन्द्रनीलश्च बन्हिश्च पीतं श्यामश्च कापिलम्,
श्वेतं विद्युत्प्रभं तारं कृष्णं रक्तं क्रमेण तत्।
श्यामं शुक्लं तथा पीतं श्वेतं वै पद्मरागवत्,
शङ्खवर्ण पाण्डुरश्च रक्तं चासवन्निभम्।
अर्कवर्णसमं सौम्यं शङ्खाभं श्रोतमेव च। *GP* 15.5-7

13. *Sk.P, Āvantya Khanḍa, Revā Khanḍa,* 200.7

14. *Sk.P, Avantya Khanḍa,* 200.10
बाला बालेंन्दु-सदृशी रक्तवस्त्रानुलेपना
उषः काले नु ध्यातव्या संध्यासंधान उत्तमे।

15. *SkP, Ābantya khanḍa, Revā Khanḍa* 200 6-7.

16. *SkP, Abantya khanda, Reva Khanda* 200 7-8.

17. Thomas B. Coburn, *Devi Mahataya, Crystalization of the Goddess Tradition,* MLBD, Delhi, Varanasi, 1984, P. 146.

18. S.K.Lal, *Female Divinites in Hindu Mythology and Ritual,* p. 56.

19. *Linga P.* 1.13.5-7

20. चतुर्मुखी जगद्योनिः प्रकृर्तिगोः प्रतिष्ठिता। *Vāp.,* ch. 23-50.

21. रक्ता भवति गायत्री सावित्री शुक्लवर्णिका
कृष्णा सरस्वती ज्ञेया सन्ध्यात्रमुदाहृतम्।
Sk. P 11.2.34-44 गायत्री वैष्णवी वा वै। *Guruda P* 1, 36.11

22. प्रातर्बाला च मध्याहने यैबनस्था भबेत्पुन.
बुद्धा सायं भगबती यिन्त्यते मुनिभिः सदा.
हंसस्था गरूडारूदा तथा बुषभबाहिती.
ऋग्वेदाध्यायिनी भुमौ दुश्यते या तपस्विमिः। *PB* 12.5.Y

23. *Padma-Purāṇa* 46. The details of the twenty-four different Gāyatri Mantras have been appended.

24. *Linga-P* 48.

25. *Sk.P* 35.192.

26. *Varāha P* 34.19.ed. Hrishikesha Shastri, *Bibliotheca Indica,*Calcutta, 1888. द्रुपदा नाम गायत्री जजत. जल हरः
27. S. Bhattacarjee, *The Indian Theogony,* P. 347; J.N. Banerjea–*The Development of Hindu Iconography,* srd Ed, Munshiram Manoharlal, 1974.
28. *AP* XLIX.15
29. *MP* CCLX1.24
30. *Ibid.,* - CCIX.40; *Ibid* CCLX. 44
31. *Puranic Encyopaedia-Vettommari*
32. खि केच्त्पिठन्ति स्म शच्फिरुपं पठन्ति च.
केचिन्सूर्य केचिदग्निं वेदगा आग्निहोत्रिणः।।
AP 111, M. M DVTI, Cosmo Publications
33. उतरे शिखरे जाता भुभ्यां पर्वतवासिनी।
व्रह्मणा समातुज्ञाता गच्द्द देजी यथासुखम्।। *Gp* 1. 205 70-72
34. *The Muhabharata* 3.227-282 BORI, Poona; *DBP,* I-20; *BrVais* P. 23-26.
35. *Savitryupanisad* 1.1-8; *Upanisatsamgraha,* Motilal Vanarasi Dass, Delhi, 1970.

7

Method of Sandhyā Worship of Gāyatrī and its Advantages

Oṁ is *Sabda-Brahman,* represented by the *Vedas,* and the *Gāyatrī-Mantra* is considered as the elaboration of *Oṁ* and the spiritual 'Boon conferring mother of the *Vedas'* (*Varadā Vedamātā*), the *Vedas* being held as further elaboration of the Gāyatrī. Because of its supreme spiritual significance, the *Gāyatrī-Mantra* has been incorporated as the very core of a daily prayer-ritual known as *sandhyā.* Being in the nature of contemplation the ritual is classed as *upāsanā* or spiritual contemplation. This *upāsanā* is to be performed thrice a day at the conjunction (*Sandhi*) times of the night and dawn, forenoon and afternoon, and evening and night, lasting fourty-eight minutes at each conjunction[1].

As the *upāsanā* is done at the conjunction time (*Sandhyā*), it is designated as the *Sandhyā-upāsanā.* It is also called *Sandhyā-Vandanā* (adoration or worship) and often merely *Sandhyā.* It can be practised by all without distinction of caste, colour, creed or sex.[2]

The morning *Sandhyā* is to be done early in the morning while the stars are visible. When the sun is in the meridian, the mid-day *sandhyā* is to be performed, and while the Sun is visibly going down, the evening *Sandhyā* is to be recited over. Distinctions are again made in the above three *Sandhyās.* The morning *Sandhyā* is seen best with stars, stars disappear with middling, and inferior with the Sun risen above the horizon. So the evening *Sandhyā* again is of three kinds the best, the middling, and the inferior. When the sun is visibly disappearing, the evening *Sandhyā* is the best, when the sun has gone down the horizon, it is middling and when the stars are visible, it is inferior.[3]

The *Sandhyā-upāsanā,* with the visible sun in the sky as the symbol, is a *sāndhanā* (spiritual practice) to bring about the conjunction (*Sandhi*) of the individual self with the cosmic self to realize the unity of both. So the *Sandhyā*-ritual incorporates the elements or features of all the four main types of *Yoga-Karma, Bhakti, Dhyana,* and *Jñāna.*

Sandhyā is a specially devised efficient spiritual ritual for the realization of the divinity of the self (*Ātman*). It is therefore not a *Kāmya Karma i.e.* optional ritual to be performed occasionally for the attainment of worldly fulfillments. It is, on the other hand a *Nitya karma* or an obligatory daily ritual whose objective is to bring about self purification and attainment of cosmic reality. It is a wonderful mental exercise to elevate and equip the mind for this purpose. It is an all-round complete ritual which incorporate the principles of the *Supreme Divinity* (*Brahman*), cosmic creation and deities nature and spirit and spiritual union or liberation (*Yoga* or *Mokṣa*). As a result of its daily practice with proper spirit, the mind is made pure, its present weaknesses and inertia are eliminated, and its inherent spiritual power come into manifestation. The different aspects of the ritual are conducive to physical and mental health and vigour. Thus *Sandhyā* is devised to lead to both physical and spiritual advancement.[4]

In the elaboration of the *Sandhyā* ritual the main purpose of spiritual elevation and visualization of the union of the individual and universal is always kept in view. Hence ritualistic procedures are devised for the removal of the physical, mental and psychic obstacles within to enable one to rise mentally step by step above the ego-centered life to the divine consciousness. Each part of the ritual is meant to give expression externally to an internal mental attitude and spiritual feeling. The main item, of course is the repetition (*Japa*) of the *Gāyatri Mantra* and meditation on it, others coming in as auxiliaries. Appropriate vedic *mantras* are prescribed to be recited with these concrete ritualistic procedures for the purification of the mind and the personality, and for generating the mental attitude helpful for concentration of divine truth.

Japa is preceded by a simple ceremony. Flowers and leaves of *Bilva* are gathered and put into a water pot. The water in that pot is offered to the Sun in the morning with the recitation of the *Mantra,* आ कृष्णेन रजसा वर्तमान: (*RV* 1.35.2). On the appearance of the disc of the Sun, the *Mantra* 'उदुत्वं जातवेदसम्' (*RV* 1.50.1) and 'चित्र देवानाम्' (*RV* 1.115.1) are recited up to a fixed number. In the morning the *japa* is to be performed with both the hands, turned downwards, and at the noon with both the hands placed near the chest. *Japa* of the *Gāyatri-Mantra* forms an important part of the worship. *Japa-sādhanā* of *mantras* is normally regarded as a sacrifice or *Yajña.* In the Gitā it is told that *Yajñānām japa yajñosmi.* As per *Mbh* the disciplined chanting of *mantras* is indeed important without any other requirement and is sufficient for realising the love (Asva, 44/8). *Liṅga-purāṇa* prescribes that–'One who sincerely performs *japa* would never face any calamity' (*LP* 8/5/124-125).

The Bharadvāja Gāyatrī *vyākhyā,* particularly prescribes the gravity of Gāyatrī *japa* in detail. The following is the cream of the description.

रूद्धा प्राणमपानश्च जपोन्मासं शतत्रयम्।
यदिच्छेत्तदवाप्नोति सहस्रात्परमाप्नुयात्।।

A devotional *japa* of thousand *Gāyatrī-mantra* per day continuously for a month along with proper controlling of *Apāna, Prāṇa* during the *japa* fulfils all worthy desires of the devotee.

Regarding the *japa* of the hundred *Gāyatrī-mantras* it is started that–

एकपादोजपेदुर्ध्वं वाहुरूद्धानिलावशः।
मासशतमवाप्नोति यदिच्छेदिति कौशिकः।

The *japa* of hundred *Gāyatrī-mantras* per day performed regularly for a month - under the discipline of standing on one leg alone, keeping both the arms up towards the sky and restraining the respiration to the maximum possible extent during this daily practice, takes the devotee to the desired noble goal.

However, while describing the method of *Sandhyā* worship of *Gāyatrī,* we should follow the seven sections of ritual practise. They are (1) visualized meditation (*Dhyāna*), (2) explication of *Mantra,* (3) ritual worship procedure (*Pujā vidhih*), (4) eulogy (*Stotra*),

(5) protective armour (*Kavaca*), (6) essence (*Hṛdaya*) and (7) japa (Recitation) *i.e.* (*i*) one-hundred and eight names, (*ii*) one thousand names.

Visualized Meditaion of Gāyatrī as described in the following Verse :

मुक्ता-विद्रुम-हेम-निल-धवलाद्दार्यैत्रक्षणै
युक्तम् इन्दु-निवद्ध-रत्न-मुक्तां तत्त्वार्थवर्णात्मिकाम्
गायत्रीं वरदाभयङ्कुश-करां शुभ्रं कपालं गदाम्
शङ्खचक्रमथारविन्दयुगलं हस्तै वहन्तीं भजे।। *DB*. Ch. 12(10)

Explication of the Mantra

In Indian civilization, the role of the sound and the word has been investigated since the time of the *Vedas* to the present. In most *Hindu* rituals, *Mantras* have a prominent part. An etymology for *Mantra* is the root *'Man'* which is associated with thought, will and intention, and the suffix *'tra'* which means an instrument of that which precedes it *i.e.* an instrument of intention. Another meaning is that *'Man'* is related to mind and *'tra'* means protection, hence a protection for the mind. The *prapañcasāratantra* V.2, states that 'by meditation on the place of ultimate principle (*tattva*) one is saved, thus it is named *Mantra*. Each deity has a specific *Mantra* and *vija* (seed syllable) which represents his/her essence. This Gāyatrī is composed of twenty-four syllables, each letter corresponding to an important deity in the *Hindu* pantheon (which will be discussed in ch. 1,2).

Ritual Worship Procedure (*Pujāvidhi*)

These are the procedures involving–(1) *Āc amana,* (2) *Apamār-janam,* (3) *Prāṇāyama,* (4) *Punar-ācamanam,* (5) *Punarmārjanam,* (6) *Aghamarṣaṇam,* (7) *Suryopāsthānam,* (8) *Gāyatrī upāsanām,* (9) *Visarjanam and* (10) *Antya prakaraṇān.*

The following procedures are illustrated in the *Purāṇas* like, *Agni-purāṇa, Skanda-purāṇa, Garuda-purāṇa, Padma-purāṇa, Brahmavaivarta-purāṇa* and *Devī-Bhāgavata-purāṇa.*

The Agni-Purāṇa

The *Agni-purāṇa* mention that first of all the sound '*Oṁ*' is to be uttered, then the name of the seer *i.e.* Viśvāmitra, is to be uttered, then the name of the *chandas* (Gāyatrī) and the deity *i.e.* Sāvitrī is to be recited.

गायात्री प्रणवश्चान्ते जपे चैवमुदाहृतं।
विश्वामित्र ऋषिच्छन्दो गायत्रं सविता तथा।। *AP.* 215

The gods who preside over different letters constituting the *Mantras* are the fire god, the wind god, the Sun, the lightning, the god of death, Lord of the water (ocean), the Jupiter, the god of rain, the Indra, the Gāndharva, the Puṣan, the Mitra, the Varuṇa, the Tavṣṭṛ, the Vasus, the Maruts, the Moon, the Angiras, the Visvedevās, the Asvins, the Rudraka, the Brahmā and the Viṣṇu respectively who are said to destroy sins at the time of repetition of Gāyatrī.

अग्निर्वायुरविर्विद्युत् यमो जलपतिर्गुरः।
पर्जन्य ईन्द्रा गन्धर्वः पूषा च तदनन्तरम्।। *Ibid.,* 216

मित्रोऽथ वरुणस्त्वष्ट्रा वसवो मरुतः शशी।। *Ibid.,* 217

अङ्गिरा विश्वधासत्यौ क स्तथा सर्वदेवताः।
रुद्रो व्रह्मा च विष्णुश्च क्रमशोऽक्षरदेवताः।। *Ibid.,* 218

They respectively protect the toes, ankles, legs, knees, shanks, the male organ of generation, hip, navel, belly, breasts, heart, neck, face, cheek, nostrils, eyes, the centre of the eye brows, forehead, front part of the face, the two sides in the right and left head and mouth in order.

पादाङ्गुष्ठौ च गुल्फौ च नलकौ जानुती तथा।
जङ्घ शिश्रश्च वृष्णौ कटिर्नाभिस्तथोदरं।। *AP.* 219

स्तनौ च हृदयं ग्रीवा मुखन्तालु च नासिके
चक्षुषी च भ्रुवोर्मध्यं ललाटं पूर्वमाननम्।। *Ibid.,* 220

The famous *Gāyatrī-Mantra* is enjoined to be uttered standing in water, sixteen times, then *Prāṇāyama* and offering into fire is enjoined as the morning ritual.[5]

To get rid of sins one is asked to offer sesame, along with the recitation of Gāyatrī, one who desires peace of mind should offer barley, and one who desires long life should sacrifice butter.

गायत्र्याः तु तिलै होमः सर्वपापप्रणाशनः।
शन्तिकामो चैव कुर्य्यादायुष्कामो घृतेन च।। *Ibid.*, 225

For the fulfilment of an action the offering of mustard seeds is enjoined and milk, for brilliance of knowledge, with desire of son, curds should be offered, and a person who desires corn should offer rice along with the recitation of Gāyatrī or Sāvatrī *Mantra*.

सिद्धार्थकैः कर्मसिद्धर्थै पयसा व्रह्मवर्च्चसे
पुत्रकामस्तथा दध्नाधान्यकास्तु शालिभिः।। *Ibid.*, 226

One should be oblation with twigs of *Kṣhīri* (milky) trees for the appeasement of afflictions due to planets. Then one desiring for wealth should do with *Vilva* (a kind of tree) and one who craves for prosperity should offer lotuses, whereas a person desiring health should offering *durva* grass. The same is enjoined at a calamity to ward it off.

खीरिवृक्षसमिद्भिस्तु ग्रहपीडोशान्तये।
धनकामस्तथा विल्वै श्रीकामः कमलैस्तथा।। *Ibid.*, 227

A person who desires fortune should offer guggule; a person who desires mastery over a lord should offer milk preparation in the fire.

शौभाग्येच्छुर्गुगुल विद्यार्थी पायसेन च
अयुतेनोक्तसिद्धिः स्याल्लक्षणे-मनसेसित।। *Ibid.*, 228

It is said that *durva* should be offered after being smeared with three kinds of sweets *i.e.* sugar, ghee and honey.[6]

Skanda-purāṇa

According to *SkP* the method of contemplation is mentioned as follows –

Every letter of the *mantra* is to be fixed at a part of the body.

Thus '*Tat*' at the head, '*Sa*' at the mouth, '*Vi*' at the throat, '*Tu*' at body joints, '*Va*' at the heart, '*Re*' at the both the sides, '*Ni*' at the right belly and '*Ya*' at the left '*Bhar*' at the waist, '*Go*' again at the two sides, '*De*' at the knees '*Va*' at the feet, '*Sya*' at the thumbs '*Dhi*' at the chest, '*Ma*' at the root of the knees, '*Hi*' at the private parts, '*Dhi*' at the heart, '*Yo*' at the lower lip, next '*Yo*' at the upper one, '*Nah*' at the nostrils, '*Pra*' at the eyes, '*Co*' at the eyebrows, '*Da*' at the breath and '*Yat*' at the forehead. (*SkP* VII.1, 07-29-36).

Utterance of Gāyatri metre only by the *dvijas i.e.* persons of the three upper *Varnas–Brāhmaṇas, Kṣatriyas* and *Vaiśyas,* not by a *Śūdra* would commit the sin of 'killing *Brāhmaṇ*'.

व्रह्माहत्या भवेत्सहि न तु शुद्रै कदाचन
उच्चारण धारणाद्वा नरके तति ध्रुवम्।। *SkP.* V.3.200.3

Garuḍa-Purāṇa

In *G.P,* Viśvāmitra is the *Ṛsi* and Savitā is the god. It consists of three words and eight letters and again of four words and six letters. The one of the three words should be used for the purposes of recitation and that of the four words for the purposes of adoration.

त्रिपदाष्टक्षरा श्रेया चतुष्पादा षडक्षरा
जपे च त्रिपदा प्रोक्ता अर्चने च चतुष्पदा।। *GP.* 1.35.4

GP describes the methods of *Nyāsa,* recitation, meditation, adoration, and fire by which a worshipper should use the *Gāyatī-Mantra* daily.

The devotee should assign it to the toes of the feet, in steps, knee joint, organs of excretion, scrotum, tubes, navel, belly, breast, heart, throat, mouth, palate, eyes, eye-brows, forehead, in the east, south, north, west and head.

पादाङ्गुष्ठे गुल्फमध्ये जङ्घयौविद्धि जानुनोः
ऊर्ध्वो गुह्य च वृषणे चाड्यां नाभौ तनुदरे।।

स्तनयो हृदिकण्ठौष्ठमुखे तालुनि वांशयोः
नेत्रे भृवोर्ललाटे च पूर्वस्यां दक्षिणोत्तरे।। *GP.* 15.5-6

It also clearly mentions the method of practising *Prāṇāyama* and the method of performing *Sandhyā.*

Having practised *Prāṇāyam* (suppression of vital airs), thrice the worshipper should bath at the period of conjunction. That process of *Yoga* is called *Prāṇāyama* in which a man having controlled his vital breath, reads thrice the Gāyatrī with Praṇava and *Vyāhṛtis* (*Oṁ bhur bhuvḥ svaḥ Oṁ*). By the *Yogic* process of *Prāṇāyama* a twice born destroys the impurities of mind, speech and body and therefore, practises it during all hours of the day.

स प्रणर्वासव्याहृतिः गायत्र्यौ शिरसा सह
त्रिः पठेदायतप्राणायामः स उच्यते।। *GP.* 16.2

Then reciting the *Ācamana Mantra 'Sāyam Agni'* (fire in the evening) as well as '*Prataḥ Sūrya*' (the Sun in the morning) he should drink water.

सायमग्निश्च नेत्युक्त्वा प्रातः सूर्ये तपः पिवेत्
आपः पुनन्तु मध्याह्ने उपस्पृश्य यथाविद्धिः।। *GP.* 16.4

He should perform *mārjana* (mystical wiping) with the *Rg 'Apohista'* and should rob his body with the water of *kusa* blades. Then adding to this *Mantra,* Praṇava he should sprinkle water at every step.

आपोहिष्ठेत्युया कुर्यांमार्जनं तु कुशोदकैः
प्रणवेन तु संयुक्तं क्षिपेद्वारि पदे पदे।। *GP.* 16.5

One should destroy the nine fold impurities originating from *Rajas* (darkness), *Tamas* (ignorance), *Moha,* from waking state, dreaming state and that of dreamless step and those originating from speech, mind and action.

रजस्ताम्भ. स्वमोहोत्थान जाग्रत्स्वप्नासुषुप्तिजान
वाङ्मन्त्रः कर्मजान् दोषान् नवैतान्नवाभिर्दहेत्।। *GP.* 16.6

Taking water in the joint palms and reciting the *Mantra Aghamarṣana* and throwing it quickly thrice, six, eight or twelve times destroys all sins.

समुद्धृत्योदकं पाणो जप्त्वा च दृपदा क्षिपेत्।
त्रिषडेष्टौ द्वादशधा वर्तयेदपमर्षणम्।। *GP.* 16.7

The Sun shall be worshipped with the two *Ṛks Udutyum* and *citram.* The sins committed during the day or night shall be destroyed instantly.

उदुत्युं चित्रमित्याभ्यामुपतिष्ठेदभाष्करम्
दिवारात्रौ च यत् पापं सर्वं नश्यति तत्क्षणात्।। *GP* 16.8

The *Sandhyā* prayer shall be recited in the morning in standing position and in the evening in sitting position. The Gāyatrī shall be recited with Praṇava prefixed and accompanied by *Mahāvyāhṛtis.*

It is also described that the letter ***Oṁ Bhuḥ*** to the heart, ***Om Bhuvḥ*** to the head, *Om Svaḥ* to the tuft of hair on the head.

The scholarly devotee shall fix for the first *Pāda* (group of six syllables) of Gāyatrī in the *Kavaca* and the second to the eyes. The *Anga-vinyāsa* is to be done with the third *Pāda* and fourth *Pāda* all over the body.

During the *Sandhyās* (morning, mid day and evening) Gāyatrī, the mother of the *Vedas* shall be recited after due *Nyāsas.* He shall be blessed with welfare in all limbs if the *Nyāsa* is accompanied by *Prāṇāyama* too.

At last comes the *Visarjana Mantra*–"O! Goddess born in the land of northern summit and permitted to stay on the mountain by Brahmā, please repair as please you".

उत्तरे शिखरे जाता भुम्यां पर्वतवासिनी
व्रह्मणा समानो ज्ञाता गच्छ देवी यथा सुखम्।। *GP* 16.7

Padma-purāṇa

PadP Sriṣṭkhanḍa explains in detail about the utterance of *Gāyatṛi-Mantra,* how each letter of the *Gāyatrī-Mantra* is connected with twenty-four parts of the body, *Gāyatrī Pancasiṣa Lakṣanaṁ Gāyatrī, Nyāsa,* twenty-four letters of the *Mantra* belong to twenty-four deities, and also about *Prāṇāyāma* and *Oṁkāra.*

The practitioner is to be utter the sound *AUM* first. Then the name of *Ṛṣi, Chandra,* and *Devatā.* Then *Gāyatrī* should be invoked and followed by *AUM* again.

A wise man should first assign the various letters of Gāyatrī to the twenty-four parts in his body beginning with the feet and ending with the head. The wise devotee should assign the syllable '*Tat*' to the great toe of the foot.

चतुर्विंशतिस्थानेषु आपादमस्तकेषु च।
तत्कारं विन्यसेद्योगी पदाङ्गुष्ठे विचक्षणः।। *PadP* – 46.172

One should assign the letter '*Sa*' to the region of the ankle, '*Vi*' to the shanks, '*Tu*' to the knee and '*Va*' to the region of the thighs.

सकारगुल्फदेशेतु विकारं जंघयोर्न्यसेत्।
तत्कारंविन्यसेद्योगी पदाङ्गुष्ठेन्विक्षणः।। *Ibid.*, 173

'*Re*' to the privity, '*Ni*' to the scrotum, '*Bha*' to the navel, '*Go*' to the belly. One should assign the letter '*De*' to the breasts, '*Va*' to the heart, the letter '*Sya*' to the hands, having assigned the letter '*Dhi*' to the mouth, '*Ma*' to the palate, having the letter, '*Hi*' to the tip up the nose, '*Dhi*' to the eyes, '*Yo*' in between the eye-brows and the letter '*Nah*' to the forepart of the face, the letter '*Pra*' to the right part and the letter '*Da*' to the left part of the face having assigned the letter '*Yat*' to the head.

रेकारं गुह्यदेशेतु णिकारं वृषणे न्यसेत्
यंकारं कटिदेशेतु भकारं नाभिमण्डले।। 174

गोकारं जठरेन्यस्य देकारं स्तनयोर्न्यसेत्
वकारं हृदयेन्यस्य स्यकारं कर देशे।। 175

धींकारं वदनेन्यस्य मकारं तालुकेर्न्यसेत्
हिकारं नासिकाग्रे च दिकारं चक्षुषोर्न्यसेत्।। 176

योंकार तु भ्रुवामध्ये योकारं ललाटके
नःकारं तु मुखे पूर्वे प्रकारं दक्षिणमुखे।। 177

चोकारं पश्चिमेन्यस्य दकारं चोत्तरे न्यसेत्
याकारं मुर्ध्निविन्यस्य सर्वव्यापि व्यवस्थित।। 178 (*PadP* 46)

PadP explains the method of *Prāṇāyāma* to be exercised for the deity connected with each syllable.

Apāṇa remains at the anus and *Prāṇa* in the heart of a man. So having contracted the anus one should get it (*i.e. Apāna*) united with '*Prāṇa*'. Then doing *Kumbhaka* exercise with *Puraka* and also practicing the *Prāṇāyāma,* a *Brāhmaṇa* should mutter the Gāyatrī hymn.

गुददेशेत्वपानस्याद्हृदिप्राणोस्तिदेहिनः। *PadP.* 46.158

पुरकेण तदापुत्र कृत्वा कुम्भकमुत्त्रगम्।
प्राणायाम त्रयं कृत्वा गायत्रीं स जपेद्विजः।। 158

PadP also vivid describes the methods of '*Nyāsa*' in evening prayer which is enlisted in *Srṣṭikhanda.*

The practitioner should assign '*Oṁ bhuḥ*' to the heart, '*Oṁ bhuvaḥ*' to the head, and '*Oṁ Svaḥ*' to the lock of hair on the crown of the head. He should assign '*Tat saviturvareṇyam*' to the body, '*Bhargo devasya dhīmahi*' to the eyes and '*Oṁ dhiyo yo naḥ pracodāyat*' to the hands.

ॐ भूरिति हृदयेन्यस्य ॐ भुवशिरसि न्यसेत्।

ॐ स्वः शिखायै यत्सवितुर्वरेण्यमिति कलेवरे

ॐ भर्गोदेवस्य धीमहीति नेत्रयोः।।

ॐ धियो यो नः प्रचोदयादिति करयोर्न्यसेतः।। *PadP.* 46.180-181

While reciting the hymn '*Oṁ Āpojyotirasomṛtam bhurbhuvaḥ-svarom*' he being purified from sin by merely touching water would go to *Hari* (*Viṣṇu*).

ॐ आपो ज्योती रसोमृतं व्रह्म भू भुवः स्वरोम्
इत्युदक स्पर्शमात्रेण पापात्पूतो व्रजेद्हरिम्।। 182

Having muttered Sāvitrī three times at the time of evening prayer with *Kumbhaka,* with *Vyāhṛtis* and twelve *Oṁkaras* as (*Oṁ Bhuḥ, Oṁ Bhuvaḥ, Oṁ mahaḥ, Oṁ janaḥ, Oṁ tapah, Oṁ satyam, Oṁ tatsaviturvareṇyam bhargo Devasya dhīmahi dhiyo yo naḥ pracodāyat i.e.*) we reflect upon the excellent lustre of god Savitṛ to urge our minds.

'*Oṁ Āpojyotirasomṛtam Brahma bhurbhuvaḥsvarom* and having muttered the Sāvitrī (hymn) of twenty four letters at the time of Sun worship he becomes superior with great learning and obtains *Brahmanahood.*

ॐ भूः ॐ भुवः ॐ स्वः ॐ जनः ॐ तपः ॐ सत्यम्
ॐ तत् सवितुर्वरेण्यं भर्गो देवस्य धीमहि धियो यो नः प्रचोदयात्।।
ॐ आपो ज्योती रसोमृतं ब्रह्म भू भुवः स्वरोम्
इति सव्याहृतिं स प्रणवाद्वादशोंकाशं सन्ध्याकाले कुम्भकेन वारत्रयं जप्त्वा।

PadP also tells about the characteristics of five heads of *Gāyatrī* (अथ गायत्रीपञ्चशीर्ष लक्षणम्) *i.e. Oṁ Bhuḥ Oṁ Bhuvaḥ, Oṁ mahaḥ, Oṁ janah, Oṁ tapaḥ, Oṁ satyam, Oṁ tatsaviturvareṇyam bhargo Devasya dhīmahi dhiyo yo naḥ pracodāyat.*

Having muttered Gāyatrī with *Vyāhṛtis* the practitioner again assign the letters of Gāyatrī to the various parts of the body. Being free from all sins he would go to the same heaven as of *Viṣṇu.*

सव्याहृति तु गायत्रीं पुनर्न्यासं तु कारयेत्
सर्वपापविनिर्मुक्तों विष्णुसायुज्यतां व्रजेत्।। *PadP* 46.187

The five heads of Gāyatrī are *Oṁ Bhuḥ* to the two feet, *Oṁ Bhuvaḥ* to the knees, *Oṁ svaḥ* to the waist, *Oṁ mahaḥ* to the navel, *Om satyam* to the forehead, *Oṁ tatsaviturvareṇyam* to the lock of the hair on the crown of the head.

She is described to be specially worshipped and propitiated on the full moon day of the month of Kartika (*i.e.* parts of October, November) and Jyestha (*i.e.* parts of May, June). The popularity of Gāyatrī, originally the praise of the power of Sun god *i.e.* Savitṛ, *Sāvitrī-Mantra* in the Gāyatrī metre could be seen from the practice of various gods in the same metre. (*PadP Pātalakhaṇḍa* 108.87, *LiṅgaP* 11.48.5-26.)

Brahma Vaivarta-Purāṇa

In *Brahma-vaivarta-Purāṇa* we find information about Sāvitrī's *Dhyāna*, modes of her worship, *Stotra, Mantra,* the importance of *Gāyatrī Japa* etc. with reference to king Aśvapati's acceptance of *devī* Sāvitrī as his daughter.

The methods of *japa* as described in *Brahmavaivarta Purāṇa* are as follows :

Make the palm of the right hand like a snake's hood, the fingers are all close, no holes are seen, and make the ends of the fingers bend downwards, then being calm and quite and with one's face east-ward, practice *Japa.*

> करं सर्पफणाकारं कृत्वा तद्रन्थमुद्रितम्।
> आनम्रमूर्धमलचं प्रजपेत्प्राह्मुखो द्विजः।।7।।

Then count from the middle of the ring finger and go on counting right handed till come to the bottom of the index finger. The rosary is to be the seed of white lotus, it should be consecrated and purified.

> तर्जनीमूलर्य्यन्तं जपस्यैव क्रमः करे।
> श्वेतपङ्कवीजानां स्फटिकानां च संस्कृताम्।।19।।

Japa is to be done in a sacred *Tirtha* or in a temple. Becoming self-controlled one should place the rosary on a banyan leaf or on a lotus leaf and smear it with cow dung, wash it, uttering *Gāyatrī-mantra* and perform over it one hundred times *Gāyatrī japa* intently in accordance with the rules.

> कृत्वा च मालिकां राजज्जपेतीर्थे सुरालये।
> संस्थाप्य मालामश्वत्थपत्रे पद्मे च संयतः।।20।।

> कृत्वा गोरोयनाक्ता च गायत्रया स्नापयेतसुधीः।
> गायत्रीशतक तस्यां जपेच्च विधिपूर्वकम्।।21।।

Then wash the rosary with *pancagavya*-milk, curds, clarified butter, cow urine and cow dung. Then wash it with the *Ganges* water and perform the best consecrations.

> अथवा पञ्चगव्येन स्नात्वा मालां सुसंकृताम्।
> अथ गङ्गोदकेनैव स्नात्वा वाऽति सुसंकृताम।।22।।

Then after reciting or performing ten lakhs of *Japa* everyday in morning, mid-day and in the evening Aśvapati will see the *Devī* Sāvitrī.

Sāvitrī is described to be specially worshipped on the thirteenth day of the black fortnight in the month of Jyaistha, the fourteenth day (the *caturdaśī tithi*). This vow is to be observed with great care and devotion. Fourteen fruits and fourteen plates with offerings of food on them, flowers and incense are to be offered and this vow is to be observed for fourteen years consecutively.

ज्येष्ठे शुक्लत्रयोदश्यां शुद्धे काले च संयतः।
व्रतमेतचतुर्दश्यां व्रती भक्तया समाचरेत्।।

व्रतं चतुर्दशाब्दं च द्विसप्तफलसंयुतम
दत्वा द्विसप्तनैवेद्यं पुष्पघुणादिकं तथा।। *BrhP* 23.42-43

Garments, holy threads and other articles are also offered and after the *vrata* is over, the *Brāhmins* are to be fed. The *mangala ghata* is to be located duly according to the rules of worship with branches and fruits.

वस्त्रं यज्ञोपवितं च भोज्यं च विधिपूर्वकम्।
संस्थाप्य मङ्गलघटं फलशाखासमन्वितम्।।

Ganesa, Agni, Viṣṇu Śiva and *Śivā* are to be worshipped. "गणेशं च दिनेशं च वह्नि विष्णुं शिवं शिवाम्।"

Thus reciting the *Dhyāna Mantram* and meditating on her, one is to offer *naivedyas* (offering of food) to her and then place one's fingers on one's head. One is to meditate again, and then invoke the *Devī* within the pot.

One should present fourteen things (*Ṣodaśopacāra*), uttering proper *Mantra* according to the Vedas. The fourteen articles of worship are (1) Seat (*Āsan*), (2) Water for washing feet (*Pādya*), (3) offering of rice and *Durba* grass (*Arghya*), (4) water for bath (*Snāniya*), (5) anointment with *Sandal* paste and other scents (*Anulepana*), (6) incense (*Dhūpa*), (7) Light (*Dipa*), (8) offering of food (*Naivedya*), (9) Betals (*Tāmbula*), (10) Cool water, (11) garments, (12) ornaments, (13) garlands and (14) scents, offering of water to sip and beautiful bedding.

आसनं पाद्यमर्ध्यं च स्नानीयं चानुलेपनम्
धूपं दीपं च नैवेद्य ताम्बुलं शीतलं जलम्।।53

वसनं भूषणं माल्यं गन्धमाचनींकम्।
मनोहरं सुतल्पं च देयान्येतानि षोडश।।54

While offering these articles, one is to utter the *Mantras* this beautiful wooden or golden seat, giving spiritual merit is being offered me to thee.

दारुसारविकारं च हेमादिनिर्मितं च वा
देवाधारं पुण्यप्रदं च मया तुभ्यं निवेदितम्।।53

This water from the *tirthas,* this holy water for washing thy feet, pleasant, highly meritorious pure, and as and embodiment of *pujā* is being offered by me to thee.

तीर्थोदकं च ह्लादं च पुण्यद प्रीतिद महत्
पजगभूतं शुद्धं च मया तुभ्यं निवेदितम्।।54

The holy *Arghya* with *Durba* grass and flowers and the pure water in the conch-shell is being offered by me to thee.

पवित्ररूपमर्धं च दूर्वा पुष्पदलान्वितम्
पुण्यदं शङ्खतोयोत्कं मया तुभ्यं निवेदितम्।।55

This sweet scented oil and water being offered by me to thee with devotion for your bathing purposes. Kindly accept this.

सुगन्ध गन्धतोयं च स्नेहं सौगन्धकारकम्
मया निवेदितं भक्तयां स्नानीयं प्रतिग्रह्यताम्।।56

O mother! This sweet-scented water divine like, highly pure and prepared of ***kunkuma*** and other scented things.

गन्धद्रव्योक्रद्भव पुण्यं प्रीतिदं दिव्यगन्धदम्
मया निवेदितं भक्त्या गन्धतीयं तथाऽम्बिके।।47

O Parameśvarī! This all suspicious, all good and highly meritorious, this beautiful *dhūpa,* kindly take.

सर्वमङ्गलपच सर्वं च मङलप्रदम्
पुण्यदं च सुधूपं च ग्रहाण परमश्वेरि।।58

O World mother! This is very pleasant and sweet scented, therefore I offer to thee. O mother! This light manifesting all this universe and seed as it were, to destroy the darkness is being offered by me.

जगतां दर्शनार्थायप्रदीप दीप्तिकारकम्
अन्धकारध्वंसवीज मया तुभ्यं निवेदितम्।।60

Devī! Kindly accept this delicious offering of food, highly meritorious, appeasing hunger, pleasant, nourishing and pleasure giving.

तुष्टिदं पुष्पिदं चैव प्रीतिदं क्षुद्विनाशनम्
पुण्यदं स्वादुरूपं नैतेद्य प्रतिग्रह्यताम्॥61

This betel is scented with *camphor* etc. nice, nourishing, and pleasure giving, this is being offered by me.

ताम्बुलप्रवरं रम्यं कर्पूरोदि सुवासितम्
तुष्टिदं पुष्पिदं चैव मया तुभ्यं निवेदितम्॥62

This water is nice and cool, appeasing the thirst and the life of the world. Kindly accept this.

सुशीतल चारि शीतं पिपासानाशकारणम्
जगतां जीवरूपं च जीवनप्रतिगह्यताम्॥63

O *Devī!* Kindly accept this silken garment as well as the garment made of *Kārpasa* cotton, beautifying the body and enhancing the beauty.

देहशोभास्वरूपं च सभाशो भाविवर्धनम्
कार्पासज च कृमिज वसनं प्रतिगृह्यताम्॥64

Kindly, accept these golden ornaments decked with jewels, highly meritorious, joyous, beauteous and prosperous.

कांचनादिविनिर्माण श्रींकारं श्रीचुतं सदा
सुखदं पुण्यदं रत्नभूषणं प्रतिगृह्यताम्॥65

Kindly accept these fruits yielding fruits of desires, obtained from various trees and of various kinds. Please have this garland, all auspicious and all good, made of various flowers, beauteous and generating happiness.

नानावृक्षसमुद्भूत नानारूप समन्वितम्
नानापुण्यविनिर्माण वहुशोभासमन्वितम्॥67

O *Devī!* Kindly accept this sweet scent, highly pleasing and meritorious. Please take this *Sindura*, the best of the ornaments, beautifying the forehead, highly excellent and beautiful.

सिन्दुर च वरं रम्यं भालशोभाविवर्धनम्
भूषणानां च प्रवरं सिन्दूरंप्रतिग्रह्यताम्॥68

Kindly accept this holy and meritorious threads and purified by the vedic *Mantras* and made of highly holy threads and knitted with highly pure knots.

विशुद्धग्रन्थिसंयुक्त पुण्यसूत्रविनिर्मितम्
पवित्रम्वेदमन्त्रेण यज्ञसूत्र च गृह्यताम्।।69

Uttering thus, offer the above articles that are to be offered to the *Devī,* every time the specific seed *Mantra* being uttered. Then the intelligent devotee should recite the *stotras* and subsequently offer the *Dakṣiṇās* with devotion to the *Brāhmanas.* The radical or the specific seed *Mantra* is the eight-lettered *Mantra Srīm Hrīm klīm Sāvitrī Svāhā.*

Kavaca

Kavaca literally means Armour or a coat of mail. In the *nyāsa* if refers to crossing one's arms and touching the shoulders which is also a type of protection. In this section, the practitioner protects the entire body by the recitation of specific *Mantras* at designated place of the body, beginning with head and ending with feet, and wearing amulets empowered with *Mantras.* This practice, unlike the *nyāsa* practice which transforms one's body into a divine body, protects the practitioner by requesting deities to guard certain parts of the body. These deities are summoned by the appropriate *Mantras* and are requested to remain at these parts of the body in order to neutralize negative influences, to propitiate planets, to ward off untimely death, and to provide general protection against all adverse circumstances.

The third chapter of twelfth book of *DB* deals about the Gāyatrī *Kavaca Ṛsi, Chandas. Devatā, Dhyāna* and *Nyāsa* which means is very secret. According to *DB* it destroys all sins. Therefore to recite or to hold it on one's body enables the *Man* to become free from all his sins and get all his desires fulfilled and he gets the *Sāyuya mukti* with the *Devī.*

Brahmā, Viṣṇu and Maheśvara are the *Ṛsis.* The *Ṛg,* the *Yajus,* the *Sāma* and the *Atharva* Veda are the *chandas.* The *Paramākalā* Gāyatrī of the nature of Brahmā is the *Devatā* of the Gāyatrī *Kavaca.*

ब्रह्मरूपा देवतोक्ता गायत्री परमाकला। DB. 12.6

'Tat' in the Gāyatrī is the *Vīja,* 'Bharga' is the *Śakti,* and *Dhiya* is the *kilaka,* and its *viniyoga* (application) is in getting the *mokṣa* (liberation).

तद्वीजं भर्ग इत्येषां शक्तिरुक्ता मनीषिभिः।
कीलकं च धियः प्रोक्तं मोक्षार्थे विनियोगनम्॥7

Kavaca means the first four syllables touch the heart, with the next four letters touch the tuft on the crown of the head, and with the next three letters on the armour, with the last four letters make the *nyāsa,* all over body repeating *'astraya phot',* a mystic sound.

चतुर्भिहृदयं प्रोक्तं त्रिभिर्वणेः शिरः स्मृतम्।
चतुर्भिः स्याच्छिखा पश्चाव्तिभिस्तु कवचं स्मृतम्॥8

DB Purāṇa describes the *dhyānam* or adoration of Gāyatrī in a very beautiful manner.

The Gāyatrī *devī* has five faces, one of which is of white colour, and the other four is of pearl, *vidruma,* golden and *Nilakāntamaṇi* colour respectively. Each face has got three eyes, on the head there is a crown of jewels and the digit of moon is shining there. Her body is composed of the twenty-four *tattvas.* She has ten hands, on the top right and on left hands there are two lotuses, lower down, there are disc and conch shell, lower down, there are rope and skull, lower down, there are noose and goad, and on the bottom hands right and left she is making signs of 'no fear' and 'ready to grant boons'.

मुक्ताविद्रुमहेमनीलधवल स्छायैर्मखैस्त्रिक्षणै
युक्तामिन्दुनिब्द्धरत्न मुकुटां तत्वार्थवणीत्मिककाम्॥

गायत्री वरदाभयाऽङ्कुशैशकां शुभ्रं कपालगुणं
शङ्खैव चक्रमथारविन्दयुगलं हस्तंर्वहन्ती भजे॥10

Thus meditating on Śri Gāyatrī, one is to recite the *Kavaca.* Thus let the Gāyatrī *Devī* protect the front, Sāvitrī *Devī* protect the right, the Sandhyā *Devī* the back and the *Devī* Sarasvati the left and mother Pārvati *Devī* protect the quarters.

गायत्री पूर्वतः पातु सावित्री पातु दक्षिणे।
ब्रह्मसन्ध्या तु मे पश्चादुत्तरायां सरस्वती॥11

The *DB Purāṇa* mentions that by reciting the *Gāyatrī Kavaca* one can be assured of getting protection from all the directions. Let the *Jalasāyinī* protect the southeast, *Yatudhāna Bhayankarī* protect the southeast, *Pavamānāvilāsinī* the north-west, *Rudrarupinī Rudrānī* protect the north-east. Let Brahmāṇi protect the top and Vaiṣṇavī protect the nether regions.

पार्वती मे दिशं रक्षेत्पावकी जलशायिनी।
यातुधानी दिशं रक्षेद्यातुधान भयङ्करी।।12

पावमानी दिशं रक्षेत्पवमानविलासिनी
दिशंरौद्री च मे पातुरुद्राणीं रुद्ररुपिणी।।13

उर्ध्व ब्रह्माणि मे रक्षदधस्ताद्वैष्णवी तथा
एवं दश दिशो रक्षेत्सर्वाङ्ग भुवनेश्वरी।।14

Let the word '*Tat*' in the *Gāyatrī* protect legs, "*Savituḥ*" protect knees, '*Vareṇyam*' protect the lions, '*Bharga*' the navel. Let '*Devasya*' protect the heart, '*Dhīmahi*' protect the neck, '*Dhiyah*' protect the eyes, '*Yaḥ*' protect the forehead, '*Naḥ*' protect the head and '*Pracodayāt*' protect the tuft on the crown of the head.

तत्पदं पातु मे पादौ जङ्घे मे सवितुः पदम्
वरेण्यं कठिदेशं तु नाभि भर्गस्तथैव च।।15

देवस्य तद्धृदयं धीमहीति च गल्लयो
धियः पदं च मे नेत्रे यः पदं मे ललाटकम्।।16

नः पातु मे पदं मूर्ध्निः शिखायां मे प्रचोदयात्।

Again the *Kavaca* is to recited according to syllables. First *'Tat'* of the twenty-four syllables *Gāyatrī* protect the head, '*Sa*' protect the forehead, *'Vi'* protect eyes, '*Tu*' cheeks, '*Va*' protect nostrils, '*Re*' mouth, '*Ni*' protect upper lip, '*Yah*' protect lower lip, '*Bha*' within the face, '*Rgo*' protect cheeks, '*De*' throat, '*Va*' shoulders, '*Sya*' right hand, '*Dhī*' navel, '*Ma*' heart, '*Hi*' belly, '*Yo*' loins, '*Yo*' anus, '*Naḥ*' thighs, '*Pr*' knees, '*Cho*' shanks, '*Da*' heels, '*Ya*' legs, '*At*' protect all the sides.

The divine *Kavaca* of the *Devī* Gāyatrī can baffle hundreds and thousands of obstructions and evils and can grant sixty-four *kalās* and liberation.

इदं तु कवचं दिव्यं वाधाशतविनाशनम्
चतुः षष्टिकलाविद्यादायकं मोक्षकारकम्।।24

By the glory of this *Kavaca,* man can become free from all evils and can attain the state of *Brahmā.* Moreover whoever reads or hears this acquires the fruits of making a gift of thousand cows.

Hṛdaya

This section is the 'essence' (*hṛdaya*) of the entire practice. It contains parts of all the important practices, such as *nyāsa,* visualized meditation of Gāyatrī, praises to Gāyatrī, innovation of her as one's protectors, recitation of her one hundred and eight names and one thousand names, and the results obtained by performing this *hṛdaya* practice.

DB puraṇa describes the subject on the *Hṛdaya* of Gāyatrī. It is explicitly written in the *Atharvaveda.* Narāyaṇa said to Nārada that at first consider the Gāyatrī the *Devī,* the mother of the Vedas as of a cosmic form (*virat rūpa*), and meditate all the *Devas* as residing on her body.

The *Ṛsi* of this Gāyatrī, *Hṛdaya* is Nārāyaṇa, the *chandas* is Gāyatrī, and Śri Parameśvari Gāyatrī is the *Devatā* (presiding deity).

गायत्रीहृदयस्थाऽस्यऽव्यहमेव ॠषि स्मृतः
गायत्रीच्छन्द उद्दिष्टं देवतां परमश्वेरी।। *DB* 12.4.30

Perform the *Nyāsa* and taking seat in a lonely place, meditate intently on the *Devī* with heart and head well collected. Then the method of *Anganyāsa* is described as follows.

Meditate on the *Devatā Dyau* on your head, the twin *Aśvins* on upper and lower lips, the Agni, fire within mouth, Sarasvatī on the tongue, Bṛhaspati on the neck the eight Vasus on the two breasts, the Vāyus on the two arms, the *paryana deva* on the heart, Akāsa on the belly, *Antarikṣam,* on the navel, Indra and Agni, on the loins, the Kailasa and the Malaya mountains on the two thighs, the *Viśvedevās* on the two knees, Viśvāmitra on the shanks, the Sun's northern and southern paths, the *Uttarāyaṇa* and *Dakṣināyana* on the annus, the *pitṛs* on the thighs, the earth on the legs, the *vanaspati* on the fingers and toes, the *Ṛsi's* on the hairs of the body, the *mūhurtas* on the nails, the planets on the bones, the seasons on the blood and flesh, the *Samvatsaras* on the *Nimisa* (twinkling of eye) the Sun and the Moon on the day and night respectively.

Thinking thus repeat 'I take refuse of the divine holy Gāyatrī, the chief and most excellent one, the thousand eye and I take refuse wholly un to her.

अहोरत्रादितयश्चन्द्रमा: प्रवरां दिव्यां गायत्रीं
सहस्रनेत्रं शरणमहं प्रपद्ये।

Thus a person is to repeat 'I bow down *Tat saviturvareṇyam'*, 'I bow down to the rising sun in the east', 'I bow down to the morning Aditya', 'I bow down to the Gāyatrī, residing in the morning Sun' and I bow down to all.

अहोरात्रादित्यश्चन्द्रमा: प्रवरा दिव्यां गायत्रीं सहस्रनेत्रां शरणमहं प्रपद्ये।

Whoever recites this Gāyatrī *Hṛdaya* in the morning finds all the sins committed in night all destroyed. Whoever recites this in the evening and in the morning can rest assured to have become free of sins, he gets the fruits of all the *Tīrthas*, he is acquainted with all the *devas*, he is saved if he has spoken anything that ought not to have been sucked, if he has done anything that ought mot to have done and if he has accepted hundreds and thousands of gifts that ought never to have been accepted.

प्रातरधीयानो रात्रिकृतं पापं नाशयति। सामयधीयानो दिवसकृतं पाप नाशयति। सायं प्रातधीयानो अपापो भवति। सर्वतीर्थेषु स्नातो भवति। अवाच्यवनात्पूतो भवति। अभक्ष्यभक्षणात्पूतौ भवति। अनेन हृदयेनाऽधीतेत क्रतुसहस्रेणेष्टं भवति।

Gāyatrī is enjoined at various rituals pertaining to divine worship and also the rituals of the names. Before requesting to *Brāhmaṇas* at the *Śrādha* to take their means. Gāyatrī with *Vyāhṛtis i.e., AUM Bhuḥ Bhuvaḥ* and the *Mantra Madhu vata rtayatee* are enjoined to be uttered (*Ṛg* 1.90.7).

One Thousand Names of Gāyatrī

The *nāmastotra,* the praise of names of a deity is well known in many religious traditions. In the *bhakti* cult of ancient India *B.K. Goswami* states, 'The worship, the concentration on and the recitation of the *Mantras* and the repetition of the holy names, constitute the main part of the religious life of a *sasvata* worshipper. Most praises with the recitation of names consist of one hundred and eight, three hundred, a thousand, or a thousand and eight names. These names may be recited aloud, repeated inaudibly, mentally repeated, or sung in groups (*namakirtana*). In the *Viṣṇu-Purāṇa* (6.2.27) it is said "That which one obtains in the *kṛtyayuga* by meditation, by performing sacrifice in the Tretā, by worship in the Dvāpara, one receives in the Kaliyuga, by reciting (the names) of Keśava."

The efficacy of the recitation of a deity's name in a ritual context has its historical antecedent in the Vedas. Renou in his *Eludes Sur le vocabulaire du RV* states that "the name above all is that one of a deity", and that the beginning of language occurred when the ancient seers gave names to all objects (X.71.1). The first chapter in *RV* (1.1.155) mentions Agni's name eight times in the first nine stanzas. In the *ŚB* (6.1.3.9) receiving a name frees one from evil, and in (11.2.3. 4-6) he who knows those two great forces (name and form) of the becomes himself a great force.

Furthermore, the *BG,* instead of repeating Kṛṣṇa's or Arjuna's name, is replete with epithets for them, thereby emphasizing their diverse and accomplished abilities. In the ninth chapter stressing devotion, Kṛṣṇa is described as many things, including the father of this world, the mother and the establisher (9.17). The power of invoking a deity's name and his/her various epithets is emphasized in India's early sacred texts. One of the first specific one thousand names is that of Viṣṇu in dialogue between Bhisma and Yudhishsitra in the *Mbh* Ch. 149 of the *Anuśāsanika parvan.* From this prototype, the popularity of praising the names grew, as is evident from the numerous praises found in the *Purāṇas* and *tantras.* Some of the more famous ones are the 'Lalita Shasranāma' in the *Brahmāṇḍa Puraṇa,* the 'Gayatri Sahasranama' in the *Devī Bhāgavatam*, the 'Śiva Sahasranāma' in the *VaP* and in the *Brahma Purāṇa.*

In Gonda's monograph, 'Notes on names and the name of god in ancient India', he enumerates several ways that knowledge of a name makes one powerful. He cites the *AV* (11.8.7) "As long as the former earth remains nameless it cannot be identified as to become an object of knowledge".

Padma Purāṇa

The *PadP* has given one hundred eight names of Gāyatrī that have been appended in Appendix-III.

Devī Bhgavata Purāṇa

In keeping with the practice of the *Purāṇas,* the *DB* has given the *Sahasranāma* of Gāyatrī. The *Sahasranāma* tries to attribute a number of qualities to a particular deity. In other words, it is a list of epithets. The *Gāyatrī Sahasranāma* is arranged in an alphabetical order.

Continuous succession of the adjectives and the compounds create a musical cadence. It is prescribed to be recited daily. The epithets create an impression of awe and reverence. The *stotra* employ full grammatical sentences, whereas the list of thousand names does not contain any verb. The one thousand and eighty names of *devī* Gāyatrī begins with the syllable 'a' and goes with 'a', 'ā', 'i', 'ī', etc. in due order of Sanskrit alphabets.

Her ways and actions cannot be comprehended by intellect; she is therefore *Acintyalakṣaṇā*. She is Avyaktā, she is Arthamatre Māheśvarī, and she is Ajitā, Aparājitā, Ajarā, Ajā, Aparā and Aravindanibhekṣaṇā.[7] She beginning with the syllable 'a' and ending with the syllable '*Kṣa*' comprises of fifty syllables. So she is called as Akāradkṣakārānta. She is Adilaxmi Adiśakti. Gāyatrī is further called Āgneyī[8]. She is Ādityamaṇḍalagatā.[9] Gāyatrī is also known by the name Indirā, Iṣṭā, Indrāṇī, Irāvatī etc. She is also known as Iśvarī because she is related to Iśvara. She is Umā, Usā, Udunibhā etc. Gāyatrī Devī is also known as Ūrdhakeśī, Ṛtā, Rsī, Ṛtumatī, Ṛjudharmā, Luptadharmā etc. She is Ekākṣarā, Ekamātrā, Aindrī, Oṁkarā, Osadhī, Otā, Andamādhyāsthitā etc. She is Kātyāyanī, Kālaratrī, Kamalā, Kharbbā, Khecarī, Gangā, Gāyatrī, Gitā, Ghoṣā, Cārudantā, Chāyā, Chatreśvarī, Jātadevā, Jambudvīpābati, Jhallakī, Vādyakuśalā, Nṛpā, Taṇakabhedini, Dāmarī, Dākinī, Nirguṇā,[10] Tripadā,[11] Tharvā Dānabāntakarī, Dhānyā, Dhrubā, Phaladā, Vandyā, Brāhmī,[12] Bhagavatī, Mata, Māyā,[13] Māheśvarī,[14] Yogamāyā, Yogā, Rātī, Revā, Lolā, Lalitā, Varadā, Vaiṣṇavī etc.

She is also known as Śivā, Sarasvatī, Surasuranamasktā, Sarasvatī,[15] Sāvitrī,[16] Hiranyavrnā, Ksiralohitanayā, Kṣamā etc.

Thus the *Sahasranāma* is an attempt at identifying all that is responsible in the *Devī*. This also indicates that the *Devī* is all pervading, omnipotent power. She is not only like the *Brahman,* knowledge, truth and infinity but also directly participates in the affairs of the *Asuras,* the human beings and the heavenly personalities. The thousand names present a variegated picture of the myriad, coloured personality of the *Devī* to the devotee. In this *Sahasranāma* all the epithets are of the supreme power, who is identified with Gāyatrī.

This shows that Gāyatrī and the *Devī* are not different and the *Gāyatrī upāsanā* is *Devī upāsanā* only. The author of the *DB* has given these thousand names after describing the *tāntric* ritual of Gāyatrī worship. The epithets are formed in such a manner, as to indicate all possible majestic ideas.

On close analysis, we find that the list of thousand names contains the adjectives of *devī* only. It can be classified into some categories.

Abstract adjectives embodied in the *devī* are *Aparājitā, Cirapravagnā, Jayantī, Ghoṣā* and *Tungā* etc.

Adjectives conveying the beauty of the *devī* are *Aravinda-nivānanā, Vrdhvahupriyā, Karikumbhastanākarā, Nabajam-būnadaprekhyā* etc.

Tantra Adjectives : Adjectives describing the *devī*, after the manner of *tantra.*[17]

Asṭṛa Adjectives : Words used in the *Sahasranāma* describing the *paraphernalia* of the *devī* weapons.[18]

Adjectives conveying the connection of *devī* with certain other divine beings.

The adjectives used in this context with certain personalities.[19]

Adjectives directly identifying the *devī* with certain ladies.[20]

Adjectives indicating her various exploits, such as *Mahisāsura-mardinī, Prutunaprāṇaghatinī.*

The adjectives *Antarakaśarūpīṇī, Otaprotanivāsinī, Turiya-padagāminī, Trikalajñānadāyinī* etc. of the *devī* embodying Vedantic concepts.

Epithets describing her special qualities such as *Sāndrakaṛuṇā Ramaṇiyā, Yugadhārā Rogasramaṇī, Sādhubandhu.*

Epithets indicating her connection with different sects are sectarian aspects, such as *Akṣasūtradharā, Vaiṣṇavī, Sivakārā* etc.

Epithets identifying her with constellation such as *Vdunibhā, Citrā* and *Tarakā.*[21]

Whatever it may be the adjectives given in connection with *Gāyatrī Sahasranāma* extensive light on the various aspects of nature and qualities of the goddess.

Glory and Advantages of Gāyatrī Japa

In *Hindu* religious life, Gāyatrī as a *Mantra* as well as a divinity holds a unique place. Perhaps because of its utter simplicity, the *Gāyatrī-Mantra* has become an in separable part of the daily rites of a pious *Hindu,* irrespective of his sectarian belief. He believes that a mere repetition of this *Mantra* can bring to him an enormous spiritual and physical power, and that he can perform miracles and obtain his desired objects by means of the power thus attained.

From the vedic expositions to the contemporary spiritual literature, the grandeur of Gāyatrī has been acclaimed with grandiloquence.

In *Atharva-Veda,* the following prayer has been offered to Gāyatrī in which it has been described as one which gives longevity, energy (*Prāṇaśakti*), domestic animals, fame, wealth, and spiritual splendour (*Brahma-tejaḥ*).

स्तुता मया वरदा वेदमाता प्रचोदयन्तां पावमानीद्विजानाम्।
आयुः प्राणं प्रजां पशुं कीर्तिं द्रविणं व्रक्ष्मवर्चसम्।। *AV* 19.17-1

Almighty god in the form Vedas has stated in *AV* "may Vedamātā Gāyatrī to whom I offer prayer, purify dvijas (*Brāhmaṇas*) and grant them longevity, spiritual vital energy, animals, fame, wealth, and spiritual splendour".

According to *Manusmṛti,* Gāyatrī is the face of Brahmā.

ॐकारपूर्विकास्तिस्रो महाव्याहृतयस्तथा
त्रिपदा चैव गायत्री विज्ञेयं व्रक्षणो मुखम्।। *Manusmrti* 2.82

Gāyatrī is the essence of the whole of *Veda* as the creator milked the three lines of *Gāyatrī-Mantra* from the *Vedas* respectively.[22]

Vyāsa says that just as honey, ghrit and water of milk and taste respectively. So also *Gāyatrī-Mantra* is the essence of all the *Vedas*.

यथा मधु व न पुष्पेभ्यो घृतं दुग्धाद्रसात्पयः।
एवं हि सर्ववेदानां गायत्री सार उच्यते।।

According to Viśvāmitra *Ṛsis* and seers say that there is no other *Mantra* like *Gāyatrī-Mantra* in all the four *Vedas*. *Veda, Yajña, Dāna* (donation, charity), *Tapa* are not equivalent even to a fraction of *Gāyatrī-Mantra*.

तदित्यृचः समो नास्ति मन्त्रो वेदचतुष्टये।
सर्वे वेदाश्च सज्ञाश्च दानानि च तपांसि च।
समानि कलया प्राहुर्मुनयो न तदित्यृयः।। *Viśvāmitra*

Mahānāmyaka Upaniṣat says गायत्री छन्दसामातेति। Gāyatrī is the mother of *Vedas*.

According to *Bṛhat Parāśara Smṛti*, in old days Brahmā weighed Gāyatrī against Vedas and found that Gāyatrī weighed heavier than all the four Vedas put together.

गायत्री चैव वेदाश्च ब्रह्मणा तोलिता पुरा।
वेदेभ्यश्च चतुर्भ्योऽपि गायत्र्यतिगरीयसी।।

Manusmṛti declares god Prajāpati Brahmā created three-stepped Gāyatrī as the essence of three *Vedas*.

त्रिभ्य एव तु वेदेभ्यः पादम्पादमद्वदुहत्।
तदित्यृचोऽस्याः सावित्र्याः परमेष्ठी प्रजापतिः।।77

Ekākṣhar which means *Oṁ* is *parabrahma, Prāṇāyam* is great *Tapa*. However, nothing is more purifying than *Gāyatrī-Mantra*.

एकाक्षरं परं ब्रह्म प्राणायामः परन्तपः।
सावित्र्यास्तु परन्नास्ति पावनं परमं स्मृतम्।।83

Gāyatrī-Mantra with Praṇava and three *Vyāhṛtis* should be uttered and meditated upon because there is no *Mantra* as efficacious in destroying sins as *Gāyatrī Mantra*.

गायत्र्यास्तु परन्नास्ति शोधनं पापकर्मणाम्।
महाव्याहृति संयुक्ता प्रणवेन च संजपेत्।। वृ. पराशर स्मृति।

There is no greater charity than giving food and water to the needy, no greater austerity than non-violence, no greater *jap,* no *yajña* greater than chanting of *Vyāhṛtis.*

Gāyatrī holds the hands of a person falling in the ocean of hell and rescues him. A dvija should therefore, perform Gāyatrī *Japa* daily with a pure heart

हस्तत्राणप्रदा देवी पततां नरकार्णवे।
तस्मात्तामभ्यसेन्नित्यं ब्राह्मणो हृदये शुचिः।। वृ पराशर स्मृति।

Of all the *Sūktas,* of *Ṛk, Yaju, Sāman* and the divine *Oṁ* (Praṇava) *japa of Gāyatrī-Mantra* is the best.

सर्वेषां जपसूक्तनामृचश्च यजुषां यथा।
सामं चैकक्षरादींन्ना गायत्री परमोजपः।। वृ. पराशर स्मृति।

Upaniṣadas are the essence of the *Vedas* and Gāyatrī along with its three *Vyāhṛtis* is the essence of *Upaniṣadas.*

सारभूतास्तु वेदानां गुहयोपनिषदो मताः।
ताभ्यः सारस्तु गायत्री तिस्रो व्याहृतयास्तथा।। योगी याज्ञवल्क्यस्मृति।

Gāyatri is the mother of *Vedas.* It is the destroyer of sins. There is no other *Mantra* more sacred and purifying than *Gāyatrī-Mantra* on this earth as well as in the heaven.

गायत्री वेदजननी गायत्री पापनाशिनी।
गायत्र्यास्तु परन्नास्ति दिवि चेह च पावनम्। योगी याज्ञवल्क्य।

There are no teerth like Gangā and no god like Keśhav. So also there has been, is and will be no *japa* as beneficial as Gāyatrī *Japa.*

नास्ति गङ्गा समं तीर्थं न देवः केशवात्परः।
गायत्र्यास्तु परं जाप्यं न भूतं न भविष्यति।। योगी याज्ञवल्क्य।

Just as fire is the greatest amongst all the vedic deities, *Brāhmaṇa* is best among men and the spring is the best of all the seasons, Gāyatrī *chanda* is the best of all the vedic metres.

यद्यथाग्निर्देवानां ब्राह्मणो मनुष्याणाम्।
वसन्तऋतूनामियं गायत्री चास्ति छन्दसाम्।। गोपथ ब्राह्मण।

In the *Mbh* (Ch. 150) in *Anuśāsana parvan,* Yudhisthira questioned Bhiṣma, "What is that subject of silent recitation by reciting which, every day one may acquire the merit of righteousness in a large measure?" What is the *Mantra* for recitation which bestows success if recited on the occasion of setting out on a journey or while entering a new building, or at the commencement of any undertaking or on the occasion of sacrifices in honour of the deities or of the *pitṛs* (manes)?

What *Mantra* it is, which propitiates all malevolent influences or leads to prosperity or growth, or protection from evil or the destruction of the foes or which at the same time is consistent with the *Vedas?*

शान्तिकं पौष्टिकं रक्षा शत्रुघ्न भयनाशनम्।
जप्य यद् ब्रह्मसमितं तद् भवान् वक्तुमर्हति।। (*Anuśāsana Parva.* 150)

After hearing these, Bhisma proclaims the advantages of uttering *Gāyatrī-Mantra.* It is illustrated as follows :

Bhiṣma said that one who recites this *Mantra*, which was declared by Vyāsa and ordained by Sāvitrī day and night, never becomes stained by sin.

व्यास प्रोक्तमियं मन्त्र शृणुष्वैकमना नृप।
सावित्र्या विहितं दिव्य सद्यः पापविमोचनम्।।

(*Mbh, Anuśāsanaparva,* 150.4)

Indeed the man that hears it becomes with long life. This *mantra* was daily recited by the foremost royal sages devoted to the practice of *Kṣhatriya* duties and steadily observant of the vow of truth.

सेवितं सततं राजन् पूरा राजर्षिसत्तमै।
क्षत्रधर्मपरैनित्यं सत्यव्रतपरायणैः।। *Ibid.*8

Those monarchs with restrained senses and tranquil soul who recited this *Mantra* everyday succeeded.

इदमाह्निकमव्यग्रं कुर्वन्ननियतैः सदा।
नृपर्भरतशार्दूल प्राप्यते श्रीरनुत्तमा।।9

By reciting this excellent *Sāvitrī-Mantra* in a vehicle or in the courts of kings one attains high success.

यानपात्रे च याने च प्रवासे राजवेश्मनि च।
परां सिद्धिमवाप्नोति सावित्री ह्युत्तमां पठन्॥68

There, where this *Mantra* is recited, the fire does not burn the wood. The children do not die, nor do snakes dwell. Indeed, at such places, there can be no fear of the king, nor of goblins and demons.

अग्निर्दहति काष्ठानि सावित्री यत्र पठ्यते।
तत्र वालो म्रियते न च तिष्ठन्ति पन्नगाः॥71

The man who recites this *Mantra* ceases to have any fear of the fire, or the water, or the wind or the beasts of prey.

This *Mantra* recited duly, contribute to the peace and well being of all four orders. Those men who recite this *Mantra* with reverence become free from every sorrow and at last attain a high end. The person who recites this *Mantra* in the midst of kine sees his kine became fruitful. Either setting out on a journey or coming back home one should recite this *Mantra* on every occasion.

गवां मध्ये तु पठतो गावोऽस्य वहुवत्सलाः।
प्रस्थाने या प्रवासे वा सर्वावस्थगतः पठेत॥72

This *Mantra* constitutes a great mystery of the sages and is the very highest of those *Mantras,* which they silently recite. Even chanting of this *Mantra* bears more results for them who practise the duty of recitation and pour libations on the sacrificial fire.

All the princes belonging to the solar race and the lunar race including family like those of the Raghus and Kurus used to perform Gāyatrī *japa* daily after proper ablution.

सोमादित्यागन्वयाः सर्वे राघवाः कुरवस्तथा।
पठन्पित शुधयो नित्यं सावित्री परमागतिं॥79

AP describes that the repetition of Gāyatrī seven times would destroy one's sin and ten times would convey the person to heaven. Repeated twenty times, the Goddess would convey him to the abode of Lord Iśvara (Śiva).

शत्पावर्त्तापापहरा दशभिः प्रापयेदिवं।
विंशावर्त्ता तु सा देवी नयते हीश्वरालयं।। *AgniP* – 215.6

One would cross the ocean of the *muṇdane* existence by repeating it hundred and eight times. The Gāyatrī excels the repetition of Rudra and *Kuṣmanḍa* (*Mantras*) in its merit.

अष्टोत्तरशतं जप्त्वा तीर्णं संसारसागरात्।
रुद्र-कुष्मान्डजपेभ्यो गायत्री तु विशिष्यते।।7

There is nothing excelling Gāyatrī for repetition. There is nothing equal to *Vyāhṛtis* for doing oblations. A quarter of the hymn or a half of it or half of the hymn or the whole hymn being repeated purifies one of the sins such as the killing of a *Brāhmin,* drinking of wine, stealing of gold and cohabiting the precepter's wife.

ब्रह्महत्या सुरापानं सुवर्णस्तोयमेव च।
गुरुदारागमश्चैव जप्येनैव पुनाति स्ता।।9

It is said that on having committed a sin one should do oblations with *Sesamum* repeating Gāyatrī. After repetition of Gāyatrī a thousand times and fasting one gets rid of his sin.

पापे कृते तिलैर्होमो गायत्रीजप ईरितः
जप्त्वा सहस्र-गायत्र्या उपवासी स पापहा।।10

The killer of a cow, the patricide, the matricide, the killer of a *Brāhmin,* the defiler of the bed of preceptor, the person who has stolen gold and the drunkard get purified after repetition of this *Mantra* lakhs of times.

गोघ्नः पितृघ्नो मातृघ्नो ब्रह्महा गुरुतल्पगः।
ब्रह्मघ्नः स्वर्णहारी च सुराषो लक्षजपतः।।11।।

One would get rid of his sin by drinking water consecrated by the repetition of Gāyatrī hundred times.

When one repeates the Tapa hundred times Gāyatrī destroys one's sin. That goddess repeated a thousand times would destroy the minor offences (उपपातक).

शतं जप्त्वा तु गायत्री पापोपशमनी स्मृता।
शहस्त्रं जाता सा देवी उपपातकनाशिनी।।13

नित्ये नैमित्तिके काम्ये तृतीये तपवर्धने।
गायत्र्यास्तु परं नास्ति इहलोके परत्र च।।

One who understands Gāyatrī (which is also known as Sāvitrī) attains heaven. Therefore one should, after taking bath, perform *Gāyatrī-japa* with a calm collected mind since it destroys all sins.

सावित्रीजपतो नित्यं स्वर्गमाप्नोति मानवः।
तस्मात् सर्वप्रयत्नेन स्नातः प्रथममानसः।।
गायत्रीं तु जपेत् भक्त्या सर्वपापप्रणशिनीम्।।

In *Mbh* (*Anuśāsana Parva*), it is stated that this *Mantra* constituted a great mystery the sages and occupied top most position among the *Mantras* they used to recite silently. Even chanting of this *Mantra* bore more results for them, than those who practised recitation and poured libations on the sacrificial fire.

It is no exaggeration to state that mastery in Gāyatrī *Sādhnā* is Kāmadhenu (wish fulfilling cow) for the twice-borns (Dvijas).

वहुना किमिहोक्तेन यथावत् साधु साधिता।
द्विजन्मनामियं विद्या सिद्धिकाम-दुधा स्मृता।।

Gāyatrī is the Sun and substance of all the *Vedas*. Gāyatrī is Brahmā. Gāyatri is almighty god.

सर्ववेदोद्घृतः सारो मन्त्रोऽयं समुदाहृतः।
ब्रह्मादिदेवा गायत्री परमात्मा समीरितः।।

Gangā is known as such because it incorporates all the *teerthas.* It is a form of Brahma Gāyatrī.

या नित्या ब्रह्मगायत्री सैव गंगा न संशयः।
सर्वतीर्थमयी गंगा तेन गंगा प्रकीर्तितः।।

With context to different *teerthas* mentioned in *Vana-Purva* (*Tīrtha Yātrā,* Ch. 85.28-31) *Pāṇḍavas* proceeded to the *teertha* known as Gāyatrī celebrated over the three worlds. By staying there for twelve nights one's soul is cleansed of all sins.

उष्यद्वादशशत्रतुपुतात्मां च भवेन्वरः।
तत व च गायत्र्या स्नानं त्रैलोक्यपूजितम्।।28 *(Vana-Purva)*

Staying there for three nights, one acquires the merit of giving away a thousand kine. A strange phenomenon is seen to occur there in respect of *Brāhmaṇas.*

त्रिरात्रमुषितस्तत्र गो सहस्त्र फलं लभेत्।
निदर्शनं च प्रत्यक्षं ब्राह्मणानां नराधिपः।।29

If a *Brāhmaṇa*, whether born of a Brāhmaṇi or any other women, recites the Gāyatrī there, the recitation becomes rhythmic and musical, while a person who is not a *Brāhmaṇa* cannot adequately hymn it all.

अब्राह्मणस्य सावित्रीं पठतु स्तु प्रणश्यति।।3

In *Svargārohaṇa Parva,* there are four *slokas* at the end of the *Mahābhārata*, which are collectively called *Bhārata-Sāvitrī.* It is stated that *Bhārata-Sāvitri* used to be recited every morning by pious *Brāhmins* as a part of what is called the *Prātaḥsmaraṇa* or morning prayer.

न जातु कामान्न भयान्न लोभाद्धर्म
त्यजेज्जीवितस्यापि हेतोः।
नित्यो धर्मः सुखदुःखे त्वनित्ये
जीवो नित्यो हेतुरस्य त्वनित्यः।। स्वर्गारोहरण-पर्व.50

इमां भरतसावित्री प्रातरुत्थयय: पठेत्
स भारतफलं प्राप्य परं ब्रह्मधिगच्छति।।51

Agni-purāṇa also states that the Gāyatrī known as the Ajapā is of the form of Brahmā, Viṣṇu and Maheśvara. There is no re-birth for one that repeats the *Ajapā-mantra.*

अजपा नाम गायत्री ब्रह्माविष्णुमहश्वरी।
अजपां जपते यस्तां पुनर्जन्म न विद्यते।। *AP* 216-26

According to the *Garuḍa-purāṇa,* if it is recited ten times, Gāyatri removes the sin of this birth, if recited hundred times, it destroys the sins of previous births, and if recited a thousand times, it removes the sins of three *Yugas.*

दर्शभिर्जन्मजनितं शतेन तु पुराकृतम्।
त्रियुगं तु सहस्त्रेण गायत्री हन्ति दृश्कृतम।। *GP* 16,10

Garuḍa-purāṇa also clarifies that the one who recites three times daily three main rites *i.e.,* there *Sandhyā* shall burn off the nine sorts of defects arising from *Rajas* (Passion), *Tamas* (Ignorance) and *Moha* (Delusion) from waking state dreaming state of dreamless step originating from speech, mind and action.

रजस्तम्भः स्वमोहोत्थान् जगुत्स्वप्नसुषुप्तिजान्।
वाङ्मन्तः कर्मजान् दपषान् नवैतान्नवाभिर्दहेत्।।6

Chapter twenty-six of *Garuḍa-purāṇa* eulogized Gāyatrī named as Gāyatrī Kalpa as follows :–

The great goddess Gāyatrī gives enjoyment and emancipation. All the great sins of the person who recites Gāyatrī are destroyed.

गायत्री परमा देवी भुक्तिमुक्तिप्रदा च ताम्।
यो जपेन्नस्य पापानि विनश्यन्ति महान्त्यपि।। *GP* 26-1

Having recited it one thousand and eight times or one hundred and eight times, at the three periods of junctions one repairs to the region of *Brahma.*

अष्टोत्तरं सहस्त्रं वा अथवाऽष्ट शतं जपेत्।
त्रिसन्ध्यं ब्रह्मलोकी स्याच्छतजप्तं जलं पिवेत्।।2

Having invoked the twelve names of the goddess such as Gāyatrī, Sāvitrī, Sarasvatī, mother of the *Vedas,* Sanskṛtī, Brahmāṇī, Kauśikī, Sādhvī, Sarvārthasadhinī and Sahāsrākṣī with her own *Mantra Bhuḥ, Bhuvah, Svaḥ* destroys all sins at the period on junction.

गायत्रैः नमः सावित्र्यै सरस्वत्यै नमो नमः।
वेदमात्र च सांस्कृत्यै ब्रह्माणी कौशिको क्रमात्।।4

The devotee offers in the fire the *Ājya* (melted ghee) and *Havisyaka* (food offering) with *Bhuḥ Bhuvaḥ Svaḥ,* to get all virtues and desired objects; he utters the *Mantra* one thousand and eight time.

After worshipping the idol made of sandalwood or gold, the devotee shall repeat the *Mantra* one hundred thousand times, taking only milk, bulbous roots and fruits, and pouring twenty thousand *ahutis* he shall obtain all desires.

यथा लक्षं तु जप्तव्यं पयोमुलफलाशनैः।
अयुतद्वयहोमेन सर्वान् कामनावाप्नुयात्।।7

Matsya-purāṇa describes that how should a king perform *Lakṣa-homa* and *Koti-homa* the dispellers of all evils. In this context, it is said that "Ten thousand sacrificial offerings should be made by reciting the sacred Gāyatrī, and six thousand by reciting the formulae *manastokenau*, thirty-thousand by reciting the prescribed formulae of *Navagrahas* and four thousand by reciting the formulae sacred to Viṣṇu."

गायत्र्यां दशासाहस्त्रं मानस्तोकेन षडगुणाः।
त्रिंशद्ग्रहादि मन्त्रैश्च चत्वारो विष्णुदैवतैः।। *MP* 136.16

According to *PadP,* he who assigns the twenty-four letters to the various parts of the body-beginning with the feet and ending with the head obtains Brahmā's world. Knowing the deity in every letter he would, obtain the same heaven as that of Viṣṇu.

चतुर्विंशतिस्थानेजपादादौमस्तकातके।
चतुर्विंशत्यिक्षरं न्यस्यब्रह्मलोकं सविंदति।। *PadP* Ch. 46.141

A *Brāhmaṇa,* remaining in water, should mutter twelve or eighteen letters beginning with Agni and ending with the sky. He is thereby feed from not only a crore of minor sins but also from great sins like the murder of a *Brāhmaṇa.*

सप्तपंचतथाब्रह्म यजुरष्ठादशाक्षरम्।
ज्वलनादिहकारातं जले स्थित्वा शतं जपेत्।।143

उपपातककोटयानु तथापि पातकैरपि।
भ्रह्महत्यादिभिः पापैर्भुक्तायातिममालयं।।144

Having muttered with head bowed and prayed especially with the utterance of '*Oṁ*' having three syllables he will be undoubtedly purified.

प्रणवेनत्रिमात्रेणसार्द्धजप्त्वा निशेषतः।
पूताः सर्वेनसंदेहोजप्त्वा मां शिरसा सह।। *Ibid. 17.278*

She has remained in the eight syllables of Gāyatrī metre and the best *Brāhmaṇas* will attain success by muttering her names with devotion. Gāyatrī herself declared that, "This world is pervaded by me and adorned with all the words I am the mother of the Vedas". A well controlled *Brāhmaṇa* just having the essence of Gāyatrī is better than one knowing the four *Vedas,* eating everything and selling all things.

गायत्री सारमात्रोऽपि वरं विप्रः सुसंयतः।
नायंत्रितचतुर्वेदी सर्वाशीसर्वविक्रयी।।281

Well-settled in *Prāṇāyama* the *Brāhmaṇas* destroy blemishes and sins as the wind destroys a cloud in the sky.

He who mutters the Gāyatrī hymn endowed with *Prāṇāyama* and having its letters united with deities assigned to the various parts of the body, becomes free from all sins committed even during crores of his existence and attaining *Brahmaṇ,* goes beyond *Prakṛti.*

गायत्रीं यो जपे नित्यं प्राणायाम-समन्विताम्।
प्रत्यक्षरामरैर्युक्तां स्वाङ्गे विन्यस्यतामपि।।155

सर्वपापाद्विनिर्मुक्तो जन्मकोटिकृतादपि।
ब्रह्मणः पदविं प्राप्य स गच्छेत्प्रकृतेः परम्।।156

That man, who knowing the sound of each syllable, assigns it to the various parts of the body reaches *Brahmaṇahood.* He who knows this Gāyatrī endowed with all the mystical letters forming the essential part of the (Gāyatrī) hymn, knows the four *Vedas* and has the knowledge of mediation and of the three muttered prayers.

इमां यो वेति गायत्रीं सवेवीजसमन्विताम्।
सर्वेतिचतुरवेदान् योग-ज्ञानं जपत्रयम्।।190

He who does not hear Gāyatrī is beyond a *Śūdra.* To such an impure *Brāhmaṇa* the presents made at the time of *Śrāddha* should not be given.

य एनां नैव जानाति स शूद्रात्परतः स्मृतः।
तस्यापूतस्य विप्रस्य न देयं पितृपार्वणम्।।191

His bath is useless, every thing about him would be fruitless. Like a pure flower at an impure place all his learning, wealth, birth are fruitless.

Gāyatrī is said to be superior to the *Vedas* and the giver of final bliss. If Gāyatrī hymn is recited ten times, it destroys the sin committed from birth, if it is recited a hundred times it destroys the sin of the previous birth and if it is recited a thousand times it destroys the sin committed in every birth in the three *Yugas*.

चतुर्वेदश्च गायात्री पुरावैतुलितमया।
चतुर्वेदात्परागुर्वी गायत्री मोक्षदा स्मृता।।193

He who mutters the Gāyatrī in the evening and in the morning by counting the beads of rosary, undoubtedly gets the fruit of recitation.

गायत्रीमक्षरमालायां सायं प्रात यो जपेत्।
चतुर्णामपि वेदानां फलं प्राप्नोत्यसंशयम्।।195

He who everyday mutters the Gāyatrī hymn thrice a day for one year the sin committed during a crore of his existence.

गायत्र्युच्चारमात्रेण पापकूटात्पुनीति च।।197

Brāhmaṇa who recites or reads it to others or explains it to people, is not reborn and obtains inexhaustible heaven.

यः पठेत्पाठयेद्वापि उपद्रेष्टाजनस्य च।
न तस्य पुनरावृतिः स्वर्गमक्षयमश्नुते।।207

In this world he would also obtain wealth, grains, royal enjoyments, and sound health and also a good son and auspicious fame and in heaven he enjoys like a god.

धनधान्यं लभेदराज्य भोगाननरोगताम्।
सत्सुतं च शुभां कीर्तिं देवेद्रमते दिवि।।208

The twelfth chapter of the *DB* is entirely devoted to the glorification of the Gāyatrī.

Gāyatrī is considered as the mother of the *Vedas* and she was first worshipped by Brahmā. Then the *Vedas* worshipped her. Subsequently the learned men worshipped next the king Aśvapati worshipped her in India and then the four *Varnas* worshipped her.

ब्रह्मणा वेदजननी प्रथमे पूजिता मुने।
द्वितीये च वेदगणैस्तत्पश्चात् विदुषां गणैः।। *DB* 34.3

One hundred Gāyatrī *Japa* destroy one month's sins. One thousand *Japa* destroy one year's sins and one lakh destroys the sins of the present birth and ten lakh destroy the sins of all births.

सकृज्जपश्च गायत्र्याः पापं दिनभवं हरेत्।
दशवारं जपेनैव नश्येत्पापं दिवानिशिम्॥14

शतवारं जपेनैव पापं मासार्जितं हरेत्।
सहस्त्रधा जपश्चैव कल्मषं मत्सरार्जितम्॥15

लक्षो जन्मकृतं पापं दशलक्षोऽन्यजन्मजम।
सर्वमन्शकृतं पाप शतलक्षाद्विनश्यति॥16

If one is impure and devoid of *Sandhyā,* one has no right to do any action, and even if one performs an action, one does not get any fruit thereby.

सन्ध्याहींन्रोऽशुचिर्नित्यमर्हः सर्वकर्मसु।
यदह्ला कुरुते कर्म न तस्य फलभाग्भवेत्॥24

He who does not do the morning *Sandhyā* and the evening *Sandhyā,* is driven away from all the *Brāhmiṇic Karmas* and he becomes like *Śūdras.*

नोपतिष्ठति यः पूर्वा नोपास्ते यस्तु पश्चिमास।
न शूद्रवद्वहिष्कार्यः सर्वस्माद् द्विजकर्मणः॥26

He who does *Sandhyā* three times through out his life, becomes like the Sun by his lustre and brilliance of *tapas.*

यावज्जीवनपर्यन्तं त्रिसन्ध्यां यः परोति च।
स च सूर्यसमो विप्रस्तेजस तपसा सदा॥27

The earth is always purified by the dust of feet. The *Brāhmaṇa* who does his *Sandhyā Bandanā* and remains pure, becomes energetic and liberated while living.

तत्पादपद्मसजसा सद्यः पूता वसुन्धरा।
जीवन्मुक्त स तेजस्वी सन्ध्यापूतो ही द्विजः॥28

The *Brāhmaṇa* who becomes void of *Sandhyā* three times a day, the devas do not accept his worship nor do the *pitṛs* accept his *pinḍs.*

न गृहणन्ति सूरा पूजां पितरः पिण्डतर्पणम्।
स्वेच्छया च द्विजातेश्च त्रि सन्ध्यारहितस्य च॥30

He who has no *Bhakti* towards the *mulaprakṛti,* who does not worship the specific seed *Mantra* of *Māyā* and who does not hold festivities in honour of *mulaprakṛti,* know him verily to be an *Ajagara* snake without poison.

मूलप्रकृत्यभक्तो यस्तमन्त्रस्याप्यवर्चकः
तदुत्सवविहींत्रस्य विषहींत्रो यथोरगः।।31

Devoid of the *Viṣṇu-Mantra,* of the three *Sandhyās* and of the fasting on the *Ekadasi Tithi* (the eleventh day of the fortnight), the *Brāhmin* becomes a snake devoid of poison.[23]

विष्णुमन्त्रविहींत्रश्च त्रि सन्ध्या रहितो द्विजः
एकाएशीविहिनश्च विषहीनो यथोरगः।।32

One can rather avoid worshipping Śiva or Viṣṇu because that is not only done as obligatory, but the *Sandhyopasanā* ought to be done daily. The Gāyatrī of the great *devi* is the essence of all the *Mantras* in the *Vedas.* In the *Veda Śāstras,* the worship of Gāyatrī is most definitely pronounced. Brahmā and the other *devas* meditate in the *Sandhyā* times on *devī* Gāyatrī and make a *japam* of her. For this reason the Gāyatrī has been mentioned as the object of worship by the Vedas. The *Brāhmaṇas* are called *Śāktas* in as much as they worship the primal *Śakti* Gāyatrī, the mother of the *Vedas.* They are not *Śaivas* nor *Vaiṣṇavas.*[24]

The *Japa* of the *Gāyatrī-Mantra* brings unmatched power. This is illustrated by means of the following legend (*BhaP* 10.13.37).

There was a demon named Aruṇa. He murmured the *Gāyatrī-Mantra* for one thousand years. As a result of this, through blessings of Gāyatrī, he acquired great strength. Fire issued forth from his body and burnt the entire earth. Gods and men were frightened and ran to Brāhmā. Brahmā went to the demon. The demon asked Brahmā for a boon that he would not be killed in battle, by man or a woman, by any weapon or by gods to battle. The gods, being frightened went to Brahmā, but Brahmā could not help. Then they went to Śankara. In the meantimes, the *daitya* army had already reached *Amarāvati.* Sarasvatī finally told the gods that, if the demon gave up Gāyatrī he would be killed. Bṛhaspati went to the demon and deluded him. The demon gave up Gāyatrī. The moment he gave up Gāyatrī, he became lustreless and powerless. The goddess (*Devī*) took the form of a bee (therefore she is known as *Bhramari Devī*) and with an army of bees, attacked the demon and finally killed him.

BrVaiP state that, "One *japa* of Gāyatrī, destroys the days sins. Ten *japas* of Gāyatrī destroy day and night's sins.".

सकृज्जपश्च गायत्र्याः पापं दिनभवं हरेत्।
दशवारं जपेनैव नश्येत्पापं दिवानिशम्।। Ch. 23.14

If one be impure and devoid of *Sandhyā,* one has no right to do any action and even if one performs an actions, one does not get any fruit.

सन्ध्याहींन्नोऽशुचिर्नित्यमर्हः सर्वकर्मसु।
यदह्ना कुरुते कर्म न तस्य फलभाग्वेत्।।25

He who does not do the morning *Sandhyā,* and the evening *Sandhyā,* is driven away from all the *Brāhmiṇic Karma* and he becomes like *Śūdras.*

स शूद्रवद्वहिष्कार्यः सर्वस्माद् द्विजकर्मण।
यावज्जीवनपर्यन्तं त्रिसन्ध्यां यः करोति च।।26

He who does *Sandhyā* three times throughtout his life, becomes like the sun by his luster and brilliance of *tapas.*

स च सूर्यसमो विप्रस्तेजसा तपसा सदा।।27

The *Brāhmaṇa* who does his *Sandhyā Bandanam* and remains pure, becomes energetic and liberated while living. By his contact all the *teerthas* become purified. All the sins vanish away from him as snakes fly away the sight of Garuda.

तीर्थानि च पवित्राणि तस्य संस्पर्शमात्रः।
ततः पापानिप्यान्त्येव वैनतेयादि केरगाः।।29

An Assimilation

As mentioned earlier, *japa* or chanting of divine hymns has been regarded as an important spiritual practice in almost all the religions of the world. In the Indian scriptures of yore the *japa-Sadhanā* of *Mantras* has been designated as a *Yajña.* God Kṛṣṇa has therefore indicated it a paramount *Yajña* by stating in the holy Gitā *Yajñānāṁ Japa Yajñosmi*.

References

1. Swāmi Mukhyānanda, *Oṁ Gāyatrī and Sandhyā*, p. 40.
2. *Sukla –YV* (XXVI-2).
3. *DB Purāṇa* – XVI (1-8).
4. Mukhyānanda Swāmi, *Om Gāyatrī and Sandhyā*, p. 41-42.
5. *AP* 199-2.
6. *AP.* 280.5. त्रिमथुराप्लुतम्।
7. *SK.P. A.R.* 200-3.
8. *TS*, 5.7.1.1
9. *Kālikā P*, 23.18-19
10. *DB* 12.8.75
11. *GP* 1.35.4
12. *Devi Māhātmya* P. 146
13. *DB* 12.8.66
14. *Liṅga P* 13.5-7
15. *Sk. P. A.R.* 200.7-8
16. *Sk. P.* 200-3
17. *Iḍāpingalacārinī, Yakāradihakārāntā, Guhyamaṇḍalāvartinī.*
18. *Khadgakhetakarā, Dhakkāhastā, Tankabāṇasamāyuktā.*
19. *Tumburusūtā, Trisankuparitā, Naradāpriyakārīnī, Manustutā.*
20. रेवती, रेणुका, रम्भा, रुक्मिणी, पार्वती, वृन्दा।
21. Lalye P.G., *Studies in DB Purana*, p. 207-208.
22. 165 *Manusmṛti* 2.77.
23. *Brahma Vai. Purāṇa* 23.32
24. *DB* XII. 8-10.

8

Tāntric Mode of Worship of Gāyatrī

The *Tantra* school originated somewhere in the Gupta period and later flourished in almost all parts of India, particularly in eastern India. Though the word *Tantra* now represents a particular type of literature, its real meaning is quite different.

The word is derived from the root '*tan*' which means 'to spread' with the addition of the suffix *tran*[1]. The word '*Tantra*' is also used in the sense of 'a loom' derived from the same root. In the *Aśvālāyana Śrauta Śūtra*[2], it is used in the sense of 'procedure' containing many parts. Kautilya used the word '*Tantra-yuktih*' and *Suśruta*[3] also has used it in the sense of 'treaties'. *Sabara,* a commentator of the *Purva mimānsā Sūtras,* has defined *Tantra* as 'one which performed once, helps many[4]. Śankara has used the word in the sense of 'system'[5].

The *Mahābhārata* has also employed the word in the sense of 'system'[6].

The '*Īśana Sva gurudeva padhati',* gives the derivation of the word[7]. The Nepal manuscript of '*pingalimata*' gives the extended meaning[8]. The *Śabdakalpadruma* quotes *Varahī tantra,* where *tantra* is defined as one which gives account, among other things, of places of pilgrimage, origin of gods, royal duties and mythological stories. There are four sections in the particular work–*Vidyā, Kriyā, Yoga,* and *Carya* as described by *Bāṇa,* the author of Kādambari refer ring to rites similar to those of *tantras.*

Though the antiquity of *tantricism* cannot be traced out definitely, some early traits can be found in the literature and inscriptions of the Gupta period. Dr. J.N. Banerjee has pointed out that the word '*Tantra*' occurs in an inscription of the first quater of the fifth century A.D. found in the village of Gangadhar (Jhalwar, Madhya Pradesh).

In the lines 22-23 of this, it is described about the creation of the very terrible abode of the divine mother full of *Dakīnīs*... Who stir up the very oceans with the mighty winds rising from the *Tantric* rites of their religion[9].

It is clear that in early literature, the word does not mean any cult of *Śakti* or *Tantra.* From the days of the *Śabara* onwards, the word *Tantra* lost its wider meaning and came to be applied to a particular system, which dealt with the worship of the female principle – '*Śakti*'.

Some western scholars try to assign an extra-Indian origin to the *Tantras.* The deities eulogized in the *Tantras,* are not unknown to Indian literature, as shown before. The concept of '*Śakti*' can be traced to the *vedic* literature. The *ṚV.* frequently mentions magicians, who were mostly non-*vedic* and are described as *aveda* (godless). and *anṛtadevā* (who worship false gods). The *ṚV* people were afraid of black magic[10] and *raksas* (evil spirit). In the tenth *manḍala* of *ṚV,* we get the famous *Devī Sūkta,* containing hymns to Durgā, another name of *Śakti,* the main deity of the *Tantras* and of *tantric* faith.

As the illustrious commentator of Manu, Kalluka Bhatta states, that the *tāntrika* cult is part and parcel of *Śruti-'Vaidika Tantrika chaib dvibidhā Śrutiḥ Kirtita".* (There are two classes of *Sruti-Vedic* and *Tantric*[11]).

Kane has cited a number of passages from *AV, Sukranītīsāra* and *Vājasaneyī Saṁhitā,* to which *tāntric* conceptions can be traced[12].

Again in the *AV* we meet with many rites and rituals which were quite similar to what we find in the *Tantras.* These go to support the view that the underlying principles of the *Tantras* are enshrined in the *Vedas* as well. The *upaniṣads* contain seeds of the *tāntric* form of religion. For instance, the *Praśnopaniṣat* refers to *Ṣatcakra Veda,* one of the most important subjects of discussion in the *Tantras.*

In the *BṛhU* there occur some *Mantras* for chastising enemies carrying off wives, which in many respects are a kin to *tantric mantras.* Kātyāyana, the seer to the *AV* is mentioned to have worshipped the primordial energy, more popularly known as *Śakti* in the name of Mahiṣāmardinī. The great Saint Dattātreya, Viśvāmitra, Vaśiṣṭha, Śri Kṛṣṇa, Nārada, Gautama, Kapila were all conversant with the *tāntric* principle[13].

In *Śrimad-Bhāgavata,* we find the *Braja Gopis* worshipping Yogamāyā for obtaining Śri Krṣṇa as their Lord and there are ample references to *tāntric* gods and goddesses in it. That the *tāntric* system was also in vague in the days of the *Purāṇas* is also very much clear in the *Mārkendaya-Purāṇa,* the *Liṅga-Purāṇa* etc. The initiation ritual is found in a number of *Purāṇas* like *GP* 1.9, *PadP* 31.8.75, *AP* 27, 81-89 chapt. In the *VarāhaP* (181-186) the sectarian *Mantra* is often used together with the *Purāṇic* and *Vedic Mantras.* In the *GP,* this ritual is full of *Nyāsas* and the *Tāntric-mantras*[14]. A mystic *tāntric* performance of Gāyatrī *Uddhāra* is also described in the *Kurma Purāṇa*[15].

The origin of *tantras* and gradual development are divided into three broad classes *i.e. Āgama, Saṁhitā,* and *tantra.* Each of these classes belongs to a particular sect. The *tāntric* works of the *Śaivas* are called *Āgama,* those of the *Vaiṣṇavas* and *Śākas* are respectively designated as *Saṁhitā* and *Tantra.* These works are also divided into *Hindu (Brāhmaṇical) Tantras* and *Baudha Tantras.* In accordance with the predominace of the deities in them, they are classed as Saka, Śaiva, Saura, Ganapatya and Vaiṣṇava[16].

The origin of *Tantras* is so shrouded in obscurity that it is difficult to ascertain exactly when they came into being. Some modern indologists think that the original *Tantras* were probably composed in or after the fifth or sixth century A.D.

Nothing definitely is known about the provenance of the *Tantras.* It is however, supposed that the works of the *Āgama* and *Tantra* classes originated in Kashmir and Bengal respectively. The works of the *Saṁhitā* classes are believed to have originated partly in *Bangal* and partly in the *Deccan.* Some scholars think that the fundamental doctrines of the *Tantra* were borrowed by India from China.

There are numerous works on *Tantra.* The traditional number of *Tantras* is sixty four. The names of *Tantras* differ in different sources. Besides original treaties, there is a number of digests and commentraries.

A few of the chief works of the *Saṁhitā* class are *Ahirbudhnya Saṁhitā, Iśvara-Saṁhitā, Jñānamṛtasura Saṁhitā and Parmā*

Samhitā. Similarly, some important works of the *Tantra* class are *Mahānirvāṇa, Tantra-raja, Śaradā-tilaka, Kulārṇava, Prapañcasāra* and *Tantrasāra* etc.

Arthur Avalon, one of the greatest oriential scholars on the *Tantric* cult, has drawn the conclusion that there is no justification in favour of the argument that the *Tantras* are the off-shoots of the *Buddhist Mahāyāna* cult. This is fully corroborated by Swami Śankarānanda, that the *tāntric* worshippers formed a big part of the *Āryan* society and acted as the standard bearers of the *Āryan* culture. In fact the ritual side of the *Vedas* and the practical *kriyās* for the attainment of spiritual unfoldment constitute what we now designate as the *Tantras*[17].

However, from the above discussion it is clear that the *Tāntric* mode of worship incorporate *Yoga* as well as *Tantra.* Unlike the other *Puraṇas* mentioned above, the *DB Purāṇa* describes the *tantric* performance of *devī* Gāyatrī. It is an extremely secret method. The whole of XI chapter of the *DB Purāṇa* is related to the *Gāyatrī-tantra.* There is symbolic description about achieving money, progeny, women, health position, victory over enemies and sway over others by enchanting the *Mantras* through *Tāntric Sādhanā.*

Achievement Obtains by Gāyatrī-Sādhana

The sage Viśvāmitra says to Nārada that standing on one leg, with both hands raised and controlling Vāyu the man who repeats daily one hundred Gāyatrīs for one month gets all his desires fulfilled.

एकपादो जपेदुर्ध्वं वाहुः स्थित्वा निराश्रयः
मासं श्मत्रयं विप्रः सर्वान्कामानवाप्नुयात्। (*DB* XI.76)

Submerged under water, if one repeats Gāyatrī as many as times as mentioned above, he gets everything. If one year with hands uplifted and without holding anything, anyone stands on one leg, controls one's breath and repeats *Gāyatrī-Mantra* three hundred times or thousand times, eating *Haviṣyānnam* only in the night time, he becomes a seer. This thing repeated two years gives infallible speech, three years gives knowledge of the present, past and future, four years will enable to see face to face the solar god, five years will give the eight *siddhis,* lightness etc. Six years will enable one to assume forms as he desires. Seven years gives immortality, nine years gives *Manuhood,* ten years gives *Indrahood,* eleven years gives *Brahmahood,* and twelve years gives the state of *Purāṇa Brahma*[18].

By these practices of *Tapasyā* the seers have been able to conquer three *lokas* (regions).

For Attainment of Health, Wealth, Happiness and Peace

As the *Śabda-Kalpadruma Koṣa* remarks that *Tantra* is a science that deals with the creation and dissolution of the Universe and performance of six activities, *i.e. māraṇa, uccātana, vaśikaraṇa, stambhana, śānti* and *videṣaṇa.*

So emphasing this view let us discuss the above points. While doing this *Śānti Karma,* the *Brāhmaṇas* are to perform the *Homas* with fuel soaked in milk (*Payaḥ*). If the fuel of the *Śami* tree is to be offered in *Homa* ceremony, then diseases caused by planets are cured.

आद्रार्भि क्षीरवृक्षस्य समिभिदर्जुहुयाद द्विजः
जुहुयाच्छकलैर्वाऽपि भूतरोगादिशान्तये।।11.4.

If the *homa* is performed with wet *Aśvattha* or *Udumbara* or other *Ksīra* trees, the diseases caused by demons and hob-goblins are cured. If one offers *Tarpaṇam* with one palmful of water, repeating the *Mantra "Sūryam Tarpaṇami namaḥ",* the pending evils and troubles are also averted. The repetition of the *Gāyatrī-Mantra* with knees immersed in water averts all evils.

The repetition of Gāyatrī with body immersed in water upto the throat, averts the danger to life, and the same with the whole body immersed grants all success. This is the best of all the *Śānti Karmas,* the act that brings health, wealth, happiness and peace. While performing *Homa,* light in the fuel of vessel made of gold, silver, copper, or wood of *Ksira* trees, or in the vessels made of earth, without any knot or crack, while utterring the *Gāyatri-Mantra* can offer one thousand *homas.* Sprinkle thousand times with water at every offering, touching the *pancagavya* with *Kuśa* grass, and then offer the sacrifice there, where calamities or nuisances are seen and meditate on the highest *Devatā.* Thus all the magic spells used by other persons for a malevolent purpose will be rendered any nugatory. By controlling *Deva yoni or Bhuta yoni* or *Piśāca yoni* who causes troubles, one can get them out of the house, villages, city, way and even his kingdom.

Now, there is the description of preparing is drawn the sacrificial altar. This altar is made up with sand and a square is placed on it. A *Śula* in its centre and it is plastered with *Aṣṭagandh.* For the sake of averting all the evils, repeat *Gāyatrī-Mantra* thousand times and impregnate it with the *Mantra.* Place on the level ground or *Sthāṇḍila ajar* or *Navaphala,* a fruit made of gold or silver or copper or a newly made mud *jar* and enclose it with thread. Then have the sacred water brought from the several *Tīrthas* by the *Brāhmins* and fill the *jar* while repeating the *Gāyatrī-Mantra.* The *jar* should be filled with *twigs of Cardamom* tree, *Sandal* tree, *Karpura* tree, Jati, Aparajtā, Pātala, Mallikā flowers, *Bel* leaves, Rice, Barley, Til, Mustard, Aśvattha and Udumbara trees. Doing all these, prepare one *Kuśa Kurcha* made up of twenty-seven *Kuśa* grass in the form of a braid of hair and tied in a knot and place it there. After taking bath repeat the *Gāyatrī-Mantra* one thousand times with full concentration. Then, the *Veda* knowing *Brāhmaṇas,* would recite the *Saura Mantra* and sprinkle the man attacked by the demon with water and also make him drink the water saturated with the *Mantra* and also bathe him with that. Then the person will be disposed of the devil and be happy.

Even when the man, (possessed by a devil) is going to die, he gets his life again if he drinks this water saturated with this *Mantra* and have his bathe with that. So a wise king must do this, with the desire to have a long life and after he is sprinkled with this *Mantra* changed water he has to give one hundred cows to the *Brāhmins* as the *Dakṣinā*[19].

Wealth is attained if the *Homa* is performed with red lotus or fresh *Jati* flower or with the *Sali* rice or with the fuel of *Bel* trees, leaves, flowers, fruits or roots.

If for one week the oblations are offered with fuel of *Bel* tree mixed with *Pāyasa* or with ghee one hundred times, then Lakṣmī *devī* will be surely attained. If for one week the oblations are offered with *lāja* (fried rice) mixed with curd milk and ghee, the daughter will be attained.

शतं शतं च सप्ताहं हुत्वा श्रियमवाप्नुयात्
लाजैस्त्रिमधुरोपेते होमै कन्यावाप्नुयात्।।42

If the oblations of *Pāyasānna* be offered to the solar deity and the *Prasādam* (remnant) he has given to one's wife under menstruation to eat, then excellent sons will be obtained. If for one week, the *homa* is performed with red lotus, gold is obtained. If the *homa* is performed with *Anna, Anna* is obtained[20].

Attainment of Longevity

If the *homa* be performed with the fuel of wet and pointed *Kṣīra* trees, longevity is attained. If *homa* be performed with the fuel of *Palāśa* tree, pointed and wet and mixed with curd, milk, and ghee for one hundred times consecutively, longevity and gold are attained. If for one week the *homa* ceremony be performed with the fuel of *Śamī* tree mixed with food, milk or ghee one hundred times of each or if for one week the *homa* be performed with the fuel of *Nyogradha* tree and afterwards one hundred *homas* be made with *pāyasanna,* the fear of unnatural death is removed[21].

Eradication of Enemies and Natural Calamities

If there be a earth quake or if there be seen flashes of lightnings, *homa* is to be performed with the fuel of *Vana Vetasa* and the whole kingdom will be happy. If one surcharges any piece of iron with *Gāyatrī-Mantra* repeated hundred times and if one throws it in any direction then no fear will arise from that quater out of fire, air or any other enemy. If one be imprisoned and if he repeats the Gāyatrī mentally, he will be liberated from the prison. If one touches the man possessed by a devil, disease and sorrow with the *Kuśa* grass and repeat the *Gāyatrī-Mantra,* and thus charge him with divine electricity, that man will be liberated from the fear.

For Cure of Diseases

For the cure of all diseases, one has to perform the *Mṛutyunjaya homa.* One will have to do *homa* with the *Gulancha creeper,* soaked in milk and deducting the knots thereof. For purification of fever, mango leaves soaked with milk ought to be used in the *homa* ceremony. The wasting diseases are cured if *homa* be performed with the leaves of the *Vaca* soaked in milk *phthisis* or consumption is cured. If the *homa* be performed with curd, milk and ghee, and this offerings being given to the solar deity and if *Pāyasānnam* be given to him his diseases will be cured. Leprosy disease is cured if one made *homa* with the flowers of the *Sāmkhya* tree. If the *homa* be done with the seed of *Apāmārga,* the *mirgis* or the hystric and epileptic fits are cured. So if *homa* he performed with the fuel of *Kṣ īra* trees, *lunacy* is cured; if with the fuel of *Udumbara, meha* is cured, if with sugarcane juice *gonorrhea* is cured, if with curd, milk and ghee or with the ghee of *Kapilā* cow, the *homa* be performed, the *masunika* disease or small pox will be cured and if *homa* be performed with the fuels of Udumbara, Vata and Aśvattha, then the diseases of cows, elephants and horses are cured. If the trouble caused by many ants and ant-hill *(Madhu Valmika)* then perform the *homa* ceremony with the fuel of *Śamī* tree one hundred times and with the food prepared from ghee one hundred times and offer sacrifices with the rest of the food, then the above troubles will cease[22].

Purification and Expiation of Sins

For the expiation of the sin incurred in stealing gold, one is to repeat three thousand Gāyatrīs daily for one month. By this act also the sins incurred by drinking or going to one's *Guru's* wife are destroyed. The sin incurred by killing a *Brāhman* (*Brahmahatyā*) is destroyed if one erects a shed in a forest and living there, repeats three thousand Gāyatrīs daily for one month. Those *Brāhmaṇas* that have committed the great sins *(Mahāpātakas),* will become free, if they repeat one thousand Gāyatrīs daily for one month. By controlling speech and by practicing *Prāṇāyāma,* if one repeats three thousand Gāyatrīs daily for one month, one will be free from the *Mahāpātakas.* If one practices one thousand *Prāṇāyāmas* repeating the Gāyatrī, one also becomes free of *Brahmahatyā.* If one practices this *Prāṇāyāma* one thousand times for one month, the lord of the earth becomes freed of all sins. If any *Brāhmaṇa* incurs the sin of killing a cow, for twelve days he is to repeat three thousand Gāyatrīs daily for expiation. All sins are destroyed by performing one hundred *Prāṇāyāms* with Gāyatrī[23].

Besides these attainments and eradications, by repeating Gāyatrī twenty-four thousand times is equal to performing the *Krichara Vrata* and to repeat sixty four thousand Gāyatrīs duly is equal to performing the *Candrāyaṇa, Homa* with milk or drinking *Brahmarasa,* charged with the *Mantra* increases the intellect and the *homa* with ghee gives *Buddhi* (Intelligence).

An Assimilation

The ritual functions of the *Vedas* and the practice of psycho-physical action for the attainment of spiritual enfoldment constitute the *Tantra.* This is no doubt, of Indian origin and added the Aryan culture. The *Tantric* performance of *Devī* Gāyatrī is traced, though in different frames and forms in the *Vedas,* the *Brāhmaṇas,* the *Upaniṣads* and the *Purāṇas* etc. The *DBP* gives an special approach on the *Tantric* performance of *Devī* Gāyatrī. The repetition of recitation of Gāyatrī is emphasized therein. This is as good as a *Tapasyā.* For attainment of health, wealth, peace and pleasure one should practice it. According to *DBP,* one can easily attain long life by the penance of Gāyatrī performance. Eradication of inner and outer enemies, natural calamities, severe diseases and sins is possible through this performance. It may be concluded that *Gāyatrī-Mantra* leads not only to self-realization but also to material achievement.

References

1. *Kasika quotes the Sutra* तित्रुत्रतपसि सुरूकसेषु च (VIII.2.9). By the Aunadika rule सर्वषातुर्म्यष्ट्रण् Vacaspati, Anandagiri and Govindananda derive the word from the root तात्रि or तत्रि in the sense or origination of knowledge.
2. *Asvalāyana Śrauta Sūtra* 1.15.1.
3. सुश्रुतसंहिता, (I. 3.13).
4. यत्सकृत्कृतं वहुनामुपकरोति, तत् तन्त्रमिन्युच्चते Sabara on *Purvamimansasutra* (11.4.1).
5. स्मृति श्च तन्त्राख्या परमर्षिप्रणीता, *Śankara* or *Brahma Sūtra.*
6. न्यायतन्त्रायेन कानि तैस्तैरुक्तानि वादिभिः *Mbh* XIII. 76.63.
7. *Isana sva gurudev paddhati.* Part III P. 21.
8. तनुते त्रायते नित्यं तन्त्मित्थं विदुर्वुधाः।
9. J.N. Banerjea - *Development of Hindu Iconography* p. 194.
10. Bagchi, *Studies in Tantra* PP. 45-55.
11. P.G. Lalye, *Studies in Devi Bhāgavat* P. 111.
12. *Hindu Dharma Śāstra,* Vol. III, pp. 1037-38 (*a*).
13. Bose, D.N., *Tantras their Philosophy and occult secrets.* p. 67.
14. *GP.* - 1.22.1

15. *Kurma Purāṇa* - 11, 14. 57-61.
16. Banerji, Suresh Chandra, *A companion to Sanskrit Literature.* p. 56.
17. Bose, D.N., *Tantras their Philosophy and Occult Secrets.*
18. *D.B. Purāṇa*, Ch. XI (67-77).
19. *DIS Purāṇa* XI 2-20.
20. *DB Purāṇa* XI (38-45).
21. *Ibid.,* 49-52.
22. *DB Purāṇa* XI (21-44).
23. *DB Purana,* XI (78-90).

9

Conclusion

According to the *Vedic* and *Purāṇic* literature Gāyatrī is the name of a *Vedic* metre. The *Vedas* themselves along with the *Purāṇas* have personified Gāyatrī as a female divinity. In *Vedic* literature, Gāyatrī is the most sacred verse of the *ṚV* and addressed to the Sun God as Savitṛ, the generator, but the *Purāṇas* personified Gāyatrī as a goddess, she is the wife of Brahmā, mother of the four *Vedas* and also of the twice born.

In *Vedic* times, the worship of image or icons seems to be absent. In the later times Savitṛ was represented as a goddess, sometimes with one face, sometimes with five faces sitting on a lotus or standing on the waters, the standard symbol of divine energies. One pair of her hands has the conch (*śankha*) and the wheel (*cakra*) in the other symbolizing the creation. The second pair carries the mace and the axe representing her forces to battle the demons. In another pair, she carries the bowl of *madhu,* the wine of delight, *ānanda,* the secret of creation. Another pair displays her benediction to all her devotees. The remaining pair carries two lotuses.

This *Mantra* is used for *Japa* in the *Sāndhya* worship of all Hindus where the invocation is meant for three goddesses, Gāyatrī, Sāvitrī and Sarasvatī. In *Vedic* literature, the *Mantra* gets its name from that of the metre, but in *Purāṇas,* Gāyatrī and Sāvitrī are different from each other. There is no symbol *AUM* or *OM* in the beginning of the *Mantra* in any of the *Vedic Saṁhitās* before. The tradition of beginning the recitation with the sacred syllable *Om* developed later.

Om is regarded as the ultimate word in the *Hindu* tradition. Surprisingly *Om* is not in the *RV* text. However *RV* contains its cognates like *Omasaḥ ṚV* (1.3.7) *Omānam Samyor* (1.34.6) etc. *Om* appears explicitly in *Śukla YV Mādhyandina Vāja-saneyī Samhitā* (40.15) ओउम् क्रतो स्मर, क्लिवे स्मर, कृतँ स्मर। The last part of the *Mantra* (40.17) of the same book states ओउम् स्वं ब्रह्म *(Om* is the highest Reality*)*. Several centuries later, Manu in the *Dharmaśāstra* (2.74) states that '*Om* is to be added at the beginning of each *Mantra* as well as at the end'[1].

It is pointed out the *Gāyatrī-Mantra* though originally addressed to the god Savitṛ became an independent one in the days of *Brāhmaṇas.*

The *Brāhmaṇas* are famous for establishing mystic correspondence between the physical things and metaphysical conceptions and thus they identified Gāyatrī with *Prāṇa,* Agni, *Brahman, Brahmavarcas, Śyena, Dyāu* etc.

The three lines beginning with *Tat Savitur,* is addressed to the god Savitṛ, the spiritual sun god. Here Savitṛ is not the physical Sun we seen in the sky, but the Supreme effulgence in the highest firmament above, beyond the lower triple creation. According to the traditional interpretation of Sāyaṇa, Gīta and some other *Purāṇas* the word *Tat* which is in opposition to the Bhargah indicates the highest reality.

Colebrooke's translation is 'Gāyatrī is Earth, Sky, Heaven. Let us meditate on the most excellent light and power of that generous, sportive and resplendent sun, it may guide our intellects'. Wilson's version in his translation of the *RV* says 'we meditate on that desirable light of the divine Savitri who influences our pious rites'[2].

Observations

Keeping with the practice of the *Purāṇas, DB Purāṇa* has given one thousand epithets of Gāyatrī. The *PadP* has also given one hundred eight epithets of Gāyatrī. The description in *DB Purāṇa* is an exceptional one, because it is arranged in alphabetical order. On close analysis, we find that the list of thousand names presents a varied picture of the myriad coloured personality of the *devī* to the devotee. All the epithets are of the supreme power who is identified with Gāyatrī.

There is a highly ornate description of *Devī* in each and every *Purāṇa.* Mainly *Garuḍa, Padma* and *SkPs* give more details about the appearance of *devī.* She is superior to Brahmā, Viṣṇu and Śiva. So she herself is known as *Trayī*[3]. In the *purāṇic* literature describing the form of *devī* Gāyatrī there are a series of epithets. They are extended according to the contemporary ideas of glory or decoration. So in the *Purāṇas,* particularly in *DB Purāṇa,* all the epithets of Gāyatrī are much comprehensive in connotation.

Sampurnananda has pointed that, "The *Devatās* are not the separate entities, as the ocean of power is indivisible"[4]. The Gāyatrī in the *Purāṇas* has been glorified by legendary richness. It is said that the king Asvapati of Madra was blessed with a daughter. Nature of Gāyatrī was explained to the King by the sage Parāśara. He described the method of Gāyatrī *japa* before the king. A verse from *Manusmṛti* was quoted by him during his description[5].

The worship of Viṣṇu or Śiva are not mentioned anywhere in *Vedas.* But the priest worshipped Bhagavatī Gāyatrī daily during the three *Sandhyā* times[6].

Importance of *Gāyatrī-Mantra* in Later Period

Why is it that so much important is attached to this particular *Mantra* in the *Vedic* literature? This question arises in our mind repeatedly. Kāṇe says 'the fame was due to its grand simplicity and to its adaptability to an idealistic conception of the world as emanating from all pervading intelligence'[7].

According to P.G. Lalye, "Till the *Vedic* age, the knowledge imparted to the student was purely literal. Much exercise of the intellect was necessary to make it sharp enough to receive and retain the instruction of the preceptor. The human tendency (especially that of the *Vedic* people) is to approach reverentially (for knowledge) to a person who has abundant quantity of it. As brilliance was the outstanding possession of the sun, it was felt that he alone should be approached to keep one's own intellect brilliant[8].

The *AV* gave currency to the belief that Gāyatrī is the mother of all the *Vedas,* and is capable of conferring long life, glory, children etc.[9]. In *Purāṇas,* Gāyatrī is also described as Vedamātā, Baradā, etc[10]. This idea was also further elaborated in the *Dharmaśāstra*[11].

The *Gāyatrī-Mantra* is only one which is to be uttered along with seven *Vyāhṛtis*. This *mantra* is not only given high importance not only in the major *Purāṇas* but also in the whole cultural and literary gamut of the *Vedic* and *Purāṇic* India. Even in the contemporary India the Gāyatrī worship is assuming wide popularity day by day spearheaded by groups of dedicated workers, which many believe will bring eternal peace and harmony in the personal and social life throughout the world in future.

The popularity of *Gāyatrī-Mantra* has crossed the frontiers of *Hinduism*. It was an eclectic first when U.S. senate opened with the recitation of the *Gāyatrī-Mantra,* 'a prayer that mentions no sectarian God head, a prayer every American who goes to *yoga* studio in the U.S.A. or an *Āśhram* in *Haridwāra* would not mind saying'[12].

The process of *Mantra-japa* smoothly encompasses the following four aspects of training and improvement of mind as described by the modern psychologists namely (i) memorizing by repetition (ii) retention and recalling (iii) learning by experience (iv) believing by conviction. These are the gradual steps during the enlightened march of the individual-self towards the realization fo divine-self.

The *Gāyatrī-Mantra* enfolds the basis principles of all the religions of mankind in a compact compilation of just twenty four special syllables/words of Sanskrit. That's why this *Mantra* is also described as the shortest and the most ancient religious scripture which can guide the entire human society towards a life, full of everlasting, global peace, progress and happiness if its *Japa-sādhanā* is performed as a scientific experiment collectively by more and more people under adept disciplines and with unperturbed perseverance and sincere faith.

In the present times of technological developments the physical powers and electronic devices are used to produce ultrasonic vibrations. During the ancient era of research on *Mantras* the seers used to generate, perceive and extract the power of external sound in the *Mantras* with the help of their own body and mind. The vital energy that enables functioning of the body system and the spiritual power of the inner sentiments and the unconscious mind were the principal source of their experiments on *Mantra-sādhanās.* Among the spiritual saints of the modern India, the revered names of Raman Maharsi and Maharshi Aurobindo are often cited in the context of creative use of boundless power of *Śabda* hidden in one's thoughts and sentiments.

Sri Aurobindo's mental waves are said to have invited, inspired and controlled a large number of great souls who have descended in India to initiate and successfully excel India's non violent struggle for freedom. Raman Maharshi similarly is described to have had the super natural power to influence the thoughts and sentiments of others by his mental and latent spiritual messages. Many people have witnessed the demonstrations of his power–he was even able to communicate, guide and share the sentiments with the animals around him in his *Āśrama.*

Sri Rāma Śharmā Ācarya in his super science of Gāyatrī also analyses the deeper sense of the *Mantra.* He mentions that experts of *mantra* science view that words are uttered by different parts of the mouth such as throat, tongue, teeth, lips and the root of the tongue.

During speech, the nerve-fibres of the particular parts of the mouth from which sound emits stretch upto different parts of the body or *cakra* and put pressure on the corresponding glands.

Yogis know that some specific energies lie hidden in these glands, *Ṣatcakras* (six energy centres) related to the *Suṣumnā* are quite well known but there are several other such glands in the body. The uttrance of different words has its impact on different glands and by such impact the energy of these glands gets stimulated. *Mantras* have been composed on this basis.

There are twenty-four letters in *Gāyatrī-Mantra* which are related to twenty-four glands located in the body which on getting stimulated, activate and awaken the powers of righteous wisdom.

The flow of sound of these twenty-four letters of the *Mantra* is of deep significance. The masters of the science of sound know the powers hidden in sound and the results which can be achieved by its subtle vibrations. Sound is synonymous with *Brahma.* As *Bhartṛhari* says :

अनादिनिधनं ब्रह्म शब्दतत्त्वं यदक्षरम्
प्रवर्त्ततेऽर्थभावेन प्रक्रिया जगतं यतः।। (वाक्यपदीय - ब्रह्मकाण्डम्)

It is *Brahma* from whom the original first creative vibration issues forth resulting in seven time chanting of *OM.*

Later three main waves of *Sattva, Rajas* and *Tamas* relating to *Hrīm, Srīm* and *Klīm* elements respectively flow in this current.

Deep study reveals that the twenty-four letters of Gāyatrī hit at twenty-four Vital centres and activate them. Thus the twenty-four letters of *Gāyatrī-Mantra* which are divine and are presided over by various gods fill the votary with spiritual energy. A detailed description of the letters with the centres and the powers attained is as follows :

Sl.No.	*Letters*	*Granthi or Power of Centres*	*Power of Energy Attained*
1	*Tat*	*Tāpini granthi*	Success
2	*Ss*	*Saphalatā granthi*	Bravery
3	*Vi*	*Viśva granthi*	maintenance
4	*Tur*	*Tuṣti granthi*	well being
5	*Va*	*Varadā granthi*	*yoga*
6	*Re*	*Revatī granthi*	love
7	*Ni*	*Sukśmā granthi*	money
8	*Yam*	*Jñāna granthi*	brilliance
9	*Bhar*	*Bharga granthi*	defence
10	*Go*	*Gomatī granthi*	intellect
11	*De*	*Devikā granthi*	suppression
12	*Va*	*Varahī granthi*	devotion
13	*Sya*	*Sinhāni granthi*	*dhāraṇā*
14	*Dhī*	*Dhyāna granthi*	*Prāṇa*
15	*Ma*	*Maryādā granthi*	Self restraint
16	*Ti*	*Sphuta granthi*	*tapas*
17	*Dhi*	*Medhā granthi*	far sightedness
18	*Yo*	*Yogamāyā granthi*	*Jāgṛti*
19	*Yo*	*Yoginī granthi*	production
20	*nah*	*Dharanī granthi*	*Sarasatā* (Sweetness)
21	*Pra*	*Prabhava granthi*	*ideal*
22	*Cho*	*Uṣma granthi*	*courage*
23	*Da*	*Drsya granthi*	wisdom
24	*Yat*	*Nirañjana granthi*	*Sevā*

The *Gāyatrī-Mantra* is taken not only as an ancient ritualistic practice, but also an experience by many to have contained scientific basis. The regular articulation of makes a practitioner more intelligent, far sighted as it generates an unseen power for the development of the brain facilities enriching a healthy and superior personality.

Perhaps for these reasons *Gāyatrī-Mantra* has been revered and given such importance by the traditional *Brāhmin* community. Personalities like Swamī Vivekānanda, Mahātma Gāndhi, Rabindranāth Tagore and Sri Aurobindo of the modern era have also revered this great *Mantra* as the eternal source of righteous intellect an inspiration for the foundation of a world religion and culture of high human values.

References

1. Rao Ramachandra, *OM : The Ultimate Word-Sāksi,* 2005.
2. Iyengar, T.R.R. : *Dictionary of Hindu Gods and Goddess,* P. 77.
3. *SKP. Kāśī Khanda* 4.9.58.
4. Sampurnananda, *Evolution of Hindu Pantheon,* P. 24.
5. *Manusmṛti* 11.103.
6. *GD* 37.3.
7. Kane, P.V. *History of Dharmaśāstra,* Part - 2, P. 303
8. Lalye P.G., *Studies in the DB,* P. 208.
9. *AV.* XVIV, 71.1.
10. *DB* 12.4.4
11. *Manu Smṛti,* 11.77.83.
12. DAS Ranjit Kumar, *RV. Belongs to World, not just India,* The New Indian Express, Bhubaneswar, dt. 1.8.2007.

APPENDICES

APPENDIX - I

Analogous *Gayatri Mantras* observed in the *Linga Purana* in Praise of other Deities

गायत्रीभेदाः

(लिङ्गपुराणोत्तरभाग 48 अध्यायान्तर्गताः)

Linga Puranam Ed. by Prof. J.L. Shastri, M.L.B.D, p. 989-990

1. शिव गायत्री : तत्पुरुषाय विद्महे। वाग्विशुद्धाय धीमहि। तन्नः शिवः प्रचोदयात्
2. गौरी गायत्री : गणाम्किाये विद्महे। कर्मसिद्धये धीमहि। तन्नो गौरी प्रचोदयात्।
3. रुद्र गायत्री : तत्पुरुषाय विद्महे। महादेवाय धीमहि। तन्नो रुद्रः प्रचोदयात्।
4. गणेश गायत्री : तत्पुरुषाय विद्महे। वक्रतुण्डाय धीमहि। तन्नो दन्ती प्रचोदयात्।
5. स्कन्द गायत्री : महासेनाय विद्महे। वाग्विशुच्दाय धीमह। तन्नो स्कन्दः प्रचोदयात्।
6. शिव-वृषभ गायत्री : तीक्ष्णशुङ्गय विद्महे। वेदपादाय धीमहि। तन्नो वृषः प्रचोदयात्।
7. नन्दी गायत्री : हरिवक्त्राय विद्महे। रुद्रभक्ताय धीमहि। तन्नो नन्दी प्रचोदयात्।
8. विष्णु गायत्री : नारायणाय विद्महे। वासुदेवाय धीमहि। तन्नो विष्णुः प्रचोदयात्।
9. लक्ष्मी गायत्री : महाम्बिकायै विद्महे। कर्मस्थ्यै च धीमहि। तन्नो लक्ष्मीः प्रचोदयात्।

10. राधा गायत्री	:	समुद्युतायै विद्महे। विष्णुनेकेन धीमहि। तन्नो राधा प्रचोदयात्।
11. गरुड़ गायत्री	:	वैनतेयायै विद्महे। स्वर्ण्णपक्षाय धीमहि। तन्नो गरुड: प्रचोदयात्।
12. स्रष्टा गायत्री	:	पद्मोद्भवाय विद्महे। वेदवक्त्राय धीमहि। तन्न: स्रष्टा प्रचोदयात्
13. वाच गायत्री	:	शिवास्यजायै विङ्हे। देवरुपायै धीमहि। तन्नो वाचा प्रचोदयात्।
14. शक्र गायत्री	:	देवराजाय विद्महे। वज्रहस्ताय धीमहि। तन्न शक्र: प्रचोदयात्।
15. अग्नि गायत्री	:	रुद्रनेत्राय विद्महे। शक्तिहस्ताय धीमहि। तन्नो वृह्नि: प्रचोदयात्।
16. निऋृति गायत्री	:	निशाचराय विद्महे। खड्गहस्ताय धीमहि। तन्नो निऋृति: प्रचोदयात्।
17. यम गायत्री	:	वैवस्वताय विद्महे। गदाहस्ताय धीमहि। तन्नो यम: प्रचोदयात्।
18. वायु गायत्री	:	सर्वप्राणाय विद्महे। यष्टिहस्ताय धीमहि। तन्नो वायु: प्रचोदयात्।
19. यक्ष गायत्री	:	यक्षश्वेराय विद्महे। गदाहस्ताय धीमहि। तन्नो यक्ष: प्रचोदयात्।
20. रुद्र गायत्री	:	सर्वेश्वराय विद्महे। शूलहस्ताय धीमहि। तन्नो रुद्र: प्रचोदयात्।
21. दुर्गा गायत्री	:	कात्यायन्यै विद्महे। कन्याकुमार्य्यै धीमहि। तन्नो दुर्गा प्रचोदयात्।
22. रुद्र गायत्री (II)	:	सवर्श्वेराय विद्महे। शूलहस्ताय धीमहि। तन्नो रुद्र: प्रचोदयात्।
23. ब्रह्मा गायत्री	:	चतुर्मुखाय विद्महे। हंसारुढ़ाय धीमहि। तन्नो ब्रह्मा प्रचोदयात्।
24. हयग्रीव गायत्री	:	वाणीश्वराय विद्महे। हयग्रीवाय धीमहि। तन्नो हयग्रीव: प्रचोदयात्।

APPENDIX - II

Gayatri Sahasranama as described in *Devī Bhāgavata Puraṇa*

गायत्रीसहस्त्रनाम
(देवीभागवतान्तर्गतम्)

भगवन्! सर्वधर्मज्ञ! सर्वशास्त्र-विशारद!
श्रुति-स्मृति-पुराणानां रहस्यं त्वन्मुखाच्छ्रुतम्।।1।

सर्वपापहरं देव! येन विद्या प्रवर्त्तते।
केन वा ब्रह्मविज्ञानं किं नु वा मोक्षसाधनम्।।2।

ब्राह्मणानां गतिः केन केन वा मृत्यु-नाशनम्।
ऐहिकामुष्मिकफलं केन वा पद्मलोचन्।।3।

वस्तुमर्हस्यशेषेण सर्वं-निखिलमादितः।
साधु साधु महाप्राज्ञः! सम्यक्पृष्टं त्वयाऽनघा।।4।

श्रुणु वक्षामि यत्नेन गायत्र्यष्ट-सहस्त्रकम्।
नाम्नां शुभानां दिव्यानां सर्व-पाप-विनाशनम्।।5।

सृष्ट्यादौ यद् भगवता पूर्वंप्रोक्तं ब्रबीमि ते।
अष्टोत्तर-सहस्त्रस्य ऋषिर्ब्रह्मा प्रकीर्त्तितः।।6।

छन्दोऽनुष्टुप् तथा देवी गायत्री देवता स्मृता।
हलो बीजानि तस्यैव स्वराः शक्तय ईरिताः।।7।

अङ्गन्यास-करन्यासावुच्येते मातृकाक्षरैः।
अथ ध्यानं प्रवक्ष्यामि साधकानां हिताय वै।।8।

रक्तश्वेत हिरण्य नील धवलैः युक्तां त्रिनेत्रोज्ज्वलां
रक्तां रक्तनवस्त्रजं मणिगणैर्युवतां कुमारीमिमाम्।
गायत्रीं कमलासनां करतलव्यानद्धकुण्डाम्बुजां
पद्माक्षीञ्च वरसजञ्च दधतीं हंसयाधिरूढां भजे।।9।

अचिन्त्यलक्षणाव्यक्ताऽप्यर्थमातृमहेश्वरी।
अमृतार्णवमध्यस्थाऽप्यजिता चाऽपराजिता।।।10।

अणिमादिगुणाधाराप्यर्कमण्डलसंस्थिता।।
अजराऽजाऽपराधर्मा अक्षसूत्रधराऽधरा।।11।

अकारादिक्षकारान्ताप्यरिषड्वर्गभोदिनी।
अञ्जनादि-प्रतीकाशाऽप्यञ्जनाद्रिनिवासिनी।।12।

अदिश्चिाऽजपा विद्याप्यरविन्दनिभेक्षणा।
अन्तर्बहिः स्थिताऽविद्याध्वंसिनी चान्तरात्मिका।।13।

आजाचाऽजमुखावासाऽप्यरविन्दनिभानना।
अर्धमात्राऽर्थदानज्ञाऽप्यरि-मण्डलमर्द्दिनी।14।

असुरघ्नी ह्यमावास्याप्यलक्ष्मी घ्नन्त्यजार्चिता।
आदिलक्ष्मीश्चाऽऽदिशक्तिराकृतिश्चायतानना।15।

आदित्यपदवीचाराप्यादित्यपरिसेविता।
आचार्यावर्तनाचाराप्यादिमूर्त्तिनिवासिनी।।16।

आग्नेयी चामरी चाऽऽद्या चाऽऽराध्या चाऽऽसनस्थिता।
आधासरनिलयाधारा चाकाशान्तनिवासिनी।17।

आद्याक्षरसमायुक्ता चान्तराकाशरुपिणी।
आदित्यमण्डलगता चान्तरध्वन्तनाशिनी।।18।

इन्दिरा चेष्टदा चेष्टा चेन्दिवरनिभेक्षणा।
इरावति चेन्द्रपदा चेन्द्राणी चेन्दुरूपिणी।।19।

इक्षुकोदण्डसंयुक्ता चेषुसन्धानकारिणी।
इन्द्रनीलसमाकारा चेड़ापिङ्गलरूपिणी।20।

इन्द्राक्षी चेश्वरो देवी चेहात्रयविवर्जिता।
उमा चोशा ह्युडुनिभा उर्वारुकफलानना।।21।

उडुप्रभा चोडुमती ह्युडुप्राह्युडुमध्यगा।
ऊर्ध्वा चाप्यूर्ध्वकेशी चापयुर्ध्वाधोगति भेदिनी।।22।

ऊर्ध्वबाहुप्रिया चोर्मिमाला वाग्ग्रन्थदायिनी।
ऋतञ्छर्षिर्ऋतुमती ऋषिदेवनमस्कृता।।23।

ऋग्वेदाऋणहत्रीं च ऋषिमण्डलचारिणि।
ऋद्धिदा ऋजुमार्नस्था ऋजुधर्मा ऋतुप्रदा।।24।

ऋग्वेदनिलया ऋज्वी लुप्तधर्मप्रवर्तिनी
लूतादिस्वरसम्भूता लूतादि विषहारिणी।।25।

एकाक्षरा चैकमात्रा चैका चैककनिष्ठिता।
ऐन्द्री हैरावतारूढ़ा चेहिकामुष्मिकप्रदा।।26।

ओङ्कारा ह्यौषधी चोता चोतप्रोतनिवासिनी।
और्वा ह्यौषधसम्पन्ना औपासनफलप्रदा।।27।

अण्डमध्यस्थितादेवी चाकारमनपुरूपिणी।
कात्यायनी कालरात्रिः कामाक्षी कामसुन्दरी।।28।

कमला कामिनी कान्ताकमदा कालकण्ठिनी।
करिकुम्भस्तनभना करवीरसुवासिनी।।29।

कल्याणी कुण्डलवतमी कुरुक्षेत्रनिवासिनी
कुरुविन्ददलाकारा कुण्डली कुमुदालया।।30।

कालिजिह्वा कालास्या कालिका कालरूपिणी।
कमनीयगुणाकान्तिः कलाधाराकुमुद्वती।।31।

कौशिकी कमलाऽकारा कामचारप्रभाञ्जिनी।
कौमारी करुणापाङ्गी ककुर्वेन्ता करिप्रिया।।32।

केशरी केशवनुता कदम्बकुसुमप्रिया।
कालिन्दी कालिका काञ्ची कलशोद्भवसंस्तुता।।33।

काममाता क्रतुमती कामरूपा कृपावती।
कुमारी कुण्डनिलया किराती कीरवाहना।।34।

कैकेयी कोकिलालापा केतकीकुसुमप्रिया।
कमण्डलुधनरा काली कर्मनिर्मूलकारिणी।।35।

कलहंसगतिः कक्षा कृतकौतुकमङ्गला।
कस्तुरीतिलका कम्रा करीन्द्रगमना कुहूः।।36।

कर्पूरलेपना कृष्णा कपिला कुहराश्रया।
कूटस्था कुधरा कम्राकुक्षिस्थाऽखिलविष्टपा।।37।

खड्गखेट-खरा खर्वा खेचरी खगवाहना।
खट्वाङ्गधारिणी ख्याता खगराजोपरिस्थिता।।38।

खलघ्नी खण्डितजरा खण्डाख्यानप्रदायिनी।
खण्डेन्दुतिलका गङ्गा गणेशगुहपूजिता।।39।

गायत्री गामती गीता गान्धरी गानलोलुपा।
गोमती गामिनी गाथा गन्धर्वाऽप्सरसेविता।।40।

गोविन्दचरणाकान्ता गुणत्रयविभाजना।
गन्धर्वी गह्वरी गोत्रा गिरीशागहनागमी।।।41।

गुहावासा गुणवती गुरुपापप्रणासिनी।
गुर्वी गुणवती गुह्या गोप्तव्या गुणदायिनी।।42।

गिररिशा गुह्यमातङ्गी गरूड़ध्वजबल्लभा।
गर्वापहारिणी गोदा गोकुलस्था गदाधरा।।43।

गोकर्णनिलयासक्तगुह्यमण्डलवर्त्तिनी।
धर्मदा घनदा घण्टा घोरदानवमर्द्दिनी।।44।

घृणिमन्त्रमयी घोषा घनसम्पातदायिनी।
घण्टारवप्रिया घ्राणा घृणिसन्तुष्टिकारिणी।।45।

घनारिमण्डला घूर्णाघृताची घनवेगिनी।
ज्ञानधातुमयी चर्चा चर्चिता चारुहासिनी।।46।

चटुला चण्डिका चित्रा चित्रमाल्यविभूषिता।
चतुर्भुजा चारुदन्ता चतुरा चरितप्रदा।।47।

चूलिका चित्रवस्त्रान्ता चन्द्रमाकर्णकुण्डला।
चन्द्रहासा चारुदात्री चकोरी चन्द्रहासिनी।।48।

चन्द्रिका चन्द्रधात्री च चौरी चोरा व चन्डिका।
यञ्चद्वाग्दायिनी चन्द्रचूड़ाचोरविनासिनी।।49।

चारुचन्दन-लिप्ताङ्गी चञ्चच्चामरबीजिता।
चारुमध्या चारुगतिश्चन्दिला चन्द्ररूपिणी।।50।

चारुहोमाप्रिया चार्वाचरिता चक्रबाहुका।
चन्द्रमण्डलमध्यस्था चन्द्रमण्डलदर्पणा।।51।

चक्रवाकस्तनी चेष्टा चित्रा चित्रा चारुविलासिनी।
चित्स्वरूपा चन्द्रवती चन्द्रमाश्चनन्दनप्रिया।।52।

चोदयित्री चिरप्रज्ञा चातका चारुहेतुकी।
छत्रयाता च्छत्रधरा च्छाया च्छन्दः परिच्छदा।।53।

छायोदेवी च्छिद्रनखा च्छन्नेद्रियाविसर्पिणी।
छन्दोऽनुष्टुप्प्रतिष्ठान्ता चच्छिद्रोपद्रवभोदिनी।।54।

छेदा च्छत्रेश्वरी चच्छिन्ना च्छुरिका च्छेदनप्रिया।
जननी जन्मरहिता जातवेदा जगन्मयी।।55।

जाह्नवी जटिला जेत्री जरामरणवर्जिता।
जम्बूद्वीपवती ज्वाला जयन्ती जलशालिनी।।56।

जितेन्द्रिया जितक्रोधा जितामित्रा जगत्प्रिया।
जातरूपमयी जिह्वा जानकी जगती जरा।।57।

जनित्री जह्नुतनया जगत्त्रयहितैषिणी।
ज्वालामुखी जपवती ज्वरघ्नी जितविष्टपा।।58।

जिताकान्मयी ज्वाला जाग्रती ज्वरदेवता।
ज्वलन्ती जलदा ज्येष्ठा ज्याघोषा स्फोटादिङ्मुखी।।59।

जाम्भिनी जृम्भणा जृम्भा ज्वलन्माणिक्यकुण्डला।
झिंझिकाझणनिर्घोषा झंझामारुतवेगिनी।।60।

झल्लरी वाद्यकुशला अरूपा चाभुजा स्मृता।
टंकवाणसमायुक्ता टंकनी टंकभोदिनी।।61।

टंकीगणकृताघोषां टंकनीयमहोरसा।
टंकारकारिणि देवी ठठ-शब्दनिनादिनी।।62।

डामरी डाकिनी डिम्बाडुण्डमारैकनिर्जिता।
डामरीतन्त्रमार्गस्था डमड्डामरूनादिनी।।63।

डिण्डी-रवसहा डिम्भलसत्क्रीड़ापरायणा।
ढुण्ढिपिघ्नेशजननी ढक्काहस्ता ढिलिव्रजा।।64।

नित्यज्ञाना निरूपमा निर्गुणा नर्मदानदी।
त्रिगुणा त्रिपदा तन्त्री तुलसी तरुणा तरुः।।65।

त्रिविक्रमपदाक्रान्ता तुरीयपदगामिनी।
तरुणादित्यसंकाशा तामसी तुहिनातुरा।।66।

त्रिकालज्ञानसम्पन्ना त्रिवली च त्रिलोचना।
त्रिशक्तिस्त्रिपुरा तुङ्गा तुरङ्गवदना यथा।।67।

तिर्मिंगिलगिला तीव्रा त्रिस्त्रोता तमसादिनी
तन्त्रमन्त्रविशेषज्ञा तनुमध्या त्रिविष्टपा।।68।

त्रिसन्ध्या त्रिस्तनी तौषासंस्था तालप्रतापिनी।
ताटकिनी तुषाराभा तुहिनाचलवासिनी।।69।

तन्तुजालसमायुक्ता ताराहारावलिप्रिया।
तिलहोमप्रिया तीर्था तमालकुसुमाकृतिः।।70।

तारका त्रियुता तन्वी त्रिशङ्कुपरिवारिता।
तिलोदरी तिलाभूहा ताटंकप्रियवाहिनी।।71।

त्रिजटा तित्रिरीतृष्णा विविधा तरुणाकृतिः।
तत्तकाञ्चनसंकाशा तत्तकाञ्चनभूषणा।।72।

वैयम्बका त्रिवर्गा च त्रिकालज्ञानदायिनी।
तर्पणा तृप्तिदा तृप्ता तामसी तुम्बुरुस्तुता।।73।

ताक्ष्यरशा त्रिगुणाकारा त्रिभुङ्गी तनुवल्लरिः।
थात्कारी थाखा थान्ता दोहिनी दीनवत्सला।।74।

दानवान्तकरी दुर्गा दुर्गासुरनिवर्हिणी।
देवरीकितर्दिवारात्रि द्रोपदी दुन्दुभिस्वना।।75।

देवयानी दुरावासा दारिद्याद्भेदिनी दिवा।
दामोदरप्रिया दीप्ता सततं दिग्विमोहिनी।।76।

दण्डकारण्यानिलया दण्डिनी देवपूजिता।
देववन्द्या दिविषदा द्वेषिणी दानवाकृतिः।।77।

दीनानाथस्तुता दीक्षा दैवतादिस्वरूपिणी।
धात्री धनुर्धरा धेनुर्धारिणी धर्मचारिणी।।78।

धुरन्धरा धराधारा धनदा धान्यदेहिनी।
धर्मशीला धनाध्यक्षा धर्मवेदविशारदा।।79।

धृतिर्धन्या धृतपदा धर्मराजप्रिया ध्रुवा।
धूमावती धूमकेशी धर्मशास्त्रप्रकाशिनी।।80।

नन्दा नन्दप्रिया निद्रा नृनुता नन्दनात्मिका।
नर्मदा नलिनी नीला नलीकण्ठसमाश्रया।।81।

नारायणप्रिया नित्या निर्मला निर्गुणा निधिः।
निराधारा निरूपमा नित्यशुद्धा निरञ्जना।।82।

नादविन्दुकलातीता नादाविन्दुकलात्मिका।
नृसिंहिनी नरधरा नृपनागविभूषिता।।83।

नरकक्लेशशमनी नारायणपदोद्भवा।
निरवद्या निराकारा नारदाप्रियकारिणी।।84।

नानाज्योतिः समाख्याता निधिदा निर्मलात्मिका।
नवरूपधरा नीतिर्निरूपद्रवकारिणी।।85।

नन्दजा नवरत्नाढ्या नैमिषारण्यवासिनी
नवनीतप्रिया नारी नीलजीमूतनिस्वना।।86।

निमेषिणी नदीरूपा नीलग्रीवा निशीश्वरी।
नामावलिर्निशुम्भघ्नी नागलोकनिवासिनी।।87।

नवजाम्बूनदप्रख्या नगलोकाधिदवता।
नूपुराक्रान्तचरणा नरचित्तप्रमोदिनी।।88।

निमग्ना रक्तनयना निर्घातसमनिस्वना।
नन्दगोद्यानिलया निर्व्यूह-परिचारिणी।।89।

पार्वती परमोदारा परब्रह्मात्मिका परा।
पञ्चकोशविनिर्मुक्ता पञ्चपातकनवाशिनी।।90।

परचित्तविधानज्ञा पञ्चिका पञ्चरूपिणी।
पूर्णिमा परमा प्रीतिः परतेज-प्रकाशिनी।।91।

पुराणी पौरुषी पुण्या पुण्डरीकनिभेषणा।
पातालतलनिर्मग्ना प्रीति प्रीहतिविवर्धिना।।92।

पावनी पादसहिता पेशला पावनाशिनी।
प्रजापतिः परिश्रान्ता पर्वतस्तनमण्डला।।93।

पद्मप्रिया पद्मसंस्था पद्माक्षी पद्मसम्भवा।
पद्मपत्रा पद्मापदा पद्मिनी प्रियभाषिणी।।94।

पशुपाशविनिर्मुक्ता पुरन्ध्री पुरवासिनी।
पुष्कला पुरुषा पर्वा पारिजात-सुमप्रिया।।95।

पतिव्रता पवित्राङ्गी पुष्पहासपरायणा।
प्रज्ञावतीसुता पौत्री पुत्रपूज्या पयस्विनी।।96।

पट्टीपाशधरा पङ्क्तिः पितृलोकप्रदायिनी।
पुराणी पुण्यशीला च प्रणतार्त्ति-विनाशिनी।।97।

प्रद्युम्नजननी पुष्टा पितामह-परिग्रहा।
पुण्डरीकपुरावासा पुण्डरीकसमानना।।98।

पृथुजङ्घा पृथुभुजा पृथुपादा पृथूदरी।
प्रवालशौभा पिङ्गाक्षी पितवासाः प्रचापला।।99।

प्रसवा पुष्टिदा पुण्या प्रतिष्ठा प्रणवा-गतिः।
पञ्चवर्णा पञ्चवाणीः पञ्चिका पञ्जरस्थिता।।100।

परमाया परज्योतिः परप्रीतिः परागतिः।
पराकाष्ठा परेशानि पाविनी पावकद्युतिः।।101।

पुण्यभद्रापरिच्छेद्या पुष्पहासा पृथुदरी।
पीतागङ्गी पीतवसना पीतशय्या पिशाचिनी।।102।

पीतक्रिया पिशाचघ्नी पाटलाक्षी पटुक्रिया।
पञ्चभक्षप्रिया चारा पूतना प्राणपातिनी।।103।

पुन्नागवनमध्यस्थ पुण्यतीर्थनिषेविता।
पञ्चाङ्गा च पराशक्ति परमाह्लादकारिणी।।104।

पुष्पकाण्डस्थिता पूषा पोषिताऽखिलविष्टपा।
पानप्रिया पञ्चशिखा पंनगोपरिशायिनी।।105।

पञ्चमात्रात्मिका पृथ्वी पथिकापृथुदेहिनी।
पुराणन्यायमीमांसा पाटली पुष्पगन्धिनी।।106।

पुण्यप्रजा पारदात्री परमार्गेकगोचरा।
प्रवालशोभा पूर्वाशा प्रणवा पल्लवोदरी।।107।

फलिनी फलदा फल्गु फूत्कारी फलकाकृति।
फणीन्द्रभेगशयना फणिमण्डलमण्डिता।।108।

बालवाला बहुमता बालातपनिभांशुका।
बलभद्रप्रिया वन्द्या वड़वा बुद्धिसंस्तुता।।109।

वन्दीदेवी विलवती बद्धिशघ्नी बलिप्रिया।
बान्धवी बोधिता बुद्धिर्बन्धूककुसुमप्रिया।।110।

बालभानुप्रभाकारा ब्राह्मी ब्राह्मणदेवता।
बृहस्पतिस्तुता वृन्दा वृन्दावनविहारिणी।।11।

बालाकिनी बिलाहारा बिलंवासा बहूदका।
बहुनेत्रा बहुपदा बहुकर्णाऽवतंसिका।।112।

बहुबाहुयुता बीजरूपिणी बहुरूपिणी।
बिन्दुनादकलातीता बिन्दुनादस्वरूपिणी।।113।

बद्धगोधाङ्गुलित्राणा वदर्याश्रमवासिनी।
वृन्दारका वृतहत्स्कन्धा वृहती वाणपातिनी।।114।

वृन्दाध्यक्षा बहुनुता वनिता बहुविक्रमा।
बद्धपद्मासनासीना विल्वपत्रतलस्थिता।।115।

बोधिद्रुमनिजावासा वड़स्थिा विन्दुदर्पणा।
बालाबाणासनवती बड़वानलवेगिनी।।116।

ब्रह्माण्डबहिरन्तास्था ब्रह्मकङ्कणसूत्रिणी।
भवानी भीषणवती भाविनी भयहारिणी।।117।

भद्रकाली भुजङ्गाक्षी भारती भारताशया।
भैरवी भीषणाकारा भूतिदा भूतिमालिनी।।118।

भामिनी भोगनिरता भद्दा भूरिविक्रमा।
भूतवासा भृगुलता भार्गवी भूसूरार्चिता।।119।।

भागीरथी भोगवती भवनस्था भिषग्भरा।
भामिनी भोगिनी भावा भवानी भूरदक्षिणा।।120।।

भर्यात्मिका भीमवती भवबन्धविमोचनी
भवनीया भूतधात्री रंजिता भुवनश्वरी।।121।।

भुजङ्गवलया भीमा मेरुगाढा भागधेयिनी।
माता माया मधुमती मधुजिह्वा मधुप्रिया।।122।।

महादेवी महाभागा मालिनी मीनलोचना।
मायातीता मधुमती मधुमांसा मधुद्रुवा।।123।।

मानवी मधुसम्भूता मिथिलापुरवासिनी।
मधुकैटभ-संहत्री मेदिनी मेघमालिनी।।124।।

मन्दोदरी महामया मैथिलि मसृणप्रिया।
महालक्ष्मीर्महाकाली महाकन्या महश्वरी।।125।।

माहेन्द्री मेरूतनया मन्दारकुसुमार्चिता।
मञ्जुमञ्जरीचरणा मोक्षदा मञ्जुभाषिणी।।126।।

मधुरद्रविणी मुद्रा मलया मलयान्विता।
मेघामरकतश्यामा मागधी मनेकात्मजा।।127।।

महामारी महावीरा महाश्यामा मनुस्तुता।
मातृकामिहिराभासा मुकुन्दपदविक्रमा।।128।।

मूलाधारस्थिता मुग्धा मणिपूरकवासिनी।
मृगाक्षी महिषाऽऽरूढ़ा महिषासुरमर्द्दिनी।।129।।

योगाऽऽसना योगगम्या योगा यौवनकाश्रया।
यौवनी युद्धमध्यस्था यमुनायुगधारिणी।।130।।

यक्षिणी योगयुक्ता च यक्षराजप्रसूतिनी।
यात्रायानविधानज्ञा यदुवंशसमुद्भवा।।131।।

यकारादिहकारान्ता याजुषी याज्ञरूपिणी।
यामिनी योगनिरता यातुधानभयङ्करी।।132।।

रुक्मिणी रमणी राजा रेवती रेणुका रतिः।
रौद्री रौद्रप्रियाकारा राममातारतिप्रिया।।133।।

रोहिणी राज्यदारेखा रमाराजीवलोचना।
राकेशी रूपसम्पन्ना रत्नसिंहासनस्थिता।।134।।

रक्तमाल्याम्बरा रम्या रक्तगनधानुलेपना।
राजहंसमाऽऽरूढ़ा रम्भारक्तबलिप्रिया।।135।।

रमणीययुगाधारा राजिताऽखिलभूतला।
रुरुचर्मपरीधाना रथिनी रत्नमालिका।।136।।

रोगेशी रोगशमनी राविणी रोमहर्षिणी।
रामचन्द्रपक्रान्ता रावणच्छेदकारिणी।।137।।

रत्नवस्त्रपरिच्छन्ना रथस्था रुक्मभूषणा।
लज्जाधिदेवता लोला ललिता लिङ्गदारिणी।।138।।

लक्ष्मीर्लोला लुप्तविषा लोकिनी लोकविश्रुता।
लज्जा लम्बोदरी देवीललना लोकधारिणी।।139।।

वरदा वन्दिता विद्या वैष्णवी विमलाकृतिः।
वाराही विरजा वरलक्ष्मीविलासिनी।।140।।

विनता व्योममध्यस्था वारिजासनसंस्थिता।
वारुणौ वेणुसम्भूता वितिहोत्रा विरूपिणी।।141।।

वायुमण्डलमध्यस्था विष्णुरूपा विधिप्रिया।
विष्णुपत्नी विष्णुमती विसालाक्षी बसुन्धरा।।142।।

वामदेवप्रिया वेला वज्रिणी वसुदोहिनी।
वेदाक्षरपरीताङ्गी वाजपेयफलप्रदा।।143।।

वासिनी वामजननी वेकुण्ठनिलया वरा।
व्यासप्रिया वर्मधरा वाल्मिकी परिसेविता।।144।।

शाकम्भरी शिवा शान्ता शारदा शरणागतिः।
शातोदरी शुभचारा शुम्भसुरविमर्द्दिनीं।।145।।

शोभावती शिवाकारी शङ्कराद्धं शरिरीणी।
शोणाशुभाशया शुभ्रा शिरः सन्धानकारिणी।।146।।

शरावती शरानन्दा शरज्ज्योत्स्ना शुभानना।
शरमा शूलिनी शुद्धा शवरी शुकवाहना।।147।।

श्रीमती श्रीधरा नन्दा श्रवणानन्ददायिनी।
शर्वाणी शर्वरीवन्द्या षड्भाषा षड्ऋतुप्रिया।।148।।

षड़ाधारस्थिता देवी षुण्मुखप्रियकारिणी।
षडङ्गरूपसुमतिः सुरासुरनमस्कृता।।149।।

सरस्वती सदाधारा सर्वमङ्गलकारिणी
सामगानप्रिया सूक्ष्मा सावित्री सामसम्भवा।।150।।

सर्वावासा सदानन्दा सुस्तनी सागराम्बरा।
सर्वश्वर्यप्रिया सिद्धिः साधुबन्धुपराक्रमा।।151।।

सप्तर्षिमण्डलगता सोममण्डलवासिनी।
सर्वज्ञा सान्द्रकरुणा समानारधिकवर्जिता।।152।।

सर्वोतुङ्गा सङ्गहीना सद्गुणा सकलेष्टदा।
सरधा सूर्यतनया सुकेशी सामसंहतिः।।153।।

हिरण्यवर्णा हरिणी हींकारी हंसवाहिनी।
क्षौमवस्त्रपरीताङ्गी क्षिराब्धितनया क्षमा।।154।।

गायत्री चैव सावित्री पार्वती च सरस्वती।
वेदगर्भा वरारोहा श्री गायत्री पराम्बिका।।155।।

इति साहस्त्रकं नाम्ना गायत्र्याश्चैव नारद।
पुण्यदं सर्वपापघ्नं महासम्पत्तिदायकम्।।156।।

APPENDIX - III

Savitri Aṣtottaraśatanāma according to *Padma Purāṇa*

सावित्र्यष्टोत्तर-सहस्त्रसनाम
(पद्म-महापुराण-सृष्टिखण्डान्तर्गतम्)

The Padmamahapurāṇam ed. Ksemaraj Sri Krsnadas, Nag Publishers, p. 50-51

विष्णुरुवाच।।

सर्वगा सर्वभूतेषु द्रष्टव्या सर्वतोद्भूता।।181।।

सदसच्चैव यत्किञ्चिद् दृश्यं तन्न विना त्वया।
तथापि येषु स्थानेषु दृष्टव्या सिद्धिमीप्सुभिः।।182।।

स्मर्तव्याभूमिकामैर्वातत्प्रवक्षामि तेऽग्रतः।
सावित्री पुष्करे नाम तीर्थानां प्रवरे शुभे।।183।।

वाराणस्यां विशालाक्षी नैमिषे लिङ्गधारिणी।
प्रयागे ललितादेवी कामुका गन्धमार्दने।।184।।

मानसे कुमुदानाम विश्वकाया तथाम्बरे
गोमंते गोमती नाममन्दरे कामचारिणि।।185।।

भद्रोत्कटा चैत्ररथे जयन्ती हस्तिनापुरे।
कान्यकुब्जे तथा गौरी रम्भा मलयपर्वते॥186॥

एकाम्रके कीर्त्तिमती विश्वाविश्वश्वरी तथा।
कर्णिके पुरुहस्तेति केदारे मार्गदायिका॥187॥

नन्दा हिमवतः पृष्ठे गोकर्णे भकालिका।
स्थाण्वीश्वरे भवानी तु बिल्वके बिल्वपत्रिका॥188॥

श्रीशैले माधवीदेवी भद्रा भद्रेश्वरी तथा।
जया वराहशैले तु कमला कमलालये॥189॥

रुद्रकोट्या तु रुद्राणी काली कालंजरे तथा।
महालिङ्गे तु कपिला कर्कोटे मङ्गलश्वरी॥190॥

शामिलग्रामे महादेवी शिवलिङ्गे जलप्रिया।
मायापुर्य्या कुमारी तु संताने ललिता तथा॥191॥

उत्पलाक्षी सहस्राक्षे हिरण्याक्षे महोत्पला।
गयायां मङ्गलानाम विमला पुरुषोत्तमे॥192॥

विपाशायाममोघाक्षी पाटला पुण्यवर्द्धने।
नारायणी सुपार्श्वे तु त्रिकूटे भद्रसुन्दरी॥193॥

विपुले विपुला नाम कल्याणी मलयाचले।
कोटवी कोटितीर्थे तु सुगन्धा माधवीवने॥194॥

कुब्जाम्रके त्रिसन्ध्या तु गङ्गद्वारे हरिप्रिया।
शिवकुण्डे शिवानन्दा नन्दिनी देविकातटे॥195॥

रुक्मिणी द्वारावत्यां तु राधा वृन्दावने तथा।
देवकी मथुरायां तु पाताले परमश्वरी॥196॥

चित्रकूटे तथा सीता बिन्ध्ये बिन्ध्यनिवासिनी।
सह्याद्रावेकवीरा तुहरिश्चन्द्रे तु चन्द्रिका॥197॥

रमणा रामतीर्थे तु यमुनायां मृगावती।
करवीरे महालक्ष्मीरुमादेवी विनायके॥198॥

अरोगा वैद्यनाथे तु महाकाले महश्वेरी।
अभया पुष्पतीर्थे तु अमृता बिन्ध्यकन्दरे॥199॥

माण्डव्ये माण्डवीदेवी स्वाहामाहेश्वरेपुरे।
वेगले तु प्रचण्डाथचण्डिकामरङ्कटके।।200।।

सोमेश्वरे वरारोहा प्रभासे पुष्करावती।
देवमाता सरस्वत्यां पारापारे तटे स्थिता।।201।।

महालये महापद्म पयोष्णयां पिङ्गलश्वरी।
सिंहिकाकृतशौचे तु कार्तिकेये तु शङ्कारी।।202।।

उत्पलावर्तके लोला सुभद्रा सिन्धुसङ्गमे।
उमा सिद्धवने लक्ष्मीरनङ्गत भरताश्रमे।।203।।

जालंधरे विश्वमुखी तारा किष्किन्धपर्वते।
देवदारुवने पुष्टिर्मेधाकाश्मरिमण्डले।।204।।

भीमादेवी हिमाद्रौ च तुष्टिर्वस्त्रेश्वेरे तथा।
कपालमोचने श्रद्धा माता कायावरोषणे।।205।।

शंखोद्धारे ध्वनिर्नाम धृतिः पिण्डारके तथा।
काला तु चन्द्रभागायामच्छोदे सिद्धिदायिनी।।206।।

वेणायाममृतादेवी वदर्यामुर्वशी तथा।
औपधी चौत्तरकुरौ कुशद्वीपे कुशोदका।।207।।

मन्मथा हेमकूटे तु कुमुदे सत्यवादिनी।
अश्वत्थे वन्दनीया तु निधिर्वे श्रवणालये।।208।।

गायत्री वेदवदने पार्वती शिसंन्निधौ।
देवलोके तथेन्द्राणी ब्रह्मास्ये तु सरस्वती।।209।।

सूर्यबिम्बे प्रभानाम मातृणां वैष्णवी तथा।
अरुन्धती सतीनां तु रामासु च तिलोत्तमा।।210।।

चित्रे ब्रह्मकलानाम शक्तिः सर्वशरीरिणाम्।
एतद्भक्त्या मयाप्रोक्तं नामाष्टशतमुत्तमम्।।211।।

APPENDIX - IV

Glory and Advantages of Gāyatrī Japa, Worship According to Modern Philosophy

Many sages and philosophers have sung paeans in praise of *Gāyatrī.* Several concepts are prevalent in the Hindu religion and there are controversies and conflicting opinions also in respect of some of them. But in all the sects, saints and seers have accepted the pre-eminence of *Gāyatrī Mantra* with one voice.

According to *Vīśvāmitra,* there is no other *mantra* like *Gāyatrī mantra* in all the four Vedas. All the Vedas, *Yajña, Charuit. Tapas* (devout austerity) are not equivalent even to a small portion of potency of *Gāyatrī mantra.*

Manu says that, "*Gāyatrī mantra* having three phases was conceived by *Brahmā* as the essence of three Vedas. There is no other purifying *mantra* than *Gāyatrī mantra.* A person doing *Gāyatrī Japa* regularly for three years realizes God. A *Dvija* (twice-born person otherwise known as *Brāhmaṇa*) who meditates on *Gāyatrī mantra* in the morning and evening gets the benefit of reciting all the Vedas. Such a person can attain divine powers by *Gāyatrī japa* alone. Those who perform *japa* of this *mantra* a thousand time daily get rid of the ill effect of their sins just as sanke casts off its slough. A dvija who does not worship Gāyatrī deserves severest condemnation."

Yājñavalkya says, "Gāyatrī and all the Vedas were weighed in a balance. The scale was tipped in favour of Gāyatrī. The Upaniṣads are the essence of the Vedas and Gāyatrī along with its *Vyāhṛtis* has been regarded as the essence of the Upaniṣads. Gāyatrī is the mother of the Vedas, it destroys sins and there is no other greater purifying mantra than Gāyatrī on this earth as well as in the heavens. Just as there is no better place of pilgrimage than Gangā and none can excel God, the Keśava, so also there is no mantra superior to Gāyatrī mantra. One who masters Gāyatrī becomes master of all knowledge and becomes śrotriya. A Brāhmin who is not devoted to Gāyatrī is like a Śudra, although, he may be well-versed in the Vedas. He who does not know Gāyatrī gets deprived of *Brāhmaṇatva* and becomes sinful."

According to Parāśara, "of all sūktas and ved-mantras, Gāyatrī matra is the super most. Between the Vedas and Gāyatrī, the latter has an upper hand. One who performs Gāyatrī *japa* with devotion becomes pure and gets liberated. A person without Gāyatrī worship cannot be considered a Brāhmaṇa, although, he might have read Vedas, all the scriptures, Purāṇas and history."

The sage Śankha is of the view that, "Gāyatrī alone extends a helping hand and saves a person falling in the ocean of hell. There is nothing superior to it on this earth as well as in the heavens. Undoubtedly, a person who masters Gāyatrī attains heaven."

According to the sage Śaunaka, a twice born may or may not do other worships. Out he gets liberated by doing Gāyatrī *japa* alone and attains all material and spiritual boons. Performance of ten thousand *Japas* avert calamity in the hour of crisis.

Arti says, "Gāyatrī completely purifies the soul. By the glorious power of Gāyatrī deep-rooted defects and vices are cleansed out. Nothing else remains to be attained in this world by one who fully understands the substance of Gāyatrī.

According to the great thinking and compiler is the essence of all flowers similarly Gāyatrī is the essence of all the Vedas. Gāyatrī is like kāmadhenu for one who has acquired mastery in it. Gangā purifies sins committed by the physical body but Gāyatrī, the Brahma Gangā purifies the soul. There is nothing superior to Gāyatrī-sādhanā for achieving desired fruits and developing the power of devout austerity.

Ṛsi Bharadwāj says that, "even Brahmā performs Gāyatrī *japa*. It leads to God realization. A vicious man gets rid of his vices by performing Gāyatrī *japa*. A person devoid of Gāyatrī Sādhanā is worse than a Śudra.

A person, who worships Gāyatrī, observes Brahmacarya attains longevity according to the sage Caraka.

According Nārada, "Gāyatrī is devotion personified. Wherever there is Gāyatrī in the form of devotion, god-Nārāyaṇa, undoubtedly resides there."

Vasiṣṭha says, "persons who are dull, way-ward and fickle-minded become highly intelligent and steadfast and rise to great heights in worldly and spiritual pursuits by Gāyatrī sādhanā. Those who worship Gāyatrī steadfastly and piously attain self-realisation."

According to Jagatguru Śankarācārya, It is beyond human competence to describe the glory of Gāyatrī. Nothing is more important in the world than to attain spiritual wisdom, which is inspired by Gāyatrī sādhanā. Gāyatrī is the primordial mantra. Its sādhanā destroys sins and promotes virtues."

Apart from the views expressed by the ancient seers and saints, eminent persons, philosophers, spiritual masters of the present and recent past wave unequivocally praised the pre-eminence and glory of Gāyatrī mantra.

Swami Ramtirtha said, "The most important task is to attain Rama (God). The purpose of Gāyatrī is to remove intellect's craving for sensuous pleasures and inculcate in its deep interest for God. He alone can attain God whose intellect is pure and stable. There should be such purity in the intellect that it may consider Rāma greater than *Kāma* (sensuousness).

Maharsi Rāmaṇa preached that all masteries of this mantra which is extremely powerful. Marvelous results are achieved by the power of mantras. Gāyatrī is such a mantra, which bestows both material as well as spiritual benefits.

Prof. R. Shrinivasan, a senior member of Theosophical Society, was stated that Gāyatrī has been acclaimed as the most powerful mantra in the Hindu culture. Its significance is extremely mysterious and its Sādhanā gives miraculous results. It has different effects on devotees of different mental dispositions.

According to Lokamānya Tilak, "Political freedom alone will not liberate Indian people from the bonds of slavery. For this, the inner soul should be enlightened so that it may be inspired to leave the wrong path and pursue the righteous one. Gāyatrī mantra incorporates this prayer."

Ramākriṣṇa Paramhamsa stated "I tell people that it is not necessary to get engaged in complicated Sādhanās, perform simple

Gāyatrī-Sādhanā and see the results. Great siddhis are attained by Gāyatrī-sādhanā. This mantra is short, no doubt, but it is extremely powerful.

Swamī Dayananda, the founder of Ārya Samaj, was a staunch worshipper of Gāyatrī. He told the ruler of Gwalior that *Gāyatrī-puraṣcaraṇ* is better than weekly discourses of *Bhāgvata Purāṇa.* Sawamiji had taught several persons like Saccidānanda, Heeralal Rāval, Ghodal Singh etc. at Jaipur the method of doing Gāyatrī-japa. In Multan, Swamiji advocated the supremacy of this mantra and said that the origin of all the Vedas is Gāyatrī mantra. He said that all the sages used to perform japa of this mantra in the ancient times.

Vivekānanda said, "Only that thing should be begged from a king which befits his dignity. Spiritual wisdom alone is the most suitable gift, which could be asked from God. God grants spiritual wisdom, which leads to advancement on the right path and results in our happiness. One who is advancing towards the truth always remains happy. Gāyatrī mantra is instinct with spiritual wisdom and therefore it has been acclaimed the greatest of all mantras."

According to Mahāmana Madan Mohan Mālavīya, "Gāyatrī is the most precious gem which has been given to us by the *Ṛsis.* It purifies the intellect and enlightens the soul with the light of God. Countless souls have been liberated from worldly bondage by its Sādhanā. Gāyatrī has the power to inculcate feelings of devotion to God and bestows worldly abundance. Gāyatrī-Sādhanā is essential for Brāhmaṇas. A person who does not perform Gāyatrī-japa is guilty of neglecting his primary duties."

The great Indian poet Ravindranāth Tāgore says," The mantra which can awaken India is so simple that it can be uttered in a single breath. It is Gāyatrī-mantra. There is absolutely no scope for any dispute or argumentation in regard to the supremacy of this holiest mantra."

According to Mahātma Gāndhi, "Constant *japa* of Gāyatrī mantra is useful for curing physical ailments and for the upliftment of the soul. Gāyatrī-japa performed with a calm, unperturbed mind has the power of averting crisis in the hour of distress."

Sri Aurobindo, too has advocated Gayatri-japa. According to him Gayatri has extraordinary potency to accomplish great and noble aims.

S. Rādhākrisna says, "If we ponder over the Universal prayer Gayatri we will realize what superb benefits it provides. Gāyatrī is a prayer for rejuvenating the source of our life."

Swami Sivānanda of Ṛisikesh of all the mantras, the supreme and the most potent power of powers is the great, glorious Gāyatrī mantra. The regular repetition of a few *mālās* (one *mala* consisting) of repeating the Gāyatrī mantra 108 times) will bestow upon are, all that is auspicious and benevolent to him, here in and hereafter... Therefore, it is the greatest of all mantras and its presiding deity is pana Brahman.

Sadguru Sant Keśavdas, Visva Santi Asram, near Bangalore says, "The Gāyatrī mantra is the key to opening the door of cosmic consciousness. This mantra confers wisdom, prosperity, purity and liberation, removes all fears and all ills. One who repeats the mantra 108 times in each sitting will attain radiance soon and if repeated 1008 times with sincerity and devotion in each sitting will attain illumination in 40 days."

Swami Mukhyānanda, Sri Ramakrisna Matha, Mylapore, Madras says that, "Now the time has come, as declared by Swami Vivekananda in 1901 that the Vedas and the Gāyatrī mantra must be propagated among all, as before, irrespective of caste, creed, sex or religion. Women should also perform Sandhyā as in olden times. This veda is our only authority and everyone has the right to it."

Sri Chandrasekharendra Sarasvatī Swamī (The Śankarācārya of Kancipuram) says that "People who chant the Gāyatrī-mantra with affection and devotion are protected. The Gāyatrī mantra contains in itself the spirit and energy of all the vedic mantras."

According to Sri Satya Sai "The Gayatri mantra is the elaboration of the Praṇava Sabda OM and can be recited by anyone."

Thus, besides the views expressed by the ancient Ṛsi there is vast collection of opinions of several noted and eminent intellectuals of the present century on the basis of which it can be concluded that Gayatrī-sādhanā is not a blind faith but is a well tried and tested Sunlit path of spiritual growth.

Glossary

Abhaya	–	Free from fear. Abhaya is described as a hand pose of Gāyatrī Devi.
Abhirī	–	A woman of cow herd tribe.
Ācamana	–	Sipping water before religious ceremonies and before and after meals.
Ācāra	–	A custom, practice.
Acintyalaksanā	–	The woman having incomprehensible characteristics.
Ādityamandalagatā	–	Rising in the orb of the sun.
Āgneī	–	The female counterpart of Agni.
Aja	–	Existing from all internally.
Akśamālā	–	A rosary.
Āmāyah	–	Sacred tradition.
Antarakasarupinī	–	One having the form of the inner sky(F).
Anulepana	–	Anointment
Anumati	–	Generally means permission, but in rituals it means the 15th day of the Moon's age on which she rises on digit-less than full form.
Arghya	–	A respectful offering or oblation to a god or venerable person.
Astarātra	–	Astratra is the name of a sacrifice which is continued for eight at a Stretch.
Anudumbara	–	Related to udumbara of a fig tree.

Aum	–	An auspicious sound chanted before a beginning each mantra otherwise known as pranava.
Avyakta	–	Unmanifested, the primary matter which has not yet entered into real existence.
Āyus	–	Duration of life.
Bhagavatī	–	An epithet of the river Ganges of patala or lower world. Giving pleasure or delight.
Bhuṣaṇa	–	An ornament or decoration.
Brahmavarcas	–	The light or vigour of Brahma, a mystical power of achievement.
Candrāyaṇa	–	A religious observance or explatory penance regulated by the moon's age (the period of waxing and waning) in it the daily quantity of food, which consists of fifteen mouthfuls at the full moon, it diminished by one mouthful everyday during the dark fortnight tilt is educed in like manner during the bright fortnight.
Cārudanta	–	A woman having beautiful teeth.
Chāyā	–	Shadows
Dakśiṇā	–	A present or gift to Brahmanas at the completion of a religious rite, Such as a sacrifice.
Damaru	–	A sort of small drum, shaped like a hour glass and generally used by the Kapalikas.
Danabantakari	–	The killer of the demons.
Daṇḍa	–	A stick (especially of Palasa wood).
Dharmasastra	–	A code of laws, jurisprudence.
Dhuba	–	The firmed stable permanent one (F).
Dhupa	–	It is the part of Saodasopacara worship. It indicates incense or perfume.

Dipa	– A lamp
Durgatāraṇī	– One who can cross over a fort or difficult situation.
Dvija	– A twice born, a man of any of the first three castes of Hindu society a Brahmana, a Ksatriya and a Vaisya.
Ekākśara	– The monosyllabic one (F).
Gandha	– Smell or odour.
Ghṛtāci	– Night, name of Saraswati.
Gopakanyā	– A cowherd girl, consider as belonging to mixed tribe.
Gūhyam	– Which deserves to be concealed. A Secret
Hiranyavarnā	– A river of that name-a woman of golden complexion.
Japa	– Muttering prayers, repeating prayers in an undertone.
Jātavedas	– One who has given birth to the Vedas/Agni
Jhallakavādyakuśalā	– Perfect in playing cymbal, a musical instrument.
Kalpavṛkśa	– The celestial tree grown at Indra's paradise and it is supposed to grant all desires. The wish yielding tree.
Kamanḍalu	– A water pot made of earth, wood or metal and used by ascetics.
Kapāla	– The skull or skull bone
Katyāyanaosa	– Born in family of Katyayana gotraja
Kātyāyani	– An elderly or middle aged widow described in red clothes, but here Katyayani means Parvati or one of the forms of Gayatri.
Kavaca	– Kavaca means armour generally, but in worship it means a specific chant which is

		supposed to protect the physic and surroundings of the devotee.
Kharva	–	Mutilated, having numerous qualities.
Kīlaka	–	A badge or pin, a mystical protective mantra in worship.
Kśirabdhitanayā	–	Daughter of the ocean of milk.
Latikā	–	A small creeper, string of pearls.
Māyā	–	Illusion
Naivedya	–	An offering of edibles presented to a deity.
Oṃkāra	–	One who is related to aum sound.
Padmāsana	–	A yogic posture of sitting.
Phaladā	–	The result bestowing one (F).
Pralaya	–	Dissolution.
Praṇava	–	The sacred syllable aum (Rv 1.11; MS. 2.74).
Rājasūya	–	A great sacrifice performed by a universal monarch, in which the tributary princes also take part at the time of the coronation as a mark of this undisputed sovereignty.
Rāsabha	–	A donkey
Rāti	–	Pleasure, Delight.
Saguṇā	–	Possessed of qualities or attributes.
Sahasranāma	–	Thousand names or epithets of the deity.
Śakti	–	In Hinduism, the creative energy inherent in and proceeding from God. It is exemplified by the female principle, the female reproductive organs, 'Sakti' wife of Siva.
Samhitā	–	Combination. A collection. According to *Yaska*.

Samidheni – A kind of prayer recited while the sacrificial fire is being kindled or fed with fuel.

Sandhyā – Union, Morning, Noon and evening twilight meditation.

Saptani – A rival or fellow wife, having the same husband with other.

Sastram – A religious or sacred treatise. Any department of knowledge.

Savitṛ – Generating, producing, yielding. The sun, the creator of the World.

Sāyujyamukti – One of the four stages of salvation, intimate union or identification with Supreme world.

Snāna – Purification by bathing any religious or ceremonial ablution.

Sraddhā – A funeral rite or ceremony performed in honour of the departed spirits of dead relatives.

Sṛngāra – The sentiment of love, erotics.

Śudra – Aman of the fourth or the last of the four principal tribes of the Ancient India. He is said to have been born from the feet of Purusa.

Surasuranmskrta – Respected by the gods and demons.

Suryamandala-madhysthā – Existing in the orb of the sun.

Talpa – A conch, bed.

Tāmbula – The areca nut.

Tripada – Having three feet.

Turiyapadagāminī – The woman who goes through the fourth path or track.

Upāsanā – Worship, religious meditation, service, attendants.

Vaidurya – Brought from or produced in Vidura, lapis lazuli.

Vandya – Adorable(F) fit to be saluted.

Varadā – The bestower of a boon.

Varadāmudrā – Posture of hand used during the bestowing of a boon.

Vasanam – A piece of cloth.

Vigarhitā abhirī – A censured woman of cowherd tribe.

Vyāhrtis – Words uttered by every priest in performing his daily sandhya adoration. The three vyahrtis are bhuh, bhuvah and svah usually repeated after aum. According to some scholars, the are seven in numbers.

Vyāna – One of the five life force or winds or vital airs in the body, that which is diffused through the whole body.

Yajñaḥ – A sacrifice, any suffering or oblation. An act of worship. Every householder has to perform five such devotional acts everyday. They are Bhutayanja, Manusa Yajna, Pitryajna, Devi Yajna, Brahma Yajna.

Yogamāya – The magical power of yoga or the power of god or goddess in the creation of the world personified as a deity in the name of Durga.

Bibliography

Primary Sources : Original Texts and Translations

1. *Agni Purāṇa,* Sri Agni Mahāpurāṇam, Reprinted from VSP Edn., Delhi, Nag Publishers, 1985.

2. *Agni Purāṇa,* Ed. M.C. Apte, Anandashrama Sanskrit Series, 41, Poona, 1957.

3. *Aitareya Āraṇayaka,* Ed. and Tr. by A.B Keith, The Clarendon press, Oxford, 1909.

4. *Aitareya Āraṇyaka,* Anandashrama Sanskrit Series, 38, Poona, 1959.

5. *Āpastaṁba-Srauta Śūtra,* Ed. by A. Chinaswami Sastri, Oriental Institute, Baroda, 1955.

6. *Aitareya Brāhmaṇa* with the commentary of Sāyaṇa, Ed. V.G. Apte, Anandashrama Sanskrit Series, 32, Poona, 1930-31;

7. *Ṛgveda Brāhmaṇas* : *the Aitareya and Kausitaki Brāhmaṇas of Ṛgveda,* Tr. A.B. Keith, Harvard Oriental Series, 25, Cambmass, 1920.

8. *Āśvalāyana Gṛhyasūtra* (with the AGP) : Anandashrama, Poona, 1936, Tr. by H. Oldenberg. SBE. Vol.29 Reprint : MLBD, Delhi, 1964.

9. *Atharvaveda Saṁhitā,* Nag Prakashak, Delhi, 2003.

10. *Atharvaveda Saṁhitā,* Arya Sahitya Mandala, Ajmer, 1957;

11. *Atharvaveda Saṁhitā,* Tr. by W.D. Whitney and Ed. by C.R. Laxman, 2 Volumes, Harvard Oriental Series 7-8, Camb-Mass, 1905.

12. *Atharvaveda* with *Bhāṣya* of Sāyaṇa Ed. Visva Bandhu, Hoshiarpur, 1961.

13. *Bhāgavata Purāṇa* with the commentary of Sridhara P. Ramateja Sastri, Pandita Pustakalaya, Varanasi, Vs 2019 (1963).

14. *Bhaviṣya Purāṇa,* Venkateshwar Press, Bombay, 1959.

15. *Bodhāyana Gṛhyasūtra,* Ed. Sharma Sastri, Mysore, 1926.

16. *Brahma Purāṇa*, Ed. H.N. Apte, Anandashrama Sanskrit Series, 28, Poona, 1895.

17. *Brahmavaivarta Purāṇa* Ed. V.G. Apte, 2 Volumes, Anandashrama Sanskrit Series, 102, Poona, 1935.

18. *Brahymānda Purāṇa*, Venkateshwar Press, Bombay, Vs. 1992 (1936).

19. *Devī Bhāgavata,* Ed. by Ramateja Pandeya, Pandita Pustakalaya, Kasi, 1969, Tr. by Swami Vijnanananda Sudhindra Nath Vasu, Allahabad, 1921-23.

20. *Devī Māhātmya,* Durgasaptaśatī of Mārkandeya Purāṇa Gīta Press, Gorakhpur, Vs 2027.

21. *Devī Māhātmya,* Ed. and Tr. by Swāmi Jagadisvarananda, Sri Ramakrishna Math, Mylapore, 1953.

22. *Devī Purāṇa.,* Ed. by Puspendra Kumar Sharma, KSV, New Delhi, 1973.

23. *Garuḍa Purāṇa,* Ed. Ramshankar Bhattacharya, Varanasi, 1964; Prose English Translation of *Garuda Purana* by M.N. Dutta, Calcutta, 1908.

24. *Gopatha Brāhmaṇa Bhāṣyam.* Ed. by Prajnā Devī and Medhā Devī, Chaukhamba Samskrit Pratisthan, Delhi, 1999.

25. *Gopatha Brāhmaṇa* of Atharva Veda, Ed, by Rajendra Lal Mitra, Delhi, 1972

26. *Gobhila Gṛhyasūtra,* Ed. by Chintamani Bhattacharya, Munshiram Manoharlal, New Delhi, 1982. Tr. by H. Oldenberg, SBE, Vol. 30, Reprint : MLBD, Delhi,1967.

27. *Jaiminīya Brāhnaṇa* of Samaveda Ed. Raghuvira and Lokesh Chandra, Nagpur, 1954.

28. *Kālikā Purāṇa* Ed. Biswanarayan Sastri, Varanasi, 1972.

29. *Kāṇva Samhitā,* Sukla Yajurvediya Kanva Samhita, Ed. by S. Sharma Satavalekar, Aundh 1941 (Vs 1997).

30. *Kāthaka Gṛhyasūtra,* Ed. W. Calend, DAV College, Lahore, 1925.

31. *Kauṣitaka Gṛhyasūtra* with the commentary of Bhavatrata, Ed. T.R. Chintamani, Madras, 1944.

32. *Kūrma Purāṇa,* Venkateshwar Press, Bombay, Vs 1962 (1906).

33. *Liṅga Purāṇa,* Ed. Jivananda Vidyasagara Bhattacharya, Calcutta, 1885.

34. *Maitrāyaṇī Samhitā,* Yajurvedīya Maitrāyanī Samhitā, Ed. S. Sharma Satavalekar, Aundh, 1949 (Vs. 1998).

35. *The Mahābhārata,* Critically Edited by V.S Sukthankar, S.K. Belvalkar, Poona, 1933 ff.

36. *The Mahābhārata,* Tr. by K.M. Ganguly, 12 vols; Reprint Ed. by P.C. Roy, Oriental Publishing Co., Calcutta, 1952.

37. *Mārkandeya Purāṇa* Ed. Jivananda Vidyasagar Bhattacharya, Calcutta, 1879; *The Markandeya Purana,* Tr. by F.E. Pargiter, Indological Book House, Varanasi, 1969.

38. *Matsya Purāṇa*, Ed. Jivananda Vidyasagar Bhattacharya, Calcutta, 1876; *The Matsya Purāṇa,* Tr. by Taluqdar of Oudh, Allahabad, 1916.

39. *Naighantu and Nirukta,* Edited and Tr. by Laksman Sarup, 2 parts University of Punjab, 1927.

40. *Nārada Purāṇa,* Venkateshwar Press, Bombay, Vs. 1962 (1906).

41. *Padma Purāṇa* Ed. M.C. Apte, 4 Volumes, Anandashrama Sanskrit series, 131, Poona, 1894.

42. *Pāraksara Gṛhyasūtra,* Venkateshwar Press, 1938.

43. *Ṛgveda Samhitā,* Nag Prakashak, Delhi, 2000.

44. *Ṛgveda Samhitā* with the commentary of *Sāyaṇācārya,* Ed. N.S. Sontakke, C.G. Kasikar and others, 5 Volumes, Vaidika Samsodhana Mandal, Poona, 1933-51.

45. *Sāmaveda Samhitā, Nag* Prakashak, Delhi, 1994.

46. *Sāmaveda Samhitā, Samaveda* Ed. Bhattacharya Saipada Sharma Santavalekara, Bombay, 1956; *The Samaveda Samhita,* English Translation by Rev. J. Stevenson, Varanasi, 1961.

47. *Sānkhāyana, Gṛhyasūtra,* Ed. S.K. Sehgal, Delhi, 1960.

48. *Sānkhayana Śrauta Sūtra* with the commentary of Varadattasuta Anartiya, Ed. Alfred Hillebrant in Bibliotheca India, Calcutta, 1888.

49. *Śatapatha Brāhmaṇam,* Ed. B.B. Chaubey, VVRI, Hoshiarpur.

50. *Śatapatha Brāhmaṇam,* Corrected by Pt. Chinnaswami Sastri and Pt. Pattabhiram Sastri, Ed. Pt. Ramanath Dikshit, Chaukhamba Sanskrit Samsthan, Varanasi, 3rd Ed. Vs 2054.

51. *Śatapatha Brāhmaṇa,* Śrimad Vājasaneyī Mādhyandina Śatapatha Brāhmaṇa with commentary of Sayana, Ed. A. Weber, 2nd end., Varanasi, 1964; *The Satapatha Brahmana,* Tr. by Julious Eggeling, 5 volumes, Sacred Books of the East, 12, 26, 41, 44, Delhi, 1963.

52. *Śiva Purāṇa* Ed. Ramateja Sastri, Pandita Pustakalaya, Kasi, Samhat 2026.

53. *Skanda Purāṇa* Venkateshwar Press, Bombay, Vs 1966 (1910)

54. *Taittarīya Āraṇyaka* with the commentary of Sayana, Ed. V.G. Apte, Anandashrama Sanskrit Series, 36, 2 Volumes, Poona, 1927.

55. *Taittirīya Brāhmaṇa, Krsna Yajurvediya Taittirīya Brāhmaṇa* with the commentary of Sāyaṇācārya, Ed. H.N. Apte, 3 Volumes, Anandashrama Sanskrit Series, 37, Poona, 1893.

56. *Tāṇḍya Mahābrāhmaṇa, Sāmavedīya-Tāṇḍya* (*Pancavimāśa*) *Brāhmaṇa* with the commentary of Sāyaṇa, Ed. Chinnaswami

Sastri, 2 Volumes, Kasi Sanskrit Series, 105, Banaras, 1935-35; *Pancavimsa Brahmana,* Tr. W. Caland, Calcutta, 1931.

57. *Taittirīya Saṁhitā Kṛṣṇa Yajurvediya Taittirīya Samhitā,* Ed S. Sharma Satavalekar, 2nd End, Bombay, 1957 (Vs 2019); The Veda of the Black Yajus School entitled *Taittiriya Samhita,* Tr. by A.B. Keith, Harvard Oriental Series, 18-19, Camb-Mass 1914, Delhi, 1967.

58. *Upaniṣad, Īsādi nau Upaniṣad* with *Surīkarabhaṣyārtha,* Gīta Press, Gorakhpur, 2nd Ed. Sam 2060.

59. *Sixty Upaniṣads of the Veda* Vol-I and II, Tr. by. VN. Bedekar and G.B Palsule, MLBD, Delhi, 2004.

60. *Vājasaneyī Samhitā, Vājasaneyī-Mādhyandina-Śukla Yajur-veda Saṁhitā,* Ed. by Satavalekar, Paradi 1957 (Vs 2013); The Texts of the White *Yajurvaeda* by Ralph T.R. Griffith, 3rd Edition, Banaras, 1957.

61. *Vāmana Purāṇa,* Critically Edited with English Translation by A.S. Gupta, All India Kashiraj Trust, Varanasi, 1968.

62. *Varāha Purāṇa* Venkateshwar Press, Bombay, Vs 1959 (1903).

63. *Vāyu Purāṇa,* Venkateshwar Press, Bombay.

64. *Vāṣṇu Purāṇa,* Gita Press, Gorakhapur, Vs 2026 (1969); *The Vishṇu Purana,* Tr. by H.H. Wilson, 3rd End, Calcutta, 1961.

65. *Viṣṇudharmottara Purāṇa,* Venkateshwar Press, Bombay, Vs 1969 (1913).

66. *Yajurveda Samhitā,* Nag Prakashak, Delhi, 2001.

67. *Tāndyamahābrāhmaṇam,* Part-I and II, Chaukhanba Samskrita Bhawan, Varanasi, Vs. 2059.

Secondary Sources

1. Acharya, S.S. : *Eternity of sound and the science of mantra,* Yugantar Chetra Press, Haridwar, 2003.

2. Acharya, S.S, : *Super Science of Gāyatrī,* Yug Nirman Yojana Mathura, 2004; *Prajā Purāṇa,* Vol. 1-IV, Ayugaśakti Gāyatrī, Bhubaneswar.

3. Acharya, S.S. : *Gāyatrī Mantrārtha* (Oriya), Tr. by G.C. Nayak, Orissa Yuga Nirman Sahitya Prakasan Trust Bhubaneswar, 1997; *Gāyatrī Māhāvidyākā-tattava-darśan,* Ankhandajyoti Samsthan, Mathura.

4. Agrawala, V.S. : *Matsya Purāṇa-a Study,* Ist Edn., Vārānasi, 1963.

5. Agrawala, V.S. : *Gāyatrī* (Hindi), *Vedavāni*, 16(1). Nov. 1963, 15.

6. Aiyangar, Narayana : *Essays on Indo-Aryan Mythology,* Part-I and II, Madras, 1961.

7. Anandaswami : *Mahāmantra* (Oriya), Tr. B. Sahu, Padma Commercial, Bhubaneswar, 2000.

8. Arthur and Ellen Avalon : *Hymns to the Goddess,* Madras, 1964 .

9. Banerjea, J.N. : *Purāṇic and Tāntric Religion* (Early Phase), Calcutta University, Calcutta, 1966.

10. Banerjea, J.N. : *Development of Hindu Iconography,* 2nd Edn. University of Calcutta, Calcutta, 1956.

11. Bharati, Agehananda : *The Tāntric Tradition,* B.I. Publications, New Delhi, 1976.

12. Bhattacharya, N.N. : *Indian Mother Goddess,* Calcutta, 1971.

13. Bhattacharya, H.N. : *Hinduder Devadevī* (Bengali) 3 vols. Calcutta : Firma KLM Pvt., 1986.

14. Bloomfield, M.: *A Vedic concordance,* Harvard Oriental Series 10, Camb-mass, 1906.

15. Chakravarty, Chintaharana : *The Tantras, Studies on their Religion and literature,* Calcutta, 1963.

16. Chakravarti, P.C. : *Doctrine of Śakti in Indian Literature,* Calcutta, 1940.

17. Coburn, Thomas B. : *Devī Māhātmya, The Crystallization of Goddess Tradition,* Reprint, Delhi, MLBD, 1988.

18. Dange, S.A. : *Legends in the Mahābhārata,* Delhi, 1969; Dange, S.A, *Encyclopaedia of Purāṇic Believes and Practices,* Voll. Navaran, Delhi.

19. Dange, S.A. : *Sāvitrī and the Banyan, Purāṇa,* Vol.V, No. 2, July, 1963, 260.

20. Desai, S.G. : '*The Minor Deities in the Later Upaniśads", Bhāratīya Vidyā* Vol. XXVII. Nos. 1-4 (1967), pp. 25-40.

21. Deva, Raja Radhakanta : *Śabdakalpadruma,* Varanasi, 1961.

22. Dikshit, S.K. : *The Mother Goddess,* Poona, 1941.

23. Dhal, U.N. : *Goddess Lakṣmī : Origin and Development,* New Delhi, Oriental Publishers, 1978.

24. Dhai, U.N. : "*A Folk Deity in Purāṇa Literature,*" Purāṇa, Vol. XXI, No. 1 (1979) pp. 9-22.

25. Dhal, U.N. : *"The Colour Concept of a Deity",* VIJ. Vol. XXI. prs 1-11 (1983), pp. 228-32.

26. Dowson, J.A. : *Classical Dictionary of Hindu Mythology and Religion, History and Culture,* Tenth edn., London, 1961.

27. Fausboll, V. : *Indian Mythology* according to the *Mbh.* in outline, London, 1903.

28. Hazra, R.C. : *Studies in the Upapurāṇas,* Vol. II, Calcutta : Sanskrit College, 1963.

29. Hazra, R.C. : *Studied in the Purāṇic Records of Hindu Rites and Custome,* 2nd edn. Delhi, MLBD, 1975.

30. Hastings, J. : *Encyclopedia of Religion and Ethics,* 12 Volumes, Edinburg, 1908-26.

31. Hillebrandt, A. : *Vedic Mythology,* Tr. From German by S.R Sarma, Delhi, MLBD, 1980.

32. Hopkins, E.W. : *Epic Mythology,* Strassburg, 1915.

33. Igengar, T.R.R. : *Dictionary of Hindu Gods and Goddesses,* D.K. Print World (P) Ltd., New Delhi, 2003.

34. Joshi, M.N. : *Gāyatrī in Ṛgveda,* Roopa Publication, Dharwad, 2001.

35. Joshi, J.R. : *Some Minor Divinities in Vedic Mythology and Ritual,* Deccan College Post Graduate and Research Institute, Pune, 1977.

36. Jacob, G.A. : *A Concordance of the Principal Upanisads and Bhagavati Gitā,* First Reprint, Delhi, 1963.

37. Khan, M.I. : *Brahmā in the Purāṇas,* Crescent Publishing House, Ghaziabad, 1981.

38. Khan, M.I. : *Sarasvatī in Sanskrit Literature,* Crescent Publishing House, Ghaziabad, 1978.

39. Kashya, R.L. : *Sri Aurobindo Kapali Sastry Institute of Vedic Culture,* Bangalore, 2005.

40. Kane, P.V. : *History of Dharmāsāstra,* 5 Volumes, Bhandarkar Oriental Research Institute, Poona, 1930, 1930-62.

41. Kantawala, S.G. : *Cultural History From the Matsya Purāṇa,* Oriental Institute, Baroda, 1964.

42. Kinsleys, David : *Hindu Goddesses,* Delhi : MLBD, 1987.

43. Kumarappa, Bharatan : *Hindu Conception of the Deity,* London, 193.

44. Lal. S.K. : *Female Divinities in Hindu Mythology and Ritual,* University of Poona, Pune, 1980.

45. Lalye, P.G. : *Studies in Devī Bhāgavata,* Popular Prakashan, Bombay, 1973.

46. Lal, Krishna : "*Sāvitrī from Samhitās to Gṛhyasūtras,*" ABORIS 52 pts. 1-N, 1971, 1. 225-229

47. Macdonell, A.A. and Keith A.B. : *Vedic Index of Names and Subjects* Oxford, 1912.

48. Macdonell, A.A. : *Vedic Mythology,* Strassburg, 1987; Mani, Vettam, Puranic Encyoclopedia, MLBD.

49. Prem Kumar : *Gāyatrī Mahāmantra* (Hindi), Prabhat Pocket Books, Meerut.

50. Pusalkar, A.D. : *Studies in Epics and Purāṇas of India,* Bombay, 1963.

51. Sastri, Viśvabandhu : *Vaidikapadānukramakośa,* Visvesvarananda Vedic Research Institute, Lahore-Hoshiarpur, 1935-62.

52. Satapathy, C. *Kubera : Origin and Development,* Classical Publishing Company, New Delhi, 2002.

53. Sorensen, S. : *An Index to the Names in the Mahābhārata,* New Delhi, 1953.

54. Swami Sureswarananda : *Gāyatrī Arthasangraha,* Ranadhir Book Sales, Haridwar, 1986.

55. Sheth, Surabhi : *Religion and Society in the Brahma Purāṇa,* Sterling Publishers, New Delhi, 1979.

56. Swami Amritananda : *Rg Vedic Sūktas Gāyatrī and others,* Sri Ramakrishna Math, Chennai, 2006.

57. Swami M : *The Gāyatrī Mantra,* Mr. and Mrs. Pamela Gale and Anil Kumar Malhotra, Karnataka.

58. Swami Sivananda : *The Philosophy of Gāyatrī Sādhanā,* The Divine Life Society, Tehri Garhwal.

59. Swami Mukhyananda : *OM Gāyatri and Sandhyā,* Sri. Ramakrishna Math Printing Press, Mylapore, Chennai.

60. Sri Aurobindo : *The Secret of the Veda,* Sri Aurobindo Ashram, Pondichery, 1996.

61. Taimni, I.K.: *An Introduction to Hindu Symbolism,* Adyar, 1965.

62. Vaidya, C.V. : *The Mahābhārata: A Criticism,* Delhi, 1966.

63. Mishra, J.P. : *Aṣṭādasa Purāṇadarpana,* Nag Publishers, Delhi.

64. Gonda, J. : *The Indian Mantra,* Oriens, Vol. 16.

65. Gupta, Sukeshi Rani : *Śatapatha Brāhmaṇa me Gāyatrī* (Hindi) *Gurukula Patrika,* 19, 1967.

66. Vaśiṣtha, Ram Sharan : *Gāyatrī Mantra* (Hindi) *Sasvata Vani,* 2 Dec., 1962.

67. Santakavi Shri Dasa Ganu, *Sri Gāyatrī-Stava* (Marathi).

68. Pandit, M.P. : *Gāyatrī Upāsanā,* Ved. Kes, Vol. 48, 1961.

69. Yogi, Gouri Prasad : *An Introductory Eassay on the Gāyatrī Mantra of the Vedic Period,* Rishikesh, 1957.

69. Journals : *Raimundo Panikkar, Mantramañjarī,* London, 1977.

70. Kaundinya, *Samoorṇa Gāyatrī* (rendering in English) Kamakoti Vani, Vol.3, Oct. 1971. (Contains many verses as prayers to *Sarasvatī, Laksmī* etc. composed on the model of the *Gāyatrī Mantra*).

Index